Paper Citizens

Paper Citizens

*How Illegal Immigrants Acquire Citizenship
in Developing Countries*

KAMAL SADIQ

OXFORD
UNIVERSITY PRESS
2009

OXFORD

UNIVERSITY PRESS

Oxford University Press, Inc., publishes works that further
Oxford University's objective of excellence
in research, scholarship, and education.

Oxford New York
Auckland Cape Town Dar es Salaam Hong Kong Karachi
Kuala Lumpur Madrid Melbourne Mexico City Nairobi
New Delhi Shanghai Taipei Toronto

With offices in
Argentina Austria Brazil Chile Czech Republic France Greece
Guatemala Hungary Italy Japan Poland Portugal Singapore
South Korea Switzerland Thailand Turkey Ukraine Vietnam

Published by Oxford University Press, Inc.
198 Madison Avenue, New York, New York 10016

www.oup.com

Oxford is a registered trademark of Oxford University Press

Library of Congress Cataloging-in-Publication Data
Sadiq, Kamal.
Paper citizens : how illegal immigrants acquire
citizenship in developing countries / Kamal Sadiq.
p.   cm.
Includes bibliographical references and index.
ISBN 978-0-19-537122-2
1. South Asia—Emigration and immigration.   2. Southeast Asia—Emigration and immigration.
3. Pakistan—Emigration and immigration.   4. Illegal aliens—South Asia.
5. Illegal aliens—Southeast Asia.   6. Illegal aliens—Pakistan.
7. Security, International.   8. Border crossing.
I. Title.
JV8752.S33 2009
323.609172'4—dc22
2008013538

1 3 5 7 9 8 6 4 2

Printed in the United States of America
on acid-free paper

To my parents

Contents

Acknowledgments

In all versions of the tale, Superman arrived as an undocumented alien.
—Letter to the Editor, *New York Times*, July 5, 2006

There are few "undocumented" immigrants in this world. Indeed, Superman is a rare exception. Immigrants may be illegal or unauthorized, but they are rarely undocumented; the vast majority possess some form of documentation. Characterizing them as "undocumented" is suggestive of the misunderstood character of illegal immigration. So, in this book, I dig into their experiences with the tools of fieldwork to reveal the puzzle of their entry and settlement into another state. Ironically, I began my immigrant life parallel to theirs, each of us documented in our own way. Eventually they settled, just as I did, each of us possessing documents signaling our citizenship.

This book involved fieldwork, language training, illnesses, and long absences from my homes in Delhi, Chicago, and Irvine. The book also reflects an immigrant story, my story. It marks transitions from a hot climate (Delhi) to a windy chill (Chicago) and back to warm weather (southern California). Hyde Park, where fun comes to die, became a wonderful home, much like South Delhi had been earlier. This book could not have happened without the help, support, and friendship of many people who became my community. A toast to my co-conspirators at the University of Chicago (we collectively saved the International House): Paul Castle, Hilla Dayan, Patrick Crotty, Karl Fogel, Russell Miller, the late Vi Uretz, Patricia Jobe, Philip Lynch, Pinar Emre, Hank Webber, and Richard Franke. Hyde Park will be the same because of you. International House became home due to the love and warmth of Marta and Ralph Nichols (professor emeritus, anthropology), Ilan

Cooper, Brian Davis, Scott Drewianka, Constance Kim, Delores Leblanc, Pat Maslowski, Henri Pernet, Nidhi Sharma, Takahiro Watanabe, and other friends from New York, India, Israel, Greece, Turkey, Texas—places connected by the gothic facade of 1414 East 59th Street.

Intellectually, Chicago remains the place where the life of the mind never freezes over. I want to express my gratitude to my political science teachers, Susanne Rudolph and Lloyd Rudolph, William Sewell, and John Mearsheimer, for opening doors to a life of contending ideas and endless debates. Everything was questioned; indeed, I often disagreed with my teachers. All through, I had the gentle, invisible hand of Susanne and Lloyd Rudolph to guide me through the rough intellectual terrain of Chicago. Susanne and Lloyd became my teachers and friends. They prodded, disciplined, challenged, and embraced me. This book is sprinkled with their wisdom. The arrival of Saskia Sassen at Chicago literally globalized me. I was finally transcending the boundaries of my field to understand flows that were suffocating behind barriers imposed by professional disciplines. Intellectually, she opened theoretical paths to which many of us were oblivious. I joined her global conversation—both critiquing and defending state institutions—even as I tracked the invisible path of illegal immigrants through real and mythical borders in developing countries.

Following immigrant trails from Afghanistan through Pakistan, to India, Bangladesh, Malaysia, Indonesia, and the southern Philippines was a herculean task and required the generosity of many institutions. For dissertation support I am grateful to the Harry Frank Guggenheim Foundation, and the various funding units at the University of Chicago (the Mellon, the Council on Advanced Studies in Peace and International Cooperation, and the Committee on Southern Asian Studies). Encouragement came my way through the generosity of the Division of Social Sciences at the University of California, Irvine, which honored me with its 2007–2008 Social Science Assistant Professor Research Award for excellence. Similarly, the university-wide Academic Senate Council on Research, Computing and Library Resources endorsed my overseas research with its Single Investigator Innovation Grant. Substantial funding with complete intellectual freedom is rare but vital to large overseas projects. I was fortunate to be one of a select group awarded the Smith Richardson Foundation Junior Faculty Grant to "support the next generation of public policy experts, scholars, and thinkers on topics such as American foreign policy, international relations, etc." (2005–2006). I thank Allan Song and Scott Boston at the Smith Richardson Foundation for giving me complete freedom even as I became more ambitious with the goals of this project. Finally, I am grateful to several units at the University of California, Irvine, for funding my research: the Center for Global Peace and Conflict Studies, the Center for the Scientific Study of Ethics and Morality, and the Center for Asian Studies. I thank them all.

Over the years, I have incurred the debt of many people whose intellectual support and affection sustained me at different periods of my academic life: Kathy Anderson, Matt Kocher, Martin Marty, James Vaughn, and Stephen Walt (Chicago), Stephen P. Cohen (Brookings Institution), Wayne Cornelius (University of California, San Diego), Richard Friman (Marquette), Rodney Hall (Oxford), Roger Haydon (Cornell), James F. Hollifield (Southern Methodist), Tamara Kathwari (New York), Ned Lebow (Dartmouth), Bart Nedelman (Irvine), Simon Reich (Pittsburgh), and Arthur Rubinoff (Toronto). Critical feedback from James C. Scott (Yale) and Rey Koslowski (SUNY, Albany) nudged me down innovative paths. A year's worth of fieldwork in Malaysia would not have been possible without the friendship and support of A. B. Shamsul (Universiti Kebangsaan Malaysia). Shamsul was unfailing in his intellectual and institutional support. I cherish the affection of many people who welcomed me in Sabah and Bangi. My gratitude to the following in Malaysia: Iwan Hermawan, Jacqueline Kitingan, Feridah Merican, Ungku Maimunah, Peter Selestine, and Athi Sivan. Critical to this project was the multicultural milieu and warmth of Malaysia and India. In India, repeated visits were enriched by conversations with Jayanth Banthia (former census commissioner and registrar general of India), K. N. Unni (deputy registrar general of India, vital statistics), Prashant Bhushan (Supreme Court and human rights lawyer) who kindly shared his files on citizenship, Sanjoy Hazarika (leading immigration expert), and Ashish Bose (leading demographer and advisor to the government of India). Chaity Das, Rukmini Gohain, Sudeshna Dasgupta, and Rizwan Zaman provided invaluable research assistance. Over the years, the selfless support of my professors in India (K. R. Narayanan and H. S. Chopra of Jawaharlal Nehru University) has been a source of strength. I am extremely grateful to these friends and teachers from India, Malaysia, and the United States.

I migrated from Chicago to begin teaching at the University of California, Irvine. My gratitude to the excellent research assistance of my undergraduate students. Their determination and skillful data gathering from often untraceable sources were vital to accumulating a large body of evidence from Afghanistan, Bangladesh, India, Indonesia, Malaysia, Pakistan, and the Philippines. My sincere thanks to Joanna Do, Payal Pathak, Farok Zivani, Juliana Farmer, and Bing Chomprasob, who collected, organized, and updated the material. In the final run, Kristine Cimafranca—sharp, innovative, and resolute—stepped in to provide excellent research assistance.

Irvine's Mediterranean climate was enhanced by the warmth of my colleagues. Kristin Monroe embraced me as a colleague and friend; her kindness and encouragement have been a great source of strength and inspiration. For their thoughtfulness and support, I am indebted to Frank Bean, Alison Brysk, Leo Chavez, Russell Dalton, Barbara Dosher, David Easton, Bernie Groffman, Cecelia Lynch, Anthony

McGann, Patrick Morgan, Mark Petracca, Shawn Rosenburg, Etel Solingen, and Dorie Solinger. Sharing camaraderie with me were Lisa García Bedolla, Kevin Olson, and Wayne Sandholtz. In return, I selfishly subjected them to various incarnations of the manuscript, much like the Hindu god Vishnu, to which they responded enthusiastically. I cannot thank them enough.

My editor, David McBride, and his team at Oxford University Press were outstanding. David mercilessly sharpened the text even as I mourned the loss of empirical fat. The book is leaner due to his editorial efforts. The production team of Keith Faivre, Brendan O'Neill, and Merryl Sloane conjured a final product that I had barely imagined. My toast to team Oxford. The book draws on material used earlier in (1) "When States Prefer Non-Citizens Over Citizens: Conflict Over Illegal Immigration into Malaysia," *International Studies Quarterly*, 49 March 2005: 101–122 and (2) "Lost in Translation: The Challenges of State-Generated Data in Developing Countries," in Kristin Monroe (ed.), *Perestroika!: The Raucous Rebellion in Political Science* (New Haven, CT: Yale University Press, 2005), pp.181–199.

Accompanying me on this journey were my friends and family—Tom Donahue, Ryan Harvey, and Sana Zaidi—who were present at each step, alert to any mistakes, and vigorous in their editorial comments. My sincere gratitude to each of them. Above all, my deepest thanks to Ammi, Abbu, and Nunu for comforting and nourishing me with homemade Indian culinary delights. This book is a result of their unstinting love seasoned with coriander, cumin, and a dash of turmeric.

List of Acronyms

ASS	Assam Sahitya Sabha
AASU	All Assam Students Union
AGP	Assam Gana Parishad
AREU	Afghanistan Research and Evaluation Unit
AUDF	Assam United Democratic Front
BIMP-EAGA	Brunei, Indonesia, Malaysia, Philippines: East Asian Growth Area
BEOE	Bureau of Emigration and Overseas Employment (Pakistan)
BJP	Bharatiya Janata Party
BN	Barisan Nasional
BPS	Badan Pusat Statistik
BSAF	Bangladesh Shishu Adhikar Forum
CASH	Consumer's Association of Sabah
CBI	Central Bureau of Investigation (India)
CEDAW	Convention on the Elimination of All Forms of Discrimination against Women
CM	Chief Minister
CNIC	Computerized National Identity Card
CPI	Communist Party of India
CPI(M)	Communist Party of India (Marxist)
CRC	Convention on the Rights of the Child
DAP	Democratic Action Party
DDA	Delhi Development Authority
DDD	Dangerous, Dirty, and Demanding
DO	Director of Operations

DPM	Deputy Prime Minister
DRO	District Registration Office
EC	Election Commission (India)
FIA	Federal Investigative Agency (Pakistan)
FOMEMA	Foreign Workers Medical Examination Monitoring Agency
HRWG	Human Rights Working Group
IC	Identity Card
ICAO	International Civil Aviation Organization
ICC	International Criminal Court
ILO	International Labor Organization
IMDT	Illegal Migrants (Determination by Tribunal) Act of 1983
INFID	International NGO Forum on Indonesian Development
INSAN	Institute for Social Analysis (Malaysia)
IDRC	International Development Research Centre
ISA	Internal Security Act
JI	Jamaat-i-Islami
JKKK	Jawatankuasa Kemajuan dan Keselamatan Kampung
JUP	Jamiat Ulema-i-Pakistan
km	Kilometer
KPT	Kad Pengenalan Bermutu Tinggi (identity card)
LDC	Less Developed Countries
LTTE	Liberation Tigers of Tamil Eelam
MCA	Malaysian Chinese Association
MIC	Malaysian Indian Congress
MMA	Muttahida Majlis-e-Amal
MNA	Member of the National Assembly
MNIC	Multipurpose National Identity Card
MNLF	Moro National Liberation Front
MQM	Muttahida Qaumi Movement
MRP	Machine-Readable Passport
NADRA	National Database and Registration Authority
NARA	National Aliens Registration Authority
NEP	New Economic Policy
NGO	Nongovernmental Organization
NIC	National Identity Card
NRD	National Registration Department
NWFP	Northwest Frontier Province
OCI	Overseas Citizen of India
PAS	Islamic Party of Malaysia
PAT	Pakistan Awami Tehrik

PBS	Parti Bersatu Sabah
PCO	Public Call Office
PDS	Parti Democratic Sabah
P&I	Passport and Immigration
PML	Pakistan Muslim League
PML-N	Pakistan Muslim League, Nawaz
PPP	Pakistan People's Party
PR	Permanent Resident
PTI	Pakistan Tehrik-i-Insaf
SMP	Substantial Muslim Populations
SPKIA	Survei Pendidikan dan Kesehatan Ibu dan Anak
UAE	United Arab Emirates
UC	Union Council
UKM	Universiti Kebangsaan Malaysia
ULFA	United Liberation Front of Assam
UMF	United Minorities Front
UMNO	United Malays National Organization
UNDF	United Nations Development Fund
UNDP	United Nations Development Program
UNHCR	United Nations High Commissioner for Refugees
UNICEF	United Nations Children's Fund
USNO	United Sabah National Organization
UT	Union Territories
VHP	Vishva Hindu Parishad
WESS	World Economic and Social Survey

Paper Citizens

A Paradox

Illegal Immigrants as Citizens

IN THE SERVANT ROOMS OF GOVERNMENT BUNGALOWS, IN THE TINY GARAGES of the private flats built by the Delhi Development Authority, and under the tin roofs of the *jhuggis* (makeshift homes) lived a large—and illegal—Bangladeshi population. It was the 1980s and Delhi was bustling with document-wielding illegal Bangladeshis. None of the neighborhood mothers knew where the "Bengalis" came from, just that all of them were in search of work in a household that could provide them with a "ration card"—their ticket to local citizenship. As a young boy, I was privy to gossip among the neighborhood moms—my mother included—about how some of the housemaids in the neighborhood were not actually Indian Bengalis, but Bengali-speaking foreigners from across the border. A network of housemaids ran parallel to the network of housewives, relaying neighborhood gossip. Occasionally, a new girl, a Bengali "relative" from Calcutta—that distant land— would make an appearance in the neighborhood; she would usually be hard-working and willing to do household work cheaply. Everyone assumed that the new Bengali women, like earlier ones, would settle down and acquire all of the local documents of authenticity: a ration card for subsidized food grains and cooking oil, an "official" letter to enroll children in school, and so on. Soon, children would find local jobs and daughters would be married to local men. Settlement happened smoothly and was viewed as inevitable. They were Bangladeshis posing as Indians. They spoke the same language, wore the same type of sari,[1] and preferred fish curry with a distinctive smell. They too, like us, would become Dilliwallas, citizens of

Delhi. However, while we were from other parts of India, they were from across the international border.[2]

Kuala Lumpur and Kota Kinabalu, 1990s

As rainfall approached, I was playing with a team of immigrant boys, all children of Filipino illegal immigrants. We were playing soccer across the canal that divides the upscale apartments from the large illegal immigrant settlement outside Kota Kinabalu in Sabah, Malaysia. Trees and large bushes could not conceal what was slowly emerging as a large settlement of illegal immigrants. My Chinese and Kadazandusun neighbors never crossed the canal because the slum was rumored to have a concentration of criminals, vices, drugs (*syabu*), and many other kinds of illegal activities normally associated with immigrants, in this case, Filipinos. A log served as a bridge to connect members of this community to a main road, where a single bus would take them to the city. Their houses, made from cardboard and scrap wood, had electricity and water that was illegally tapped from municipal supplies. One of the houses ran a small shop which supplied basic goods, such as eggs, bread, matchsticks, candy, and rice. In the evening, under the dim lantern light, both female and male members of the community would gamble. It was a web of relationships. People gave loans, shared employment information, developed friendships, and celebrated festivals. If one wanted to send money back home to the Philippines, there were always individuals returning who could be trusted to carry the cash. Later, I rode the subway with Bangladeshi immigrants, ate burgers with "kecap" (ketchup) at food kiosks run by Indonesian immigrants, and drank "teh" (tea) served by Filipino women, all of whom had a personal story of how they immigrated and eventually settled down. During my year in Malaysia, I witnessed a pervasive illegal immigrant presence.[3] Everywhere, I saw Bahasa-speaking maids, Indonesian Bugis bus drivers and conductors, Filipino street vendors, local imams, restaurant help, plantation workers, hostesses at the local karaoke bar, and Islamic recruits involved in local Islamic organizations—all bearing identity cards that legitimized their illegal presence. It was obvious to the local people that illegal immigrants were living comfortably as citizens.

Path to Citizenship

Although these experiences piqued my curiosity about the relations between immigration and citizenship, they were hardly unique. In India and Malaysia, it is commonplace to see illegal immigrants settling down and behaving as citizens. Once settled, these immigrants become indistinguishable from those who followed legal immigration procedures and, in some cases, from native-born citizens themselves. Today the west is unaccustomed to such an outcome, where we are used to seeing the line between foreigner and citizen crisply demarcated, with legally sanctioned immigration procedures forming an orderly path from one status to the other. Something substantially different was going on in the experiences I've just narrated: foreigners made the transition to full membership without following any of the paths officially laid out for them, vanishing into the host population and becoming, in a very real sense, citizens.

This book attempts to follow the innovative though illegal paths that such immigrants have devised. They pose an important puzzle by subverting legal immigration procedures and overturning our standard concepts of citizenship. The crucial question, in this light, is: how do illegal immigrants gain access to citizenship in developing countries? To solve this conceptual puzzle, I will analyze three of the four major immigration cases recently cited by the United Nations: illegal Bangladeshis in India, Indonesians and Filipinos in Malaysia, and Afghans and Bangladeshis in Pakistan (United Nations 2004: 55).

Traditional immigration and citizenship theories assume that the receiving state has a population that can be distinguished from illegal immigrants. For example, Rogers Brubaker (1992) has clearly delineated the boundaries between immigrants and citizens in France and Germany, contrasting the two experiences.[4] Unlike legal immigrants, illegal immigrants are not even eligible for a path to citizenship in many states. In fact, most theories do not account for illegal immigrant participation in receiving states because they assume sharp distinctions between illegal immigrants and citizens. Such distinctions can only be maintained, however, by developed or authoritarian states with sophisticated surveillance capabilities. As document-bearing illegal immigrants in India, Malaysia, and Pakistan show, not all states manage to erect such insurmountable walls around citizenship. Rather, the fact that they have accessed citizenship illegally suggests that the boundaries of citizenship may be more permeable than we generally believe. This phenomenon forces us to reconsider our accepted view of citizenship and investigate its complexity in greater detail.

Citizenship is commonly understood as a legal status and is equated with a bundle of legal rights and duties. This is held to be true of citizenship in every state in the world. But there is a problem with this conception of citizenship: it is based solely on the institutional experience of Western states. How are we to square this conception with the fact that, in developing countries, illegal immigrants increasingly act as citizens? They access the privileges and rights of citizenship, confounding the standard theory that only *legal* immigrants are eligible for naturalization and full national membership. Are there no definite boundaries around the political community in developing states? How do they exclude or include outsiders? Who determines membership in their political communities? A veil shrouds the issue of citizenship in developing countries.

Who is a citizen in India, Malaysia, and Pakistan? The "who" question of citizenship identifies the subject of citizenship. Who is "in," who is "out," who is a citizen, who is not? Once the subject of citizenship has been located, we then have to understand what legal and administrative mechanisms states deploy to determine membership. What is the content of citizenship? What is citizenship? The content is centrally about the legal infrastructure of citizenship: norms and practices codified as law, accompanied by a supporting cast of disaggregated institutions such as the judiciary, bureaucracy, legislature, and border police. This infrastructure is called upon by the state to identify individuals and groups with claims on the territory of the state. It is the infrastructure of citizenship, a citizenship from above, that draws the boundaries of the political community, determines the criteria for eligibility, and embeds power and normative force in institutions meant to protect the political community and guard the territorial boundary. However, individuals have varying experiences in negotiating this infrastructure. This is precisely why citizenship is often associated with a range of meanings. Understanding membership in India, Malaysia, and Pakistan will require us to analyze both the subject and the content of citizenship. We begin with the subject of citizenship: the citizen.

The Wall

Who confers citizenship on immigrating foreigners? Traditionally, it was the sovereign king, emperor, sultan, or rajah. Today, the sovereign state confers citizenship—or so we are told by commonly accepted accounts (García Bedolla 2005; Bosniak 2006; Koslowski 2000a; Smith 2002). From this perspective, the only way for a foreigner to become a citizen is through naturalization.[5] A foreigner coming from outside has to confront and traverse the infrastructure of citizenship to become a citizen. The infrastructure of citizenship is designed to operate like a filter, separating the eligible from those who do not belong. This is a long process in which multiple state agencies verify a person's local roots, character, and loyalty. At each stage, an individual's name, location, and identity are entered into state records; the proof of their having done so is a legal document. Through such forms of verification and documentation, the state exercises its sovereign control over who becomes a member of the polity and who does not. The state thus determines political membership, identifying the political community on whose behalf it governs. This community in turn authorizes and legitimates the actions of the state. In this conception of citizenship, governance, sovereignty, authority, and state legitimacy are all vitally connected with the control of immigration.

This understanding is, of course, based overwhelmingly on the states of Western Europe and North America. In these states, the government's power to regulate entry and settlement is unquestioned. Immigration can be deliberately controlled and channeled through guest worker programs and other absorption mechanisms (Zolberg 2006). In these circumstances, illegal immigration is viewed as an anomaly and a problem to be solved, testing the resolve and institutional resources of receiving states, rather than their very understanding of citizenship itself.

All immigration and citizenship theories make a fundamental and critical assumption: that *receiving states have a population that is documented* using standardized paperwork, and thus the host population can be distinguished from immigrants—legal or illegal. The traditional literature assumes that states have the capacity to actively distinguish between citizens and noncitizens, including legal immigrants, refugees, and illegal immigrants. We can call this putative conceptual wall separating citizens from immigrants the *distinguishability assumption.*[6] As Linda Bosniak (2006: 1) writes, "The idea of citizenship is commonly invoked to convey a state of democratic belonging or inclusion, yet this inclusion is usually premised on a conception of a community that is bounded and exclusive."[7] Citizenship is inward-looking, making it "hard on the outside and soft on the inside" (Bosniak 2006: 4). The nationalism of citizenship produces this hard outside edge—the border. Drawing the borders around citizenship, demarcating the political community which defines the nation, is essential if states are to manage "the allocation and distribution of national membership" (Feldblum 2000: 475). Hence, it becomes imperative to exclude those outside the political community from the advantages of membership, such as welfare benefits, suffrage, and so forth. The infrastructure of citizenship fulfills this purpose by constructing a wall between members and nonmembers. Similarly in theories of immigration, the border is about exclusion, regulating who comes in and who stays out.[8] Who belongs within this border and who is to be excluded are determinations that state officials have to make at every point of entry. It is assumed that individual state gatekeepers have the resources, training, and capacity to distinguish between citizen and "foreigner."

The distinguishability assumption, that the state can separate citizens from foreigners, is endemic to the literature on immigration and citizenship. It is the implicit basis for a literature detailing the differential, unequal treatment that illegal immigrants receive in contrast to citizens, for instance. This literature focuses on the social, political, and economic rights of citizens (Kymlicka 1995; Marshall and Bottomore 1996); gradations of immigrant membership (Joppke 1999; Koslowski 2000a; Schuck and Smith 1985); and the erosion of the state due to global processes creating new forms of membership not tied to the nation-state (Sassen 1998, 1999; Jacobson 1997; Spiro 1998). This literature is conceptually blind, however, to the complex, poorly understood role of *documents* in bridging the divide between a citizen and a foreigner. The conceptual wall separating a citizen and an immigrant remains firm in this discussion, anchored by taken-for-granted assumptions about the legal infrastructure of citizenship.

In this book, I will challenge these assumptions about citizenship by highlighting the importance of documents in the acquisition of citizenship. This emphasis belies our commonsense idea that citizenship is a status awarded by the state through orderly immigration processes based on clear, legally specified criteria. The commonsense idea of citizenship characterizes the developed Western states well enough, but it does not work for the range of cases I will examine here. To find a more adequate description of citizenship in the rest of the world, I will develop a rather different conception: *documentary citizenship*. It emphasizes the role that documents play in acquiring citizenship, whether the documents are legal or not and whether the newly admitted citizen is a legal immigrant or not. I claim that documentary citizenship is every bit as real as the "normal" path of legally specified immigration. What's more, this conception provides a more empirically accurate description of the actual citizenship practices in countries like India, Pakistan, and Malaysia. In so doing, it challenges many of our most deeply held beliefs about what citizenship is and how it functions.

In order to make clear some of the changes that are needed in our thinking about citizenship, I will accompany documentary citizenship with another important concept. This is the idea of *blurred membership*, which is a claim to membership by long-term residents who are unrecognized or unverified by agents of the state. Official ambiguity marks the presence of such individuals. These legal nonpersons, the subjects of blurred membership, are often the poor, landless, and indigenous natives living in developing countries. Together, these concepts provide us with a new critical perspective on citizenship, one that identifies the actual mechanisms through which citizenship is acquired in the rest of the world and the consequences that this entails for our understanding of what it means to be a citizen of a state. Articulating the idea of documentary citizenship and the broader vision of state membership that it implies will be the task of the chapters to come.

The Infrastructure of Citizenship

The state's challenge to outsiders begins with a legal infrastructure meant to secure citizens from foreigners. The legal infrastructure not only has the force of law but slowly develops norms, thus setting standards for state practices. This wall, a legal "cage" (Weber 1978) of infrastructural power (Mann 2006), "disciplines" the population by drawing boundaries between them, separating and classifying them (Foucault 1977). The purpose of the citizenship infrastructure is to identify and order individual subjects so that they can be ruled by the state. Information in files that catalog the claims of citizenship are distributed in a widespread, interlocking web of citizen-identifying institutions. In the twenty-first century, paper files are being replaced by computer files as databases increase the mobility of information on citizens and interlopers. Files and databases link the Ministry of Home or Interior to the Ministry of Immigration to the Ministry of Justice, establishing norms, practices, and precedents. Citizenship, understood this way, is state making. And the state capacities that are made in this way take the form of the legal infrastructure—the Foucauldian edifice erected by the state—that makes society legible (Scott 1998).

Let us unpack this infrastructure of citizenship, which manages and circumscribes membership on behalf of the state, with a fundamental question: what *is* citizenship in India, Malaysia, and Pakistan? Or, what is citizenship supposed to be in these states? How is legal citizenship acquired? If we think of citizenship as a formal status granted by states, then there would seem to be three traditional approaches to granting citizenship: jus sanguinis, jus soli, and naturalization. What does this do to our understanding of citizenship in India, Malaysia, and Pakistan? Is citizenship inclusive in these states? Or do citizenship laws have the effect of excluding immigrants, thus securing the boundaries of citizenship?

The constitutions of India, Malaysia, and Pakistan confer a single citizenship on the members of their respective states. However, exclusionary, narrow, jus sanguinis (blood or descent-based) features are in constant conflict with inclusive, broad, jus soli (civic-based, citizenship by birth) conceptions of citizenship in these states. Citizenship in India, Malaysia, and Pakistan is torn between inclusive impulses based on the principles of jus soli and restrictions shaped by jus sanguinis in light of increasing illegal immigration.

Indian citizenship began on a civic note, as a regime of jus soli, but has evolved into a more exclusionary citizenship regime.[9] Why and how did jus sanguinis principles encroach to produce a restrictive Indian citizenship? The constitutional provisions dealing with citizenship in India are located in Articles 5–12 in part II of the constitution.[10] At independence, India ascribed citizenship at birth on the basis of the principle of jus soli. Under the Citizenship Act of 1955, and prior to the commencement of the Citizenship (Amendment) Act of 1986, any person born in India was a citizen of India, irrespective of the nationality of his/her parents. Proving one's heritage or a connection to the national identity was irrelevant; an individual's birth in the territory was sufficient for Indian citizenship (except for children of foreign diplomats and enemy aliens). These classic jus soli principles, liberal and inclusive, were the outcome of the events at the time of the partition of India and Pakistan when about a million people died and almost 12 million were displaced. Highly inclusive laws in the form of Articles 5 and 6 enabled millions of Hindu and Sikh refugees to adopt Indian citizenship. It was in this initial period that India signed treaties of friendship with two neighboring states, Bhutan (1949) and Nepal (1950), allowing millions of people to cross the border freely and seek employment, and refuge (Karnad et al. 2006: 5). Jus soli principles embedded in the Citizenship Act of 1955 fashioned an inclusive Indian citizenship for a newly independent India.

Over the years, India diluted the effect of jus soli as it introduced restrictive measures into its citizenship policies. Restrictive legislation based on the principle of descent were introduced as India increasingly debated immigration politics on the national stage. The independence of Bangladesh in 1971 and the insurgency by Tamil Sri Lankans dislocated millions of immigrants and refugees during the 1970s and 1980s into India (Karnad et al. 2006: 7). Thousands of Tamil refugees then stayed in India. While a majority of the Bangladeshi refugees returned to their homes, many Bangladeshi Hindus and Muslims stayed in India. The strengthened Bangladeshi ethnic networks facilitated large flows into the Northeast Indian region, particularly Assam. This led to tremendous anti-immigrant agitation and violence during the mid-1980s, which resulted in the Assam Accord. The centerpiece of this accord was a new section of the constitution, 6A, which was meant to exclude Bangladeshi illegal immigrants from claims to Indian citizenship. Almost forty years after independence, the citizenship law was amended in 1986 and again in 1992. Jus soli would apply only to those born prior to the first amendment; those born in India after 1986 can claim citizenship only if one of their parents is a citizen of India at the time of their birth.[11] The need to protect Indian citizenship from the encroachments of Bangladeshi illegal immigrants was made even more explicit in the 2004 amendment. A new clause was introduced into the Citizenship Act, which states that the right to citizenship by birth specifically excludes any individual whose parent was an *illegal migrant at the time of his/her birth*.[12] Those gaining Indian citizenship were now assuredly of Indian descent, coming from Indian parentage and nationality. The exclusionary impact of jus sanguinis circumscribed the *demos* of Indian citizenship from the unwanted influence of illegal Bangladeshis.

Increasingly, jus sanguinis norms undergird the acquisition of Indian citizenship. Individuals born outside India formerly could acquire citizenship by descent only if the father was a citizen of India at the time of their birth. Liberalizing this law to allow citizenship to flow from either a father or a mother of Indian descent occurred with the amendment of the Citizenship Act in 1992. Individuals born outside India on or after December 10, 1992, were now eligible for Indian citizenship if either of their parents were a citizen of India at the time of their birth. Additional limitations followed in 2004. From December 3, 2004, onward, individuals born outside India are eligible for Indian citizenship if their birth is registered at an Indian embassy within one year of the birth. Indian citizenship was broadened to embrace female gender as a source of membership even as it became more restrictive procedurally. The protective hand of the Indian state continues to harden the boundaries of formal Indian citizenship.

The Indian state maintains its boundaries in fear of the demographic impact of immigration from its Muslim neighbors, Pakistan and Bangladesh. This is reflected in its naturalization laws as well as the recent attempts to mobilize the Indian diaspora. The Citizenship Act of 1955 permits specific types of individuals to apply for Indian citizenship through registration (section 5) and naturalization (section 6): (a) someone of Indian origin who is ordinarily resident in India for a specified amount of time before making an application for registration, and (b) someone who is married to a citizen of India and has been ordinarily resident in India for a specified amount of time before applying for citizenship (Karnad et al. 2006: 9). In both cases, increasing residential requirements for potential applicants were introduced through the 1986 and 2004 amendments to the Citizenship Act. The residential period was extended to five years with the 1986 amendment and to seven years with the 2004 amendment. The amendment restricted "persons of Indian origin" to those whose parents were born in undivided India—changed from those whose grandparents were born in undivided India—thus narrowing the pool of those eligible for "Indianness" (Karnad et al. 2006: 9).

Naturalization of a foreigner with no connection to India by birth, descent, or origin is possible provided the individual has been residing in India for fourteen years (repeated amendments have increased the residential requirement from nine to twelve to fourteen years). An "overseas" citizenship was introduced through section 7 (a, b, c, d) of the Citizenship Act in 2003, based on a historical claim to Indian origin. Again, Bangladeshis and Pakistanis were ineligible, and many political rights of citizens were excluded from overseas citizens. An overseas citizen of India (OCI) is not eligible to vote, to hold public office,[13] nor to serve in any state service. Dual citizenship is not permitted by Indian citizenship law; gaining the citizenship of another state means a parallel loss of Indian citizenship.[14] Indian citizenship is precious, not to be shared with any other state. The curtailment of Indian citizenship by imposing restrictive residential requirements, narrowly defining "persons of Indian origin" to ensure their "Indian" nationality, securing the political rights of Indian citizenship from the claims of the diaspora—all reflect a growing anxiety on the part of the Indian state toward new and old outsiders. It seems that the nation has to be protected from an ever-ready stream of illegal immigrants waiting to contaminate the fabric of Indian citizenship. Central to these concerns has been the elimination of claims to Indian citizenship by Bangladeshi and Pakistani nationals (or their descendants).

Pakistani citizenship was governed by the Pakistan Citizenship Act of 1951, which was based on jus soli principles to accommodate Muslim refugees from India with Pakistani citizenship. Hence, section 4 of the Pakistan Citizenship Act of 1951 allowed any individual born on Pakistani territory after commencement to become a citizen. Citizenship was governed by jus soli principles in Pakistan. However, continued attempts to create an identity independent of, and in contrast to, India produced tension between a narrow Islamic vision of Pakistan (led by the Zia ul-Haq regime) and a more secular yet Muslim Pakistan (led by Zulfikar Bhutto, his daughter Benazir Bhutto, and recently General Pervez Musharraf). Confidence in a common national identity was shaken when Muslim East Pakistan broke away on linguistic and cultural grounds and became Bangladesh in 1971. Moreover, the idea of Pakistan as the home to South Asian Muslims was threatened by the ongoing vibrancy of two large Muslim communities in South Asia—the Indian and Bangladeshi Muslims. Insecurity marked the construction of Pakistani nationality. In response, the Pakistani state narrowed the Pakistan Citizenship Act of 1951 with additional amendments in 1952, 1972, and 1973 (twice; Karnad et al. 2006: 11). Lengthy residence periods and multiple state authentication requirements gained momentum with every amendment. An individual born outside Pakistan could only be a citizen of Pakistan by descent if the father was a citizen of Pakistan. Naturalization was permitted, but like India, the formal process required lengthy residence and tedious, often arbitrary, verification procedures. Dual citizenship was not permitted (section 14 of the Citizenship Act). In contrast, Pakistan did recognize citizenship for immigrants (section 6 of the Citizenship Act) as long as their intention was to settle permanently, and additionally allowed the spouse, children, and dependents a claim to Pakistani citizenship. Obviously, this was meant to accommodate any immigrating Indian Muslims (also known as Mohajirs in Pakistan). Indian Muslims continued to trickle into Pakistani territory until the late 1950s. Pakistan is often known for its narrow Islamic national identity and dictatorial regimes, yet on paper it displays citizenship laws that seem open and marked by inclusive principles. This poses the puzzle of explaining the apparent incongruity between Pakistan's de jure openness and its reputation for exclusion.

This discrepancy is one of appearance only. In Pakistan, there is a disconnection between formal citizenship laws and the reality of citizenship practice, in which the discriminatory treatment of women and ethnic minorities is rampant. Hence, in 1974, the Qadianis, a sect of Muslims, was declared non-Muslim, officially denying them the privileges of full citizenship by transforming them into a minority (Saigol 2003: 395). Until recently, acquiring a Pakistani passport involved affirming your belief that the Qadianis are non-Muslims. The infrastructure of citizenship gained alarming exclusionary powers during General Zia's Islamicization program, when the state sought to introduce a column for religion in the national identity cards, thus effectively separating Muslims from non-Muslims (Saigol 2003: 402n13). This Taliban-like move failed, largely due to public opposition. However, an institutionalized gender hierarchy continues to mark Pakistani citizenship. For example, the Law of Evidence of 1984 downgraded the value of women's testimony in court to half that of men, while the Qisas and Diyat Ordinance reduced the value of a female life to half that of a male life (Saigol 2003: 397). However, an amendment of the Citizenship Act in 2000 liberalized formal citizenship for women. Now, an individual born outside Pakistan on or after April 18, 2000, is eligible for Pakistani citizenship if either parent is a citizen of Pakistan (section 5)—that is, citizenship by descent comes from mothers too. Additionally, if a woman loses her nationality by marrying a foreigner and acquiring his nationality, she can now regain Pakistani citizenship by divorcing her husband and renouncing his nationality. That said, while formal gender restrictions in citizenship laws were liberalized by 2000, other judicial practices and norms continue to devalue female citizenship in Pakistan.

At the same time, Pakistan has appeared open to conferring citizenship on "foreigners." While India's formal restrictions are in line with its fear of Muslim Bangladeshi illegal immigrants, Pakistani citizenship laws appear not to be as restrictive toward illegal immigrants. Why is this the case? First, Pakistan was born during horrific partition violence that made it hostile territory for non-Muslim migrants. Partition had equally affected India, but India reaffirmed its secular and multiethnic character from the outset. Moreover, India had as big a Muslim population as Pakistan; it was not framed as a hostile territory for any religious community. On the other hand, violence, fear, and discrimination toward non-Muslims, especially Hindus and Sikhs, marked Pakistani state formation. Second, Islamic principles increasingly defined every aspect of life in Pakistan, therefore discouraging any non-Muslim claimants—especially Hindus, Sikhs, and Christians—to Pakistani citizenship. Non-Muslim illegal immigrants were unlikely to find a favorable living environment in Pakistan. Conversely, as an Islamic state, Pakistan was a welcoming territory for any Muslim. A preferred outcome of such laws is that the majority of the claims to Pakistani citizenship have arisen from fellow Muslims: Afghan and Bangladeshi illegal immigrants. This explains Pakistan's formal openness in its citizenship laws. An exclusionary nationhood is covered in a thin exterior of liberal citizenship.

Unlike the liberal features of formal Pakistani citizenship, Malaysian citizenship is explicitly restrictive toward natives and exclusionary toward outsiders. It is governed by jus sanguinis principles. The constitutional provisions regarding citizenship are in Articles 14–31 of part III of the federal constitution.[15] By law, every individual born in Malaysia before Malaysia Day in October 1962 is a citizen. An individual born after that day is not a citizen unless she/he is born in Malaysia to at least one Malaysian parent or permanent resident. Those born abroad can apply for citizenship if they have a Malaysian father. Clearly, Malaysia does not confer citizenship by place of birth (jus soli). Hence, children of illegal immigrants born on Malaysian territory are given special birth certificates marked *orang asing* (foreigner) (Olson 2007). If either of the parents are citizens of Malaysia, only then can individuals apply for citizenship.

The key legislation is the Citizenship Rules of 1964, which recognizes entry to citizenship through registration (Articles 15, 15A, 16, 16A, 18) and through naturalization (Article 19). Citizenship through registration recognizes a large number of natives who may officially lack proofs of citizenship. However, to register as a citizen, an individual has to submit a "Form A" along with supporting documentation, specifically, an identity card, a birth certificate, a parent's birth or citizenship certificate, an entry permit, any travel document, the identity cards of parents and brothers and sisters, and birth certificates of children, plus payment and three photographs. On approval, the state will charge a further 100 ringgits (3.32 ringgits are equal to US$1) for supplying the citizenship certificate. For a poor native living in the interior without any supporting documents (an unrecognized native) acquiring Malaysian citizenship is a tall order. Further, the individual is required to demonstrate an elementary knowledge of the Malay language (section 16). For the purpose of registration or naturalization, subjective language skills in the form of "elementary" or "adequate" knowledge of Malay are required. To judge Malay language skills, the state set up a Language Board. If an individual has been a permanent resident for over twelve years and has spent over ten of those in continuous residence in Malaysia, only then is she/he eligible for Malaysian citizenship. Naturalization is a burdensome process in which the individual's "Malayness" is tested and confirmed through a variety of documents and witnesses. Correspondingly, if a Malaysian citizen acquires a foreign citizenship, the state will terminate the individual's citizenship according to provisions in chapter II of the federal constitution (Articles 23–28A). In fact, if a naturalized or registered Malaysian is living overseas as a private citizen[16] and does not register his/her citizenship annually with the Malaysian consulate for five years, the individual may lose Malaysian citizenship. Malaysia, like India and Pakistan, does not permit dual citizenship.

The exclusions extend further. Though India and Malaysia are signatories to the Convention on the Rights of the Child, which requires states to confer nationality on every child, both exclude the children of foreigners born on their territory. India specifically does not confer citizenship by birth to children of illegal immigrants. While Pakistan allows jus soli citizenship, it too is reluctant to accept large numbers of Afghan and Bangladeshi children as Pakistani citizens. Additionally, in practice, Pakistani citizenship is out of reach for non-Muslim children, given the exclusionary Islamic character of Pakistani nationality. Through restrictive administrative procedures for citizenship, Pakistan is able to violate the spirit of an inclusionary jus soli citizenship.

The infrastructure of citizenship is focused on distinguishing between citizens and immigrants, especially illegal immigrants—in other words, it seeks to implement the distinguishability assumption. For many Indian, Malaysian, and Pakistani poor, uneducated, and illegal immigrants, however, the legal means to citizenship through some form of naturalization or registration are too expensive and complicated. These costs are made even more prohibitive by the need to bribe state officials. How do these segments of the population achieve the basic rights of citizenship, without actually obtaining citizenship? Do citizenship rights only come after citizenship status?

Having identified citizenship's appropriate recipient—the "who," or the subject—we have analyzed the foundation of citizenship. And yet, as I will show in chapter 1, millions of document-bearing illegal immigrants commonly access the privileges of citizenship in India, Malaysia, and Pakistan. What does this imply for citizenship? Is it a challenge to the different meanings of citizenship? What are the theoretical stakes?

The Different Meanings of Citizenship

From Status to Rights?

According to traditional scholarship, citizenship status brings with it a bundle of citizenship rights. The traditional ordering holds that citizenship is granted first, then the recipient can exercise the various rights that citizenship entails. Civil rights (freedoms of speech and association, protection from harm), political rights (franchise, public office), and social rights (employment, education, and health benefits) come with the acquisition of citizenship status. In this view, citizenship status and citizenship rights are like conjoined twins; one cannot exist without the other. Moreover, they always follow one another in a specific order: a bundle of rights is the happy result of acquiring citizenship status (Smith 2002).

In contrast to the traditional view, however, the reverse ordering is also true. In India, Malaysia, and Pakistan, people engage in some of the citizenship rights first, then use the documentary products of those to gain citizenship status. Illegal immigrants can acquire the right to sell vegetables on streets with a minor authorization document from a local authority, be gainfully employed with localized identity paperwork, send kids to schools with locally acquired birth certificates and/or recommendation letters from a local elite, and rent or buy a house or land with tenuous paperwork—thus demonstrating their local status with local documents. A range of social, economic, and cultural citizenship rights are practiced in this way by illegal immigrants and their families.

Legal status is central to citizenship in the traditional view because of its historical association with political governance. Subjects chose their rulers, who then governed over this circumscribed body of subjects. Eligibility to belong to the community of subjects brought with it a range of rights whose distribution and allocation were governed by rules, regulations, and institutions. The monarchical ruler gave way to democratic states, but each circumscribed the bundle of rights and duties to those who were members of the community of citizens. Once the state authorized entry—and only the state could authorize entry into the community of citizens—the individual became eligible for a range of rights and entitlements, many distributed by the state.

Hannah Arendt (1968) would concur with my analysis, as she often drew attention to the role of the state in conferring the right to have rights.[17] Millions were denied the right to have rights as a result of their statelessness during the two world wars. Contrary to the view in international human rights discourse that the "rights of man" are timeless, inhering in nature, the loss of citizenship rights usually means a loss of human rights (Benhabib 2004). Since rights come from the individual's legal relationship to the state, a loss of that relationship means nonrecognition of an individual's existence and, therefore, a loss of his/her rights. One has to exist, legally, to have rights. Hence, citizenship status brings with it both citizenship and human rights.

Gaining citizenship was critical to having rights in the developed Western states that were the focus of Arendt's attention. Things are somewhat different in contemporary India, Malaysia, and Pakistan, however. Only a small minority of immigrants, tourists, and visitors are granted citizenship status through official naturalization procedures (including marriage) in these countries. While data are unavailable, gaining access to Indian, Malaysian, and Pakistani citizenship through naturalization is a rare occurrence. Often, foreign spouses, many of Western origin, who are married to local elites are the beneficiaries of citizenship. These are not individuals who seek citizenship because it brings them any added economic or social benefit from the state. In such cases, citizenship status brings unquestioned membership with the attendant freedom to travel by using a passport and the political right to vote and hold office—important benefits for members of the elite. For immigrants seeking a better life, citizenship rights are an attractive bundle, making the acquisition of citizenship a worthy goal. But if citizenship conferred by the state is too cumbersome or expensive a process, bypassing the state in order to practice citizenship rights seems an attractive proposition to illegal immigrants. We know that citizenship status brings with it attendant rights. But what if document-bearing illegal immigrants actively practice citizenship rights without citizenship status? If citizenship rights come first, can citizenship status follow?

As Nationality

Citizenship is not merely about status, rights, and responsibilities. Citizenship provides an identity to its individual members as it defines the character of the nation. Citizenship is about a national imagining. Hence, citizenship involves nation building (Bendix 1996). Postcolonial states had a vision of the nation and of the body of citizens that constitutes it—an ideal typical of India, Malaysia, and Pakistan (Anderson 1991; Khilnani 1997). This vision is enshrined in their respective constitutions and is part of their educational and cultural policies. On the eve of independence, different ethnic groups in India, Malaysia, and Pakistan made a compact, a social contract in which they merged their group identities into a common national citizenship. In theory, Indian, Malaysian, and Pakistani citizenship belonged to all of their inhabitants, who were freed from colonial rule. National imaginings based on superior claims of specific groups, such as the Hindus in India, Urdu-based Muslims in Pakistan, and Malays in Malaysia, were balanced by states that constitutionally sought to assuage the anxieties of minority groups in multiethnic environments (Kymlicka 1995). Indian, Malaysian, and Pakistani civic identities would supersede any claim by a dominant nationality. The Indian state, more successfully than the Pakistani or Malaysian state, was able to successfully subsume majority group claims to a civic conception of citizenship.

Gandhi and Nehru's India was a secular state, with different cultures, religions, and castes respecting each other and living in harmony. Nehru, more than Gandhi, as the first prime minister of India, created a secular state, where religion was secured from governance, and this "modern" ideology was further embedded in the constitution, with commitments to social equality and scientism. Nonetheless, the thin fabric of a modern secular India barely masks the claims of Hindu, Muslim, and Sikh religious nationalism; caste assertions; regional autonomy movements; and so forth. Across the border, Pakistan attempted to reconcile the goals of modern development through an Islamic ideology. It failed, and the state slowly and inevitably succumbed to radical Islam in the late 1970s. Today, this Islamic fundamentalist ideology is challenged by sectarian Sindhi, Punjabi, Baluchi, Pakhtun, and Mohajir identities, further exacerbating Shia and Sunni fault lines within Islam (Wright 1991). A common Pakistani Muslim nationality is undermined by regional and sectarian claims. The protection of Sindhi culture and water resources, the preservation of Mohajir Urdu culture and their dominance in Karachi, and the alienation of religious minorities, such as the Shias, Ahmediyas, Hindus, and Christians, from an Islam-based exclusionary conception of Pakistani nationality—all underline the weak success of Pakistani nationhood. Perhaps the only time a civic Pakistani citizenship surfaces is during a war or a cricket match with India. No wonder, then, that the underlying Islamic basis of this civic carapace has begun to assert itself more and more in Pakistan. The consensus on a common Muslim nationality that overlaps Pakistani citizenship is enforced through the Islamicization of the state (Jaffrelot 2002). And yet, there are many regional and ethnic challenges within Pakistan.

As the British colonial power exited Asia, it left behind contesting visions of the nation. Nationalities were in search of a territorial home (the state) and political space (a citizenry). Malaysia was characterized by nations-in-waiting—the Malays, Chinese, Tamils, Kadazans, Dayaks—and their sociopolitical claims as ethnic groups (Shamsul 1996). A common Malaysian citizenship, understood as Malay nationality underlined by Malay language, the practice of Islam, and Muslim culture, is as alienating to the Chinese and Tamil Hindu minorities as it is to the regional non-Muslim groups based in East Malaysia. Each community—the Malays, the Chinese, and the Tamils—expresses and articulates its citizenship claims through its own political groupings (United Malays National Organization, Malaysian Chinese Association, Malaysian Indian Congress), language schools, television programs, and places of worship. Such ethnic, social, and political groups both exercise claims to Malaysian citizenship and channel civic and cultural demands and grievances. Foreshadowing interethnic balancing, a bargain was struck on the eve of independence whereby Malays kept political power while respecting Chinese economic dominance with the plea that economic measures be launched to increase Malay participation in the economy. The two goals of the New Economic Policy (NEP) were to eradicate rural poverty (Malays being the main beneficiaries as they were primarily rural) and to encourage a new class of Malay business entrepreneurs, who would progressively share the fruits of Malaysian economic growth and exports from the 1980s onward. A Malay-controlled Malaysian state succeeded in both of the economic goals, largely by having proactive affirmative action policies for the *bumiputeras*, or sons of the soil.

While such policies recognize the historical economic imbalances among the different groups, their effective discrimination against certain groups creates a hierarchical citizenship. In this hierarchy, the Malay *bumiputeras* are at the top, meaning that Malay nationality lays claim to defining Malaysian citizenship. Below are the non-Muslim *bumiputeras*, such as the native Kadazandusuns, Muruts, Penans, Orang Aslis, etc. Further down are the Chinese and Indian minorities. Kadazandusuns, Muruts, Chinese, and Tamil Indians are de facto second-class citizens. It is a peculiar outcome, since the Chinese continue to dominate the economy even as they feel like second-class citizens. Perception of second-class citizenship can come from a feeling of relative deprivation in contrast to fellow groups, members of the same political community, and can be based on economic, cultural, or religious grievances. Malay nationality firmly occupies the dominant position in the Malaysian state.

Independent India, Pakistan, and Malaysia have all sought to create a common national citizenship, which in practice is undermined by religious, cultural, caste, and regional claims of various groups. Sometimes, the nationality of a dominant ethnic group, like the Urdu-speaking Muslims in Pakistan and the Malays in Malaysia, establishes the contours of official citizenship. In contrast, official citizenship in India continues to ward off the pressure of Hindu nationalism and prevents Hindus from narrowly defining membership in the state of India.

As Privilege

According to traditional scholarship, citizenship is a privilege that comes with certain duties and responsibilities. Since acquiring citizenship status opens the path to many safeguarded citizenship rights, all of which allow an individual a voice in political governance, citizenship is viewed as a privilege. For example, notice the joyous images of immigrants who have been newly minted into citizens in Australia, France, or the United States of America. These happy scenes emphasize the privileged nature of citizenship; the new citizens are joining the rest of the political community in governing and being governed, now linked by a common fate. They can be trusted in their exercise of the franchise, hold public office, and serve in the military for the protection of the state. National interest is safe in their hands because they are now the "nation." This is why citizenship is a privilege: only the selected few share in it.

In the West, citizenship has expanded to incorporate minority groups—blacks, native people, Jews, women—as a result of social and cultural movements. Citizenship is the site for struggles over individual and minority rights. The expansion of opportunities and freedoms for neglected groups makes citizenship a sacred ground. This was not always the case. Until recently, citizenship belonged only to propertied, wealthy, white males in Western states. Citizenship was restricted; it expanded to fully encompass a range of groups only at the dawn of the twentieth century. The right of women to exercise the franchise began in 1902 in Australia, 1918 in Canada, 1920 in the United States, and 1944 in France (Isin and Turner 2002: 3). Property qualifications that only allowed wealthy individuals to possess citizenship were in place until 1901 in Australia, 1918 in Britain, and 1920 in Canada (ibid.). The rights of African Americans in the United States and Aborigines in Australia were fully recognized only after major social movements in the 1960s and 1970s.

Aware of citizenship's limited character in the constitutional history of the Western world, the visionary framers of the Indian constitution, led by Dr. Babasaheb Ambedkar, gave equal rights to women, religious minorities, castes, and tribal minorities in India at the outset. India, Malaysia, and Pakistan were born into formal equality. These states legalized a broad range of rights for their citizens at their independence from imperial rule. This happened much before advocates for "cultural pluralism" and "differentiated citizenship" in the West began to recognize historical (blacks, women, native peoples, gays and lesbians, ethnic and religious minorities) and recent (immigrants, especially from non-European backgrounds) claims to equal rights (Young 1990). In contrast, at the stroke of midnight in 1947, the Indian state began with civic equality as an integral part of its structure. The idea of civic equality enshrined in citizenship was promoted from the top down by the Indian state even as it moderated the ethnic claims of different groups. The former untouchable, the burka-clad woman, the uneducated caste farmer, the nomadic *banjara*, the tribal Naga, the turbaned Sikh, the Muslim, and the Hindu—all stood equal before the state. Each had equal voting rights and the rights to representation and public office. In short, they had equal civil, political, and social rights. The constitution said so.

Following the Indian example, Pakistan and Malaysia too sought to incorporate gender, racial, and ethnic equality into their citizenship while balancing Islamic and Malay majoritarian claims to an ethnic-based citizenship. Often, these rights for women and minority religious and caste groups were challenged by social practices at the local level. It was precisely because of this tension between a modern civic conception of citizenship and cultural practices that the states implemented several policies to protect individual rights from encroachment by local social practices. Enhancement of these rights meant empowering historically marginalized groups through affirmative action for scheduled castes and tribes in India, for Malays and other indigenous groups in Malaysia, and for regional territorial majorities in Pakistan. In this effort, the Indian and Malaysian states have been more successful than their Pakistani counterpart.

Alternatively, cynics would argue that marginalized and minority groups do not possess any meaningful citizenship, that they are bereft of any welfare benefits and civil liberties. Discrimination, prejudice, and violence against the homeless, women, and minorities have all led to a second-class citizenship for marginalized groups. However, even critics cannot ignore the rising literacy rates, improving health indicators, and the economic and political role of these groups as a result of active state intervention to enhance their citizenship rights.

If citizenship is a privilege, it requires the development of an active and responsible citizenry to protect its ideals. Hence, the Indian, Malaysian, and Pakistani constitutions emphasize certain duties and obligations for their citizens. The 1980s heralded the entry of the concept of a "good" active citizen accompanied by a "thick" understanding of citizenship. A thick view of citizenship places emphasis on the responsibilities and duties of a good citizen. A good citizen cherishes and protects the state and enhances the quality of the community of its citizens. This is in contrast to a "thin" conception of citizenship, which is focused primarily on the legal status of citizenship with its attendant bundle of rights conferred by states.[18] For almost forty years, India was characterized by a thin citizenship, focused on entitlements for the poor through antipoverty programs, social justice, and affirmative action for the lower castes, etc. Since many felt marginalized in India, the number of those seeking entitlements in the protected socialistic economy grew by leaps and bounds. India's socialist phase, which lasted until the mid-1980s, expanded the beneficiaries of citizenship, as ever-larger groups were included. The Malaysian state too was overwhelmingly concerned with economically uplifting the Malays through its *bumiputera* policies, enshrined in the NEP. Preferential policies for the *bumiputeras* in business licenses, apartments, shops, and government and university employment marked state intervention on behalf of the Malays and other *bumiputeras*. The Pakistani state tried to redress regional imbalances through affirmative action policies in education and government employment in the various states. The claims of regional identities, such as the Baluch, Sindh, Pakhtun, and Mohajir, challenged the overarching pan-Islamic vision of Pakistan, which was increasingly held together by the army. Even today, regional groups are constantly struggling to increase their share of entitlements from the Pakistani state. Since every group, including the army, wants a piece of the state, citizenship rights have expanded to other sections of society. Citizenship understood this way is primarily about the legal relationship between an individual and the state, where individuals and groups are beneficiaries of entitlements from the state. Pakistani citizenship is thin indeed, with very few groups accountable and answerable as citizens.

A thick or thin understanding of citizenship is a reflection of the imbalance between the rights and responsibilities of citizenship. A different understanding of citizenship puts the onus on individual subjects. This is the New Right's view of citizenship, where individuals have to earn their citizenship, pay their taxes, and be economically self-reliant; their civic virtue leads to active political participation and the shouldering of civic responsibilities (Kymlicka and Norman 1994: 355–357; Mead 1986). This is the new globalized citizen of India, Malaysia, and Pakistan. The emphasis on economic liberalization, less state intervention, and the reduction of welfare and wasteful expenditures are all in the service of this new, market-friendly citizen. This new citizen expects less from the state in the form of welfare allocations and disbursements and is more self-reliant. The focus is less on what benefits one's citizenship status brings with it and more on how citizenship (and the state) can be strengthened by the activities of the individual citizen—the civic duty to pay taxes, volunteer for service, and so on. Will cutting back the state's involvement increase inequality between groups? Is a decrease in the state's welfare and social policies undermining the progress by marginalized groups? Who will benefit or lose with fewer citizenship entitlements disbursed from the Indian, Malaysian, and Pakistani states? The debate on rethinking the role of the state in social citizenship is very shrill in developing countries. With an ever-increasing range of marginalized groups benefiting from state largess and intervention, a multiethnic developing state may not be able to pull back completely. A decline in citizenship rights inevitably follows a decline of the state. In developing countries, the relationship between an active state and the protection and enhancement of citizenship rights is very critical. The privileges of citizenship can protect an individual from a life of penury and exploitation. For many, citizenship is precious.

Overextended Categories

Clearly, developing states are struggling to comprehend the visibility of illegal immigrants, many of whom, with citizen-like documents, lead legitimate lives. Illegal immigrants are a global presence whom states continually attempt to distinguish from their own citizenry via identification markers, all of which is a losing battle. Ignoring the role of documentation in citizenship is to limit our understanding of the boundaries of membership that are erected to keep illegal immigrants at bay. As a result, conceptual confusion prevails in the state-determined terminology on immigration.[19] States have produced a variety of categories to try to make sense of illegal immigration, many of which are inappropriately used, including the mischaracterization of illegal immigrants as "undocumented."[20] They are illegal, but they are not undocumented.

Undocumented immigration is the most popular term and perhaps was appropriate when it was used to describe a situation when state documents were not readily available. But, given today's technology and the ease with which "coyotes" and "mafias" are able to forge passports and other identity documents, it is wrong to characterize illegal immigrants as undocumented. Illegal immigrants are rarely undocumented. At a certain level, it could be argued that paperwork makes legality, and thus these immigrants are ultimately more full citizens than are local residents who lack similar papers. I will demonstrate in chapter 3 that, like illegal immigrants in other developing countries, these immigrants will most likely have as many documents as citizens, if not more. The high propensity of illegal migrants to use fake or real documents until the time that they can acquire "legal" documents means they cannot be characterized as undocumented.

The phrase *irregular immigration* too does not capture the phenomenon. What is "irregular" about irregular immigration? Most irregular immigration happens as regularly as legalized immigration. Is it because irregular immigrants use mountains, rivers, deserts, and remote border areas to cross the border that it becomes irregular? In many cases, they may be using traditional routes of migration (particularly in developing countries), and so the term irregular does not capture the normalcy nor the regularity of the routes used by groups to cross borders. If topography is not the criterion, then is it frequency of travel? It certainly cannot be that, because in many developing countries, including India, Malaysia, and Pakistan (see chapter 1), the flow of irregular immigration is well above the legal flows.

Clandestine immigration is another weak category that is used to characterize illegal immigration. Clandestine from whom? The state knows where these illegal immigrants live in Assam, in Sabah, in Karachi, etc., because sections of the state help them to acquire the paperwork which enables their settlement in many cases. They are hired in industries, in agriculture, in plantations, in brothels, in bazaars, as hawkers on the streets, and in local households as domestic help. The state turns a blind eye to their arrival and presence when there is a labor shortage or when demand is high for cheap labor. They form a large percentage of the populations in the towns, villages, and regions (border regions especially) of the receiving area. The illegal immigration process is certainly not clandestine; it is open and everyone knows about it. The immigrants are visible everywhere; states simply choose not to see them.

Unauthorized immigration is another misfit category. If these immigrants are unauthorized, which authority has not authorized them? When hiring illegal immigrants, the "native" employers either facilitate their documents or willingly hire them with fake or no documents. Their homes, bank accounts, access to medical facilities, and educational institutions are authorized and legitimized through fake or real documentation. The street vendors, restaurant workers, mechanics, and fruit and vegetable sellers in the mushrooming informal economy in the streets of Guwahati (Assam), Kota Kinabalu (Sabah), and Karachi (Sindh) are an indication that state officials are complicit in the "authorization" that ensures their presence (refer to chapter 2). Many work as domestic helpers in the cities of Assam (India), Sabah (Malaysia), and Sindh (Pakistan), and local populations often accept their presence as a regular feature of their households. Their presence is not only visible; it is in some manner clearly authorized. At every level, they are backed by some form of authorization in the practice of citizenship—from a bank account and driver's license to permission for the street vending of fruits and vegetables.

To analyze the lives of document-wielding illegal immigrants posing as citizens in India, Malaysia, and Pakistan, a new set of categories, processes, and subjects will have to emerge. I begin the task with an outline of my approach.

The Approach

As far as case selection is concerned, India, Malaysia, and Pakistan all have histories of lively elections since their independence. While both Malaysia and Pakistan have struggled with illiberal, sometimes authoritarian, challenges to their democratic aspirations, India has continued to carve a democratic path. All three cases display typical features of multiethnic developing countries in that they are diverse multiethnic societies in Asia which have been neglected in the mainstream literature on immigration and citizenship and which are unable to control illegal immigration.

The level of institutionalization in these three states determines the effectiveness of citizenship. Of the three states, the one that is least institutionalized is Pakistan. India has some institutions which are, without question, more robust than those of Malaysia (e.g., the judiciary, especially its upper echelons, and a more democratic party system) but others that are weaker (e.g., corrupt police, local petty officials who are shameless bribe seekers because of their poor salaries). These states share a number of common features with other developing countries in terms of their institutional weaknesses (inadequate birth registration, corruption by ethnic networks, etc.) in documenting and monitoring access to citizenship, but there are also important differences among these states. The chapter on blurred membership (chapter 3) identifies the institutional weaknesses of the citizenship infrastructure in all three states. The state is much more institutionalized in India and Malaysia than in Pakistan, which is inching toward the "failing" end of the spectrum. India and Malaysia, on one hand, and Pakistan, on the other, represent the full range of weakly developed citizenship infrastructures.

Another issue emerges with the occasional identification of illegal immigrants as Muslims, which arose in response to the increasing interest in Muslim immigrants after the attacks on the World Trade Center and the Pentagon on September 11, 2001 (9/11). The West is now worried about the illegal immigration of Muslims, and these states are dealing with Muslim illegal immigrants from the theater of the "war on terror"—Afghans, Pakistanis, Bangladeshis, Indonesians, and southern Filipinos. It might be tempting to overemphasize the Muslim dimensions of the cases I will be examining. However, the Muslim reference, while catchy, is not salient to my overall argument on the role of fake or real documents. Muslim and non-Muslim illegal immigrants (such as Mexican illegal immigrants) are equally capable of acquiring citizenship through documents. Only in areas where their religion has an impact on the ethnic politics of the receiving state (such as in India or Malaysia) will I examine religion as a special subject of concern.

Finally, in order to substantiate my argument, I have collected public and confidential reports by the state governments, proceedings from parliamentary debates, evidence submitted in court cases, census data, and importantly, the large archive of local newspaper reports, local pamphlets, and reports on illegal immigrants to show that illegal immigrants do in fact gain access to citizenship. This research involved going through every locally published news report or article in India, Malaysia, and Pakistan in the last twenty years. Additionally, I conducted fieldwork for a year in Malaysia and made multiple trips to India, using both participant observations and interviews with members of the political elite to strengthen my case that illegal immigrants are voting, and thus accessing citizenship rights. I was also able to document illegal immigrants and their settlements extensively through photographs. Meeting or talking to illegal immigrants was especially difficult and sometimes dangerous, given the tenuous circumstances of their stay, their desire to remain "invisible" from the state, and the potential for harassment by police and other state institutions. Documenting the path of illegal immigrants to citizenship is the task of this book.

Mapping the Book

In this introduction, I have identified some of the theoretical misconceptions that plague our understanding of illegal immigrant citizenship in developing states. The remainder of the book is in two parts. In part I, I introduce a theory of illegal immigrant citizenship, and in part II, I strive to prove it empirically, using cases of illegal immigration to India, Malaysia, and Pakistan.

Part I is dedicated to developing a new theoretical framework that reveals the process by which illegal immigrants settle down in developing states. In chapter 1, I discuss the methodological challenges involved in the study of illegal immigration within developing countries. These methodological problems in turn have led to the neglect of the subject matter. Therefore, I make visible these illegal immigrant flows by producing a variety of data to estimate their magnitude. Revealing these flows has the advantage of making visible a critical factor in the lives of illegal immigrants: the seeping web of networks which are increasingly corroding the state, making it pliable to the needs of illegal immigrants, which I cover in chapter 2. In chapter 3, I discuss the weakly institutionalized character of citizenship in developing countries. This is another critical factor, since it too enables the silent settlement of illegal immigrants. In chapter 4, I combine the factors discussed in chapters 2 (networks of complicity) and 3 (blurred membership) to offer an alternative theory that explains the *process* by which illegal immigrants acquire citizenship. I explain the emergence of the link between individual identity and documentation, demonstrate the process of achieving citizenship, and create a classificatory grid to help us understand the role of documents in the settlement of illegal immigrants.

In part II, I provide empirical proof of illegal immigrants using documents to gain access to citizenship. In chapter 5, I test my theory with evidence of illegal immigrants voting in national elections in India, Malaysia, and Pakistan. In all three states, illegal immigrants are gaining access to citizenship rights through documents and are voting. This result, no doubt, has theoretical consequences for democratic theory and practice. Having acquired all necessary documentary proof in order to vote as Indians, Pakistanis, and Malaysians, illegal immigrants can also join other members of their adopted countries to travel abroad. In chapter 6, I show how illegal immigrants are traveling abroad under assumed citizenship and identities, thus posing a direct challenge to sovereignty and global security. Illegal immigrants are everywhere assumed to be distinct from citizens, but if they are in fact (as I contend they are) behaving as citizens, this would have major theoretical implications for citizenship, which I analyze in the concluding chapter (chapter 7).

Important theoretical implications follow from this study of illegal immigrants behaving as citizens in developing countries. Immigration and citizenship theories broadly offer two models of immigration: inclusive or restrictive. In inclusive regimes, the state welcomes immigration, and in restrictive ones, immigrants are unwelcome. The United States, Australia, and Canada are examples of the former; Germany and Japan are examples of the latter. Amid anxiety in a post–9/11 world and with the rise of anti-immigrant rightist parties, there has been a sharp rise in restrictions on immigrants and their transition to citizenship status. We are living in a world of fear—fear of illegal immigrants, refugees, potential terrorists, and other outsiders.

Ironically, India, Malaysia, and Pakistan show how, for reasons of political and economic exigency, illegal immigrants are welcomed and settled. This puts India, Malaysia, and Pakistan in the first model, but their peculiar paths to immigrant incorporation may show another way in which states that welcome immigrants incorporate them. Documents explain the easy incorporation of illegal immigrants into the citizenships of India, Malaysia, and Pakistan.

Easy incorporation has political consequences for global security: first, the fact that illegal immigrants are able to access citizenship and hold public office in their host states incites anti-immigrant hatred and ethnic conflict based on religious or ethnic differences; second, the documents that facilitate illegal immigration between developing countries are also critical to drug smuggling, gun running, and human trafficking and thus pose a severe challenge to the security of states; third, the settlement of illegal immigrants leads to tensions in bilateral relations between states, for example, between Malaysia and Indonesia, Nepal and India, India and Bangladesh, Pakistan and Afghanistan, Sri Lanka and India, and Malaysia and the Philippines. This book demonstrates the need for scholars of world politics to rethink the impact of documented illegal immigration on a global scale.

Most important, however, are the consequences of this work for our understanding of citizenship itself. In the remainder of this book, I will provide a considerably different view than the one inherited from the developed Western states. It is a vision in which state membership is blurred, the causal relation between status and benefit is sometimes reversed, and people make seamless transitions from illegal immigration to full citizenship status. Documents sometimes create citizens instead of the other way around. This upside-down view of citizenship, I will argue, is in fact much more representative of the political condition in a significant part of the world.

PART I

The Process

WHAT IF I TOLD YOU THAT ILLEGAL IMMIGRATION BETWEEN DEVELOPING countries is invisible to the state and remains neglected internationally? Most international institutions and bodies are unable to conceptually or empirically contend with illegal immigration in developing countries because they lack reliable data, and as a result, they simply ignore the immigration. Invisibility to the state is one of many hurdles that are encountered in seeking to address the following puzzle: how do illegal immigrants gain access to citizenship in developing countries? After all, if illegal immigrants are behaving as citizens in developing countries, what factors enable this counterintuitive phenomenon to occur in spite of the fact that such illegal flows are invisible to states?

To solve this puzzle, I examine two crucial factors, each in a separate chapter (chapters 2 and 3). I begin, however, in chapter 1, with an outline of illegal immigration in India, Malaysia, and Pakistan, which demonstrates the magnitude, strength, and pervasive nature of illegal immigrant networks. Significantly, these hidden networks foster complicity among crucial sections of the state, especially those responsible for guarding the territorial and membership boundaries of the state, which I examine in chapter 2. Minutely analyzing illegal immigrant networks, this chapter reveals the corrosive effect of immigrant networks on the state apparatus—a crucial factor in explaining the settlement of illegal immigrants. Then, in chapter 3, I examine a second important factor: the weakly institutionalized nature of citizenship in developing countries. I note how citizenship in developing countries differs markedly from citizenship in developed countries and thus allows more invisible absorption of illegal immigrants. Weak boundaries of citizenship provide an accommodating environment in which illegal immigrants are able to acquire varieties of identifying documents. Finally, in chapter 4, I bring together networks of complicity and weakly institutionalized citizenship to show how they collectively enable the acquisition of citizenship-indicating documents, thus enabling full membership for illegal immigrants. I provide figures to illustrate the process and thereafter categorize the world according to documents to show the global application of my conceptual argument. These four chapters present the conceptual framework of my argument, explaining how it is that illegal immigrants gain instant access to citizenship through the use of a variety of documents. This is the phenomenon of documentary citizenship.

1

Searching for Illegal Immigrants

ILLEGAL IMMIGRATION IN DEVELOPING COUNTRIES IS OCCURRING IN LARGE numbers but rarely informs theories of citizenship and immigration. Why is this the case? I contend that the reasons for this are twofold: one is a methodological problem, and the other is a conceptual one. The former hinges on the latter primarily because of the questionable validity of the data generated in developing countries. There is also a concern with the actual, physical collection of data in developing countries due to the sensitive nature of the subject. This renders the immigrants invisible at the national level, and they are thus experienced only at the local level. The "conquest" of their invisibility involves the naming, counting, and classifying of these subjects, many of whom want to escape the scrutinizing gaze of the state (Scott, Tehranian, and Mathias 2002: 7). Making them legible also renders them legitimate to those analyzing global migration. Visibility brings analytical attention. Visibility comes through partial accounts of the national infrastructure of citizenship—the imprecise surveys, censuses, and government reports—combined with vernacular accounts of illegal subjects via news and nongovernmental organization (NGO) reports.

Making these localized subjects visible is the task of this chapter. Given their mobility and their ability to consistently escape the gaze of national institutions, this is no easy task. I begin by analyzing the neglect of illegal immigration within developing countries, pointing out the troubled relationship between the state and data generation. These methodological challenges explain why illegal immigration is rendered invisible. In the next section, I lift the veil on illegal immigration in some countries, establishing the large and expanding number of illegal immigrants in India, Malaysia, and Pakistan. In particular, I focus on illegal Bangladeshis settled in Assam, Northeast India. Determining the scale and distribution of illegal flows is the first step toward uncovering the process by which these immigrant networks enable settlement in India. Thereafter, I count the invisible flows of Filipinos and Indonesians to Malaysia, paying particular attention to their pervasive networks in Sabah, East Malaysia. In the same way, illegal Afghans and Bangladeshis have been silently absorbed in Pakistan, making it necessary to give them a voice and visibility by counting them.

One can give a variety of reasons for why the study of illegal immigration *between* developing countries has been neglected: inhospitable physical living conditions, unreliable and/or unavailable data, and, sometimes, hostile illegal immigrant subjects all deter researchers. However, given that a majority of the people immigrating live in developing countries, it is possible that studying their experiences in their regions may lead to newer theories or, at the very least, to an improvement of current explanations. Illegal immigration is after all affecting both developing and developed countries. In a time of globalization when immigration is becoming easier, theoretical innovation may have important policy implications. This chapter first investigates the analytical neglect of illegal immigrants in developing countries and thereafter makes them "legible" by documenting their presence.

Immigration between Developing Countries

To understand illegal immigrants' access to citizenship, I turned to international institutions for information about the large illegal immigration flows to India, Malaysia, and Pakistan. I was met with a deafening silence in the literature. Indeed, an occasional acknowledgment of these flows without any further information is the best I came across. A typical example is the United Nations' *World Economic and Social Survey* (WESS), which cited a study by the International Labor Organization (ILO) (United Nations 2004: 55):

> [U]nauthorized migrants cross poorly patrolled borders without being controlled and merge with a country's population. By some estimates, Asia may have several million migrants in an irregular situation. The largest numbers probably involve Nepalese and Bangladeshis in India; Afghans in Pakistan and the Islamic Republic of Iran; Indonesians and Filipinos in Malaysia; and migrants from Myanmar in Thailand.

There were, however, no estimates, no data, and no brief outlines included in this report, only more of the deep silence which has pervaded my inquiry into these huge illegal immigrations in the developing world. Ignored and marginalized by the literature on immigration and citizenship, the edifice of our theories, carefully crafted over the years from a variety of Western experiences, continue to stand tall, even as waves of illegal immigrants have transformed large parts of the developing world.

Migration *between* the developing countries of Asia, Africa, and Latin America does not inform most studies of immigration. A review of immigration literature reveals a failure to explain illegal immigration as more than a by-product of (inadequate) controls on regular legal migration. It also shows the continued dependence on a South-North (poor to rich) framework for explaining immigrant movement.[1] The leading theories of immigration are written to account for patterns and problems arising in developed countries when migrants from developing countries enter. In other words, the dominant approach to immigration describes the structural forces that drive emigration *from* developing countries and immigration *into* developed countries (Massey 1999: 304).[2] Yet, according to the *World Migration Report 2000*, many more international migrants move to developing countries than to developed countries.[3] Particularly neglected in immigration literature are cases from Asia, the continent where the largest number of immigrants reside.[4] Taking these data into account, it is clear that there is a need for a distinctive argument on illegal immigration based on cases from developing countries.

Indeed, a large percentage of the migration taking place within the developing world (which I shall call the South-South flows) has been viewed (when it has been viewed at all) as irrelevant to the study of immigration. As the *World Migration Report* 2000 points out, "more than half of international migrants live in developing countries," and "a smaller share of international migrants go to developed countries" (United Nations and International Organization for Migration 2000: 6). Further, the report recognizes that "the largest numbers of international migrants are located in Asia." Importantly for my cases, most immigration takes place within the same continent or is localized. A review of immigration trends between 1975 and 1994 from Asian states shows that, excluding emigration from China, "on average well under 10 percent of the migrants left Asia," which highlights the localized nature of these flows (United Nations and International Organization for Migration 2000: 6).[5] Table 1.1 illustrates these trends from 1970 until 2000. In table 1.1, notice the dominant share of immigrants located in Asia, in contrast to other regions of the world. With regard to international immigration flows in Asia, Graeme Hugo (1997: 275), a demographer of Asian migratory flows, has noted "the increasing volume of undocumented migration, which now is at least equal in scale to, and probably larger than, regular labor migration." Ernst Spaan (1994: 93) has also claimed that there exists a "trend away from the more 'traditional' labor migration from LDCs [less developed countries] to rich, industrialized Western Europe and the relatively more recent movement to Middle Eastern oil-rich states, *to temporary*

TABLE 1.1. World immigrants by region 1970–2000 (in millions)

	1970	1980	1990	2000
World	81.5	99.8	154.0	174.9
Developing countries	43.2	52.1	64.3	64.6
Developed countries (excluding USSR)	35.2	44.5	59.3	80.8
Asia[a]	28.1	32.3	41.8	43.8
North America	13.0	18.1	27.6	40.8
Europe[b]	18.7	22.2	26.3	32.8
USSR (former)	3.1	3.3	30.3	29.5
Africa	9.9	14.1	16.2	16.3
Latin America/Caribbean	5.8	6.1	7.0	5.9
Oceania	3.0	3.8	4.8	5.8

[a]Excluding Armenia, Azerbaijan, Georgia, Kazakhstan, Kyrgystan, Tajikistan, Turkmenistan and Uzbekistan.
[b]Excluding Belarus, Estonia, Latvia, Lithuania, the Republic of Moldova, the Russian Federation and Ukraine.

Source: United Nations and International Organization for Migration (2005: 396).

migration of low-skilled labor between nations with less developed economies" (emphasis mine).

Many flows in developing countries are of illegal immigration, and many of those migrants are moving from one condition of poverty to another. Approximately 1.2 billion people in developing countries live in absolute poverty (United Nations Development Program 2000: 4).[6] Poor illegal immigrants are moving between states that do not have standardized documentation to distinguish their citizens from immigrants. Many of these developing states have limited resources to monitor and control illegal immigration. The movement of the poor across unmarked borders into poor countries with incomplete state formation is a neglected area of research marked by conceptual ambiguity.

Scholars may contend that my previous claims about the primacy of immigration between developing countries, based on the *World Migration Report 2000*, was only true until the 1990s. Five years later, the *World Migration Report 2005* would seem to contradict my claim by establishing the dominance of immigration to developed countries from 2000 onward. The 2005 report also states that, for the 1990–2000 decade, the stock of immigrants over a ten-year period rose by only 300,000 persons for *all* developing states (64.3 million in 1990 to 64.6 million in 2000; see table 1.1). It is hard to believe that, for a ten-year period, the total migratory population in the developing world averaged only 30,000 individuals per year. Just the migratory stock in South and Southeast Asia exceeds that figure for the same period. Is the interpretation of immigration data in the *World Migration Report 2005* outdated or wrong? Which *World Migration Report* should we believe?

The source of this insufficient or contradictory data is the noncomprehensive character of the national censuses upon which developing states rely for their immigration figures. In turn, developing states supply these incomplete or faulty figures to the international bodies. This marginalizes immigration within the developing world. Illegal immigration in the developing world is neglected because it poses tremendous methodological challenges, not least of which are the hurdles erected by the state.

The Challenge of State-Generated Data on Illegal Immigration

The state plays a crucial role in generating the statistics we use regarding developing countries (Sadiq 2005b). It is the best, and sometimes the only, source of data on many political phenomena.[7] Given the constraints imposed by the often necessary reliance on state data, there are several methodological issues confronting the study of developing countries. Clearly, making factual claims based on data and statistics supplied by developing states is one way of analyzing political and social realities. It also presents many challenges.

This book underscores a methodological problem for scholars: how representative are the data we use for the problems we seek to analyze? More important for a scholar of illegal immigration between developing countries: are the data a true reflection of the problem we are studying? Very often, the sophistication of the statistical techniques and the parsimonious character of the statistical output hide the quality of the data being used. In studying illegal immigration in developing countries, it is important to be careful about what we mean by data and how we acquire and operationalize it. This is a widespread problem for social sciences scholars who study the developing world, where conditions are not amenable to the collection of data. Therefore, the *politics* of data collection is as important as the operationalization of the data and its subsequent use to build larger data sets, which can then be used for broad comparisons (or large *N* analysis).

While some of these data problems have been noted as those associated with weak statistical coverage under conditions of weak immigration control in developing countries (Zlotnik 1987: ix), others highlight the varying and sometimes ambiguous definitions used in surveys as the sources of such statistical errors. For example, Manuel Garcia Griego (1987: 1246) has explained the discrepancy between the low emigration numbers in Mexican sources based on the state-supervised export of labor and the number of Mexican agricultural workers admitted by the United States as resulting from "the procedures used to operationalize the definitions established by law, though vague definitions are also often at fault."

I am highlighting problems with data collection and statistical coverage that go beyond questions of definitional ambiguity and lack of statistical control: even with tighter control, better definitions, and their operationalization, we will have to confront the challenges that gender, cultural practices, and state manipulation throw at our methods of data generation. Therefore, I assert that we have to become creative and develop methods to examine issues that do not always arise from, for, or of the state. The complexities encountered in estimating the population of illegal immigrants and the problems with the census categories that try to accommodate illegal immigrants show us the value of local knowledge.

Shifting fuzzy categories in census reports and unreliable official immigration data present problems for scholars who are researching immigration or ethnicity. Most researchers of India, Malaysia, and Pakistan take government figures on immigration and immigrant ethnic groups at face value. Sometimes, they may substantiate their national data with figures on immigration given by the ILO or regional Asian organizations. But these organizations usually take their estimates and census classifications from the Indian, Malaysian, or Pakistani governments and may back those estimates with figures given by journalists from leading magazines, such as the *Far Eastern Economic Review* or *Asiaweek*. Very rarely do researchers question the ethnic breakdown and classification in the official census or the basic immigration data.[8]

Moreover, sections of the state in India, Malaysia, and Pakistan have an interest in suppressing information about the inclusion of illegal immigrants. This is not new. All of the following states are suspected to have misreported or hidden the magnitude of portions of their populations: Bangladesh with regard to its Hindu population; Malaysia with regard to Filipinos and Indonesians; and Pakistan with regard to its immigrant Afghan populations. Hania Zlotnik (1987: ix), from the Population Division of the United Nations, has pointed out that, in the 1980s, "the political sensitivity of worker migration in the oil-rich countries of the Middle East and North Africa...led to a virtual information blackout." Every state, democratic or authoritarian, suppresses information about certain groups or phenomena. Rogers Smith's research shows us that distorting state statistics to project the preferred image of the "people" as an empirical reality is an example of this sort of politics.[9] For many social scientists who do large N work and spend just a few months or no time in each country they select, there is a tendency to uncritically accept census and other economic data provided by government agencies. Merely running regressions on immigration data provided by India, Malaysia, and Pakistan will not only give false results but also overlooks the fudging involved in the breakdown of ethnic groups, which is so important for many scholars studying immigrant groups. Also missed will be state complicity in the phenomenon being studied. That is why some scholars caution us about national data. National aggregates can be spurious, washing out regional or local circumstances and politics which may determine local inputs (Rudolph and Rudolph 1987: 347–348).

For scholars prone to doing large *N* work on illegal immigration, the results could be hiding more than they are revealing. Since data from developing countries are of questionable validity, they pose methodological problems for researchers. Ashish Bose (2005: 374), a prominent Indian economist and demographer, cautions:

> Above all, we would plead for in-depth field studies to get a realistic picture at the grass roots level. This will provide a reality check to regression analysis. In a country of India's size and incredible social, economic, cultural and demographic diversity, all generalisations may be valid or invalid depending on the level at which one is generalising!

In the sweep of generalizations that many of us seek, we could be "seeing" what the state wants us to see (Scott 1998). For this purpose, the state often has politicians, bureaucrats, and military personnel acting as gatekeepers.[10] Controlling research and data output on politically sensitive topics, such as illegal immigration, is a feature of both democratic and authoritarian regimes. The state has much to hide and lie about, and a critical social science will have to take a microscopic look at illegal immigration to be aware of any statistical manipulation of reality. Only such a focus will reveal the contours of a population that is visible locally while remaining opaque to the rest of the world.

Counting the Invisible

Invisibility is a major challenge that scholars studying illegal immigration in developing countries confront. Publicly, no one has systematic data, but if one digs deeper, the state has confidential estimates based on reports and surveys conducted by intelligence or police agencies. Dig deeper, and one comes across several civil organizations and state agencies dispersed across the country that are collecting material. The data are unorganized, uncoordinated from the center, and collected for the short-term goals of the agencies that are confronting an invisible illegal immigrant population. Invisibility of illegal immigrants is possible because the phenomenon remains unrecognized by the federal authorities often responsible for the regulation of both immigration and citizenship. Meanwhile, international agencies are unable to provide any information on these flows. In fact, the United Nations Development Fund (UNDF), the United Nations Children's Fund (UNICEF), and the ILO rely on census and other data supplied by individual governments and are the last in the information chain to have any reliable or concrete evidence on the phenomenon. Even as networks of illegal immigrants facilitate the movement of more and more people across international borders in the developing world, on the surface they remain mostly invisible.

Additionally, some critics will dismiss these illegal flows as refugee flows resulting from political violence. They are wrong. While political violence does create refugees, such as when Bangladesh declared independence from Pakistan in 1971 or during the insurgency of the 1980s in the southern Philippines, these refugee flows only augment the networks which traditional immigration flows have introduced. Once the political violence and turmoil dies down, these networks facilitate and continue the historical illegal immigration over the region. It is for this reason that believing a stable Afghanistan will stop illegal immigration to Pakistan is misguided. Also an illusion is the hope that a peace treaty in the southern Philippines will halt the illegal immigration of Sulus and Bajaus to East Malaysia. Similarly, the hope that political and economic stability in Bangladesh will curb illegal immigration to India is wishful thinking. There has been historical immigration in these areas, and those networks are only amplified and reconfigured by the refugee flow, thus leading to continued illegal immigration of Afghans to Pakistan, Bangladeshis to India, and Filipinos to Malaysia even after these states stabilize.

Uncovering the existence of illegal immigrants will (a) fill a big gap in the estimates of international institutions and the literature on illegal immigration, and (b) expose the deep ethnic networks below the surface. Exploring which features of these networks facilitate the silent, almost effortless, absorption of illegal immigrants will be the task for subsequent chapters. However, let us first give concrete and historical shape to the invisible illegal immigrant population.

Bangladeshis in India

There has been a long tradition of immigration from the area now covered by the sovereign state of Bangladesh to the area now covered by Assam and West Bengal (states within the federal union of India) as both regions were part of undivided British India. Assam, located in northeastern India along the border with Bangladesh, was sparsely populated and the colonial state was eager to see it settled so that local agricultural and commodity resources could be exploited. Hence, labor was imported from the Hindi-speaking states of North India as well as from the Bengali-speaking areas that now constitute West Bengal (in India) and Bangladesh. Sylhet, a region that now falls in Bangladesh, was a major exporter of labor to areas in Assam during the British Empire. So long as British India united these areas, this was called internal migration. Assam, Northeast India, and Bangladesh were well connected through railway, road, and port routes that animated life in this corner of the British Empire. When Pakistan and Bangladesh were carved out of the Indian subcontinent through the partitions of 1947 and 1971, what had been internal migra-tion became international—and mostly illegal—migration. New borders emerged to divide what were previously zones of free movement and free trade. The borders are "midnight's children"—paths that were legal and customary became illegal overnight as South Asia was partitioned (Rushdie 1980). Today, unregulated flows of illegal immigrants deepen traditional immigrant networks along these old migratory routes.

India and Bangladesh share a 4,096-kilometer (km) border that runs along five Indian states: Mizoram, Tripura, Meghalaya, Assam, and West Bengal (see figure 1.1); the area is largely forest, hills, small rivers, and river islands—very difficult terrain to

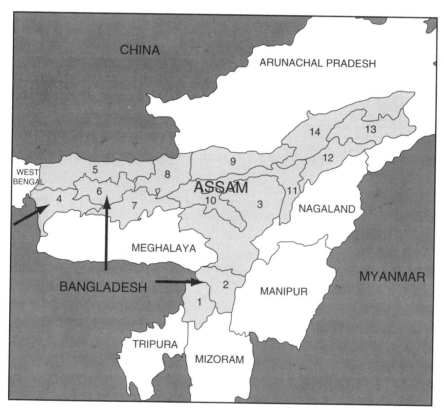

FIGURE 1.1. Illegal immigration from Bangladesh to Assam, Northeast India. Arrows indi-cate the direction of illegal immigration. Numbers denote the parliamentary constituencies in Assam: Karimganj (1), Silchar (2), Autonomous District (3), Dhubri (4), Kokrajhar (5), Barpeta (6), Gauhati (7), Mangaldoi (8), Tezpur (9), Nowgong (10), Kaliabor (11), Jorhat (12), Dibrugarh (13), and Lakhimpur (14). White areas indicate states in Northeast India: Assam, Meghalaya, Tripura, Mizoram, Manipur, Nagaland and Arunachal Pradesh. *Source*: Adapted from the parliamentary map used by the Election Commission of India (http://www.eci.gov.in/ElectionMaps/PC/S03/index_fs.htm).

regulate. Since a major river, the Brahmaputra, and its tributaries run through the Indo-Bangladesh border, many Bangladeshis immigrate by simply walking across or using a boat on the rivers. Many immigrants settle on large river islands known as *char*, using the river to go back and forth between India and Bangladesh. *Char* lands tend to be rather inaccessible, making it easier for illegal immigrants to settle and to remain invisible to state authorities. Further inland, the Barak and the Brahmaputra valley have fertile agricultural lands and ample water resources, and the latter has become the preferred destination for most illegal Bangladeshi immigrants. Bangladesh shares a 262-kilometer border with Assam, and only a limited area has been fenced. Bangladeshi illegal immigrants have already begun cutting the fence (BBC 2005).

Leading public figures from the government have given a range of estimates for the illegal immigration of Bangladeshis to India: (a) a former cabinet home minister of India, Indrajit Gupta, gave an estimate of 10 million to the Parliament;[11] (b) a former deputy prime minister, L. K. Advani, estimated the number to be 15 million;[12] and (c) a former senior bureaucrat in the government, B. Raman, has faith in an estimate of 20 million (Raman 2003).[13] With an estimated 350,000 illegal immigrants entering India annually, the illegal immigrant population in India is in the range of 15–18 million, according to a report by the Law Commission of India, which had access to every possible source in the state, including confidential figures from the Home Ministry of India.[14] It is a common perception that Assam (4 million), West Bengal (5.4 million), and the cities of Delhi and Mumbai receive most of this illegal immigration (Law Commission of India 2000: 5). However, there is no doubt that Assam is among the worst affected, and according to a confidential report sent to the president of India by the governor of Assam, the settlement of illegal Muslim immigrants is changing the demography of Assam, which may contribute to "the long cherished design of [a] greater...Bangladesh" maintained by Islamic fundamentalists (Governor of Assam 1998).[15] The chief minister of Maharashtra too supports this view by explicitly stating that "illegal Bangladeshis are a security threat."[16]

Knowing that illegal immigrants from Bangladesh prevaricate on the census, Sanjoy Hazarika (2000: 226), a leading scholar of Assam, has highlighted the "need to match religious data against birth place and actual growth rates" as one way of capturing the extent of the illegal immigration flow. Using figures on the number of Muslims in order to measure the scale of illegal immigration from Bangladesh is a strategy that has been suggested by other leading scholars. The reason for focusing on religion in India is due to one of the inherent limitations of the Indian census and other official data, a limitation that the late Myron Weiner, a distinguished scholar of Indian migration, recognized early when he argued that "people tend to lie about most things—their age, their wives, even the school they went to. Very few people lie about their religion."[17]

TABLE 1.2. States with more than 10% Muslim population, 2001

State/UT	Total population	Muslim population	Muslims (%)
India	1,028,610,328	138,188,240	13.4
Lakshadweep	60,650	57,903	95.5
Jammu & Kashmir	10,143,700	6,793,240	67.0
Assam	26,655,528	8,240,611	30.9
West Bengal	80,176,197	20,240,543	25.2
Kerala	31,841,374	7,863,842	24.7
Uttar Pradesh	166,197,921	30,740,158	18.5
Bihar	82,998,509	13,722,048	16.5
Jharkhand	26,945,829	3,731,308	13.8
Karnataka	52,850,562	6,463,127	12.2
Uttaranchal	8,489,349	1,012,141	11.9
Delhi	13,850,507	1,623,520	11.7
Maharashtra	96,878,627	10,270,485	10.6
Total	597,088,753	110,758,926	

Source: Bose (2005: 371), table 3.

In a recent article, a leading Indian demographer utilizes the latest census to disaggregate the concentration and spread of the Muslim population across India.[18] States such as Assam, West Bengal, and Delhi, which receive the bulk of Bangladeshi illegal immigration, are in the top twelve states/union territories (UTs) with the largest concentration of Muslims. Table 1.2 displays the twelve states and UTs in India with more than a 10 percent Muslim population—covering 80.2 percent of the Muslim population in India (Bose 2005).

Critics would argue that the large growth in the Muslim population of Assam (or West Bengal) may be due to natural increases in the Muslim fertility rate vis-à-vis the Hindu rate or due to the internal migration of Muslims from other regions of the country to these states. However, what these critics ignore is the long-standing tradition of immigration into this region through historic travel and trade routes from countries such as Bangladesh. Ashish Bose (2005: 371) recognizes the role of Bangladeshi immigration:

If politicians are worried about the high growth rates of Muslims in the border districts [of India], they should express their concern and make the government stop undocumented migration (comprising refugee migration and economic migration). It is nobody's point that Muslim fertility has gone up in border districts and that is why the Muslim proportion is increasing. Therefore, migration must be taken into account.

The consensus among immigration experts in India is that differences between Muslim and Hindu growth rates are explained by continuous immigration from Bangladesh.

TABLE 1.3. Assam population

Religion	% of total population (1991)	% increase during 1971–1991*	% of total population (2001)	% increase during 1991–2001
Hindus	67.13	+41.89	64.9	14.95
Muslims	28.43	+77.42	30.9	29.30

* There was no census held in Assam in 1981.

Note: Other religious communities, such as Christians (3.32 percent), Sikhs (.07 percent), Buddhists (.29 percent), and Jains (.09 percent) are small or negligible in Assam.

Sources: Adapted from Directorate of Census Operations, Assam (1999b: 4); Registrar General of India. (2004); and Office of the Registrar General and Census Commissioner, India (2007).

Indeed, immigration plays a crucial role in the changing population mix of Assam, India. Let us now examine what state sources reveal about Assam. The governor of Assam in his report to the president of India asserts that there has been over a 20 percent increase in the number of voters in as many as 45 percent (57 of 126) of the electoral constituencies between 1994 and 1997, whereas the national average for the increase in voters is about 7.4 percent. The governor further pointed out the excessive Muslim growth rate of 77.42 percent since 1971 to stress the urgency of Bangladeshi illegal immigration (Gokhale 2001). An examination of the 1991 Assam census (see table 1.3) corroborates parts of the report since the population growth rate for Muslims between 1971 and 1991 (77.42 percent) is close to double that of Hindus (41.89 percent). The percentage of Hindus fell further between the censuses of 1991 (67.13 percent) and 2001 (64.9 percent) (Registrar General of India 2004).

According to the census, the highest percentage growth rate of population for all of Assam occurred during 1951–1961 (34.98 percent), 1961–1971 (34.95 percent), and 1971–1991 (53.26 percent)—the periods with the largest illegal immigration flows into Assam from neighboring Bangladesh (see table 1.4). Dhubri, Barpeta, Kamrup, Nagaon, and Goalpara are districts in Assam that are major recipients of illegal immigration from Bangladesh, and all display high population growth rates during the periods 1951–1961, 1961–1971, and 1971–1991 (see table 1.4). Notice how the population growth rate shoots up sharply from the 1950s in these districts and continues to grow after the independence of Bangladesh. The immigration flows prior to independence in 1971, especially the very high rates of 1921–1931 in the Nagaon and Barpeta (see table 1.4) districts, established networks that enabled illegal immigrants to settle later, between the 1970s to the present. More recent census reports suggest that the population growth rate abruptly fell to 18.92 percent during 1991–2001.[19] This coincides with the implementation of many anti-immigrant schemes that followed the rise of the Bharatiya Janata Party (BJP) to power.

TABLE 1.4. Percentage decadal variation in population of Assam by district

State			District (%)			
Decade	Assam	Dhubri	Barpeta	Kamrup	Nagaon	Goalpara
1901–1911	16.99	29.97	20.02	11.10	15.84	29.97
1911–1921	20.48	26.92	34.04	7.06	31.94	26.92
1921–1931	19.91	15.76	69.02	9.38	41.35	15.76
1931–1941	20.40	14.83	44.06	19.21	15.37	14.83
1941–1951	19.93	9.25	18.77	17.17	36.65	9.25
1951–1961	34.98	27.62	32.62	37.73	35.91	37.10
1961–1971	34.95	40.51	35.81	38.80	38.99	45.88
1971–1981*						
1971–1991	53.26	56.57	43.02	65.72	51.26	54.12
1991–2001	18.92	23.42	18.53	25.75	22.30	23.07

*The census was not conducted in 1981. The figures were worked out by the Indian census using interpolation.

Sources: Adapted from Directorate of Census Operations, Assam (1997: 118–120); Unni (1999); Office of the Registrar General and Census Commissioner, India (1998a: 278). Office of the Registrar General and Census Commissioner, India (2007).

During 1991–2001, a declining population growth trend can be observed in the population of Assam overall even as falling decadal growth rates mark certain districts: Nalbari (11.98 percent), Bongaigaon (12.23 percent), and Dibrugarh (12.43 percent).[20] This has, however, not affected the districts which have been heavy receivers of illegal immigrants from Bangladesh, such as Kamrup, Dhubri, Goalpara, Karimganj, Barpeta, and Nagaon. Except for Karimganj, which lies in the Barak valley settled by Bengali Hindus, the rest of the districts are located in the fertile and heavily populated Brahmaputra valley favored by illegal immigrants (Directorate of Census Operations 1999a).[21] These districts continued to have increasing population growth rates throughout the last decade of the twentieth century. The 1991 census reveals another interesting detail: 30.29 percent of the total rural population was Muslim while only 13.55 percent of the urban population was Muslim—indicating Muslim preference for rural areas (Directorate of Census Operations 1999b: 4).[22] This supports the view that already settled Muslims (former noncitizens) and recent Muslim illegal immigrants from Bangladesh prefer to settle in rural areas of the Brahmaputra valley, where they can lead their lives with relative anonymity—outside the clutches of the authorities, who tend to be more visible in urban areas of a poorly developed state such as Assam.

The top six districts with the highest population densities and largest concentrations of illegal immigrants hardly changed their rankings between 1991 and 2001 (see table 1.5).[23] The density of population for Assam went up from 286 persons per square kilometer in the 1991 census to 340 persons per square kilometer in 2001. The

TABLE 1.5. Assam: District population density in 1991 and 2001

Rank	District	Density 1991	District	Density 2001
	Assam	**286**		**340**
1	Nagaon	476	Nagaon	604
2	Dhubri	470	Dhubri	584
3	Kamrup	460	Kamrup	579
4	Karimganj	457	Karimganj	555
5	Nalbari	450	Barpeta	506
6	Barpeta	427	Nalbari	504

Sources: Unni 1999; Directorate of Census Operations, Assam (1999a: 24). For 2001 data: Office of the Registrar General and Census Commissioner, India (2007); Assam government Web site, which has posted results of the 2001 census (population density, etc.) at http://assamgov.org/districtinfo/; and Web sites of the respective Assam districts: http://nagaon.nic.in, http://dhubri.nic.in, http://kamrup.nic.in, http://karimganj.nic.in, http://barpeta.nic.in, and http://nalbari.nic.in

density of population (in persons per square km) is highest in the immigrant-receiving and/or Muslim-populated districts of Nagaon (604), followed by Dhubri (584), Kamrup (579), Karimganj (555), Barpeta (506), and Nalbari (504). Other immigrant-receiving districts with high density include Marigaon (455), Goalpara (451), and Hailakandi (409). The areas with low population densities in Assam either are inhabited by tribal members (38 persons per square km in North Cachar Hills and 78 persons per square km in Karbi Anglong) or are overwhelmingly settled by Hindus (172 in the district of Dhemaji). These areas are avoided by illegal immigrants because they are considered to be hostile territory inhabited by native groups opposed to immigrants.

Having already examined the growth rates, we shall now interpret the religious and birth place data. In this section, I will show the extent of illegal immigration by demonstrating that at least two districts have shifted from Hindu to Muslim majorities since the late 1980s. We start by examining the growth rates at the district level for Muslims and contrast them with those of Hindus to see if there is a significant difference. In table 1.6, we look at districts where the Muslim population was already a majority or became a majority (>50 percent) between 1971 and 2001, or is fast approaching that level. Incidentally, these districts have some of the highest population densities[24] and also display a Muslim growth rate that is significantly higher than (often, more than double, and in a few instances, four or five times) the Hindu growth rate (see table 1.6). As a result of high rates of illegal immigration from Bangladesh, there are significantly high population growth rates among Muslim populations. Consequently, these districts resulted in a Hindu-majority district becoming a Muslim-majority district (see table 1.6). For example, Barpeta and Goalpara went from being Hindu-majority in 1971 to Muslim-majority in 1991, and the Muslims further strengthened their share by 2001. Nagaon and Karimganj shifted from being

TABLE 1.6. District distribution of population by religion, 1971–2001

State/ district	Census/ year	Total population	Hindus			Muslims		
			% total population	% increase 1971–1991	% increase 1991–2001	% total population	% increase 1971–1991	% increase 1991–2001
Assam	2001	26,655,528	64.89			30.92		
	1991	22,414,322	67.13	41.89	14.95	28.43	77.42	29.30
	1971	14,626,152	72.51			24.56		
Nagaon	2001	2,314,629	47.80			50.99		
	1991	1,893,171	51.73	31.19	12.96	47.19	81.91	32.12
	1971	1,251,636	59.64			39.24		
Dhubri	2001	1,637,344	24.74			74.29		
	1991	1,332,475	28.73	29.24	5.81	70.45	71.13	29.58
	1971	851,045	34.80			64.46		
Karimganj	2001	1,007,976	46.70			52.30		
	1991	827,063	50.15	29.20	13.50	49.17	57.93	29.63
	1971	582,108	55.14			44.24		
Barpeta	2001	1,647,201	40.19			59.37		
	1991	1,385,659	40.26	12.64	18.66	56.07	64.84	25.87
	1971	968,887	51.12			48.65		
Marigaon	2001	776,256	52.21			47.59		
	1991	639,982	54.56	38.69	16.14	45.31	69.42	27.45
	1971	423,901	59.36			40.36		
Goalpara	2001	822,035	38.22			53.71		
	1991	668,138	39.89	22.67	17.88	50.18	86.23	31.69
	1971	433,516	50.11			41.53		
Hailakandi	2001	542,872	41.11			57.63		
	1991	449,048	43.71	34.34	13.72	54.79	55.56	27.17
	1971	307,695	47.48			51.40		

Source: Adapted from Directorate of Census Operations (1999b: 10–16) and Office of the Registrar General and Census Commissioner, India (2007).

Hindu-majority in 1991 to Muslim-majority in 2001. Marigaon is following closely, as the Muslim population jumps every decade. In Hailakandi, the Muslim population became a majority in the 1970s and further increased its share of the population through the 1980s and 1990s. Today, more than two-thirds of the residents in Dhubri are Muslim. The 2001 census shows that not only has Assam's Muslim population jumped to almost 31 percent, but out of a total of twenty-three districts in the state, almost ten are over 30 percent Muslim (Registrar General of India 2004).[25]

There is no official state-sponsored immigration agreement or network between India and Bangladesh which lays down norms and standards about how Bangladeshi immigrants should be handled. Bangladesh has steadfastly denied that its citizens cross over to India, despite the fact that, during the 1991 census, out of a total Assam population of 22,414,332, almost 288,109 persons reported themselves as having been born in Bangladesh (Directorate of Census Operations 1998: 30, 38). This is about 84.85 percent of the foreign-born people living in Assam. A closer look at the district-level data by birth place reveals an interesting detail: most districts where "self-confessing" Bangladeshi illegal immigrants lived at the time of this census were also major immigrant-receiving areas during this period. Therefore, the Nagaon district had a large number of people (43,171) own up to having been born in Bangladesh, followed by Cachar (34,011), then Karimganj (28,568), Kamrup (21,692), Bongaigaon (21,195), and finally Barpeta (20,470; Directorate of Census Operations 1998).[26] Other areas traditionally known for receiving high illegal immigration from Bangladesh also had high figures for self-confessed Bangladeshi-born people: Dhubri, Goalpara, Kokrajhar, Darrang, and Nalbari districts. Most illegal immigrants falsify or hide any information linking them to Bangladesh, legal immigration is small, and legal naturalization is rare in India; therefore, to find 288,109 persons identifying themselves as being Bangladesh-born in just the state of Assam is remarkable in the face of official Bangladeshi pronouncements that there is no illegal immigration to India.

Since ten out of twenty-three districts in Assam have substantial clusters of Muslim, Bengali-speaking areas, these thick settlements already contain the invisible networks which Bangladeshis utilize to settle down in India. Over the decades, the networks have only deepened. The next section analyzes the parallel situation for Malaysia. In Malaysia too, the magnitude of illegal Muslim Indonesians and Filipinos is concealed from the state, meaning that it is invisible in official international and national figures. And yet, below the surface lies an intricate web of networks that enable Filipinos and Indonesians to settle in Malaysia.

Illegal Filipinos and Indonesians in Malaysia

While illegal immigrants from Indonesia and the Philippines are migrating to several states within Malaysia and are more visible in big cities such as Kuala Lumpur, the state most acutely affected is Sabah (see figure 1.2). How noticeable is the presence of illegal immigrants in Sabah? In a letter to the editor of a local daily, a citizen expressed his/her growing apprehension:

> Ours must be the only place in the world where illegals have the courage to walk about in the streets with impunity, commit crimes, use our overstretched government hospitals, steal our water, attend our schools and milk us of our resources in numerous ways. (*Daily Express* 1999a)

Migration from the Sulu archipelago in the Philippines to Sabah has a long history. Barter and trade existed as early as the ninth century; today, there is a

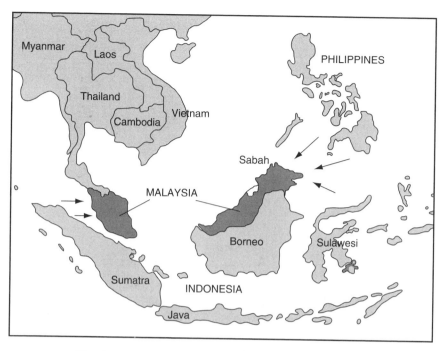

FIGURE 1.2. Illegal immigration to Malaysia from Indonesia and the Philippines. Arrows indicate the direction of illegal immigration.

regional economic trade group formed by Indonesia, the Philippines, Malaysia, and Brunei called BIMP-EAGA. The first migrants to Sabah from the Sulu archipelago arrived in the late fifteenth century when the Spanish began pushing southward toward Sulu and Tawi-Tawi in the southern Philippines. As a result, members of ethnic groups such as the Suluk and the Bajau came to straddle the modern boundaries of Sabah, Malaysia, and the southern Philippines. The second wave of migration is associated with the Mindanao insurgency in the Philippines; many refugees migrated to Sabah during 1970–1977. Thousands of Suluk and Bajau women, men, and children took to small wooden boats (*kumpits*) to flee the wartorn southern provinces of the Philippines for the relative safety of Sabah. This wave of political refugees arrived on the east coast of Sabah and settled in towns such as Sandakan, Tawau, and Lahad Datu. However, the number of 1970s refugees is small compared with the number of migrants since 1978.

It is this third phase, the post-1978 period, which witnessed a massive influx of illegal migrants. These immigrants cannot, however, be technically treated as refugees because the rebel Moro National Liberation Front (MNLF) in the southern Philippines had signed a peace agreement with the Philippines government, reclassifying the region prima facie as peaceful.[27] Thus, the latest phase of immigration to

Sabah was perceived by local observers in Sabah as the movement of mainly economic migrants seeking a better life rather than political refugees. Each wave of this historical immigration established networks in sections of the economy, the society, and, importantly for modern times, the government. New immigrants followed networks established by earlier arrivals of co-ethnics.

One of the reasons that there is such an unregulated flow of illegal immigrants is because of geographical proximity.[28] Sabah's coastline runs almost 250 miles, and its proximity to several islands in the Philippines' waters allows for easy travel across state boundaries. There are almost 200 small islands off Sabah's east coast, of which only 52 are inhabited. The Sulu Sea, a pirates' haven, separates Sabah from the Philippines, and in some places it takes less than twenty minutes by boat to reach Sabah's waters from the Philippines (*Daily Express* 2000a). Today, it is commonly known among Sabahans that the coastal town of Sandakan (in the eastern part of Sabah) is overwhelmingly Filipino, while Indonesians comprise the majority of residents in Tawau, a Sabah coastal town that borders Indonesia. According to illegal immigrants in Sabah, it takes approximately two days to reach Kota Kinabalu, the capital of Sabah, from the Philippines by boat. In fact, one of the landing points is just below the Yayasan Sabah, a skyscraper housing the chief minister's office and other key Sabahan ministries dealing with immigration and security.[29] For example, "Catherine," an illegal immigrant from the Philippines, came to Sabah twelve years ago after spending two nights on a boat.[30] She landed at Yayasan Sabah and later married a Muslim Filipino who was a legal worker and nominally converted to Islam. She says that many Christian Filipino women convert to Islam, as conversion makes it easier to become Sabahan. After a few years, she "legalized" her presence through her husband's connections and is now a legal worker. It is probable that her achievement of legal status did not preclude extralegal means to that end.

For the small number of Christian immigrants, it is easier to adopt Muslim names in order to settle down locally. The Indonesians, who are predominantly Muslim, have no such problems in assimilation or acceptance. Settlement—whether through marriages, bribery, or employment—is relatively easy for illegal immigrants. At every stage, there are co-ethnics—settlers from earlier waves of migration—who facilitate the process.

As immigrants settle, they move inward and toward bigger towns on the west coast. Both Indonesian and Filipino migrants have physical and cultural features similar to those of the Malays; the Indonesian language (Bahasa Indonesia)[31] is almost the same as Bahasa Malaysia, while southern Filipinos speak dialects common to communities in East Malaysia. In major towns of Sabah, there are very visible pockets of illegal immigrant settlements, such as Kampung BDC in Sandakan, Kampung Panji in Lahad Datu, Kampung Ice Box in Tawau, and

Kampung Pondo at Pulau Gaya, Kota Kinabalu. According to some legislators, these settlements are security threats as they violate the territorial and national sovereignty of Malaysia.[32]

Unlike the Indo-Bangladeshi case, there is no clear marker, such as religion, to separate immigrant groups from native citizens in Malaysia; however, when one examines surveys and census reports, it is clear that the illegal immigrant population is significantly altering census data. Sabah's population is growing dramatically (see figure 1.3).[33] It experienced an alarming annual growth rate of 5.7 percent between 1980 and 1991 against the Malaysian average of 2.6 percent for the same period. Despite increasing opposition to illegal immigration and despite "public" displays of deportation, Sabah had an annual growth rate of 3.83 percent compared with the low national average of 2.6 percent between 1991 and 2000. While the latest census shows a decline in the population growth rate of Sabah from 5.7 percent in 1980–1991 to 3.83 percent in 1991–2001, it remains significantly higher than most other Malaysian states, including neighboring Sarawak.[34] Interestingly, until the 1980s, Sabah's population was smaller than Sarawak's by 306,254 individuals; by 1991 the difference was reduced to 91,914 individuals, but by 2001 Sabah overtook Sarawak by almost half a million people (436,773) (Department of Statistics Malaysia 2000: 19). Sabah and Sarawak had, until recently, similar fertility and death rates. While Sarawak has a higher rate of migration from peninsular Malaysia than Sabah, Sabah's annual population growth rate during 1980–1991 was over twice that

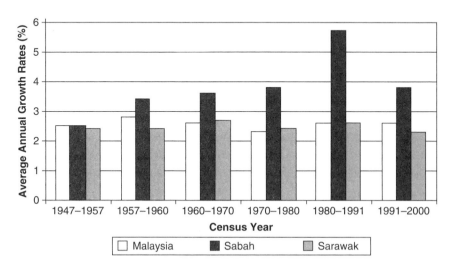

FIGURE 1.3. Annual population growth rates in Malaysia. Note: Malaysia was formed in 1963. Malaysian Peninsula is also known as West Malaysia while Sabah and Sarawak are in East Malaysia. *Sources*: Adapted from Department of Statistics (1983: 13–14); Department of Statistics (1995); Department of Statistics (2000: 20).

of Sarawak. The question of where the additional half a million people (a huge underestimation) came from when the population growth rates of both Sabah and Sarawak should have paralleled one another has become preeminently important to the "natives" of Sabah, according to Henrynus Amin, a prominent legislator of the native Parti Bersatu Sabah (PBS).[35] The obvious reference is to the rampant pervasiveness of illegal immigrants in the state.

The public perception in Sabah is that an initial trickle of refugees has now turned into a torrent of immigrants. There is a range of figures on the number of illegal immigrants in the state, clearly indicating the problems associated with estimating the illegal immigrant population. The data are scattered among various state agencies and are often unreliable. For example, while the state government estimated the population of Filipino refugees in the 1970s to be 70,000, the United Nations High Commissioner for Refugees (UNHCR) estimated their numbers to be closer to 100,000, and the local community leaders in Sabah claimed a figure in excess of 130,000 (Kurus et al. 1998: 161).[36] The state *Population and Housing Census 1991* (Department of Statistics, Malaysia 1995), however, estimates a figure of only 57,197—a huge underestimation, if not a blatant distortion (Ibid.). Sabah alone is estimated to have a stock of over a million illegal immigrants—both recent arrivals and those who came earlier and settled illegally. Yet, according to the Malaysian census, between 1970 and 1980, the net immigration from Indonesia and the Philippines to Sabah was only 45,000 Indonesians and 36,000 Filipinos.[37] The total immigration to Sabah for the same period, after counting immigrants from other countries, was only 127,000 persons out of a total population of 950,000.[38] Was Sabah only receiving about 8,000 Indonesian and Filipino immigrants per year between 1970 and 1980? No one in Sabah would accept this figure; it is a gross underestimate of reality. Later, the 1991 census in Sabah identified 207,366 persons born in Indonesia and 161,533 persons born in the Philippines out of a total of 383,076 people born outside Malaysia.[39] However, this too is a distortion in at least one way: the Filipinos are a significant presence in Sabah now, while the official figures present a different picture.

Recognizing the problems of underestimation in state data, Azizah Kassim (1998: 285) cites a former chief minister as estimating illegal immigrant numbers to be in the range of 400,000 to 500,000. Most leaders of the main opposition party, the PBS,[40] give the figure of 1 million foreigners out of an estimated Sabah population of about 2.8 million in the late 1990s.[41] Leaders of the Filipino community in Malaysia give similar estimates; their numbers in Sabah have surpassed one million, making them the "biggest concentration of Filipino illegals in any part of the world."[42] This means that almost one in every three residents of Sabah may be a foreigner. Here, "foreigner" would include both illegal migrants and legal workers.

What complicates the estimation issue further is that very often during regularization programs, many illegal immigrants get "regularized" and therefore change their illegal status.[43] Over the years, many have already made the transition from illegal status to legal citizenship. Many illegal immigrants who are deported have been known to return to Sabah within a few months, if not weeks or days. For example, Mustali, a twenty-eight-year-old Filipino who was arrested, had lived in Sabah since the age of eight (*Borneo Post* 1999c).[44] Since then, he has traveled between Malaysia and the Philippines with impunity, visiting his family several times in the Philippines. He has four children with him in Sabah; his wife returned to the Philippines to look after their older children, who are being schooled in Jolo, Philippines. The judge ordered that Mustali, as an illegal immigrant, be jailed because he "had no respect for the laws of the country by going in and out of the country as though the Philippines and Malaysia were two different states in one country" (*Borneo Post* 1999c; *Philippine Daily Inquirer* 1999). The international boundary between Malaysia and the Philippines, which should guard the territorial sovereignty of Malaysia, is nonexistent for the invisible illegal immigration taking place across the two states.

These illegal immigrant flows are not acknowledged in the vast literature on international immigration, and, importantly, they continue to be ignored by major international institutions. Only after making their magnitude and features visible can one analyze the deep workings of their networks.

Afghans and Bangladeshis Illegally Settled in Pakistan

The migration between Afghanistan and Pakistan is historical: the port city of Karachi has long provided a vital outlet for landlocked Afghanistan. Linguistic, cultural, and tribal (for example, the Pashtuns) ties straddle the border between Afghanistan and Pakistan. Similarly, Bangladeshi networks existed prior to its independence from Pakistan in 1971. Yet, the permanent character of the Afghan (and Bangladeshi) presence is rarely ever acknowledged by the Pakistani state. Meanwhile, huddled in the lanes of many shanty towns are illegal immigrants who are every day providing services that other Pakistanis refuse to undertake—the dangerous, the dirty, and the demanding (DDD). The immigrants are needed, but they remain invisible to the state. The largest wave of Afghans began to arrive in Pakistan as refugees after the Soviet invasion of Afghanistan in 1979. Legally, they are categorized as refugees fleeing conflict and persecution. According to the 2005 census,[45] almost 80.1 percent of the Afghan population came between 1979 and 1985 after the Soviet invasion of Afghanistan, followed by the second wave of refugees who came in 1985 as a result of the vicious civil war. A third wave occurred in 1990 with the rise of the Mujahideen—and the ouster of the Soviet regime—and finally, a fourth flow took place after the American ouster of the Taliban in 2001. Refugee and immigration flows among different ethnic groups vary according to the changing fortunes of which ethnic group comes to power in Afghanistan.

The Pashtun-dominated Taliban's persecution of Hazaras, Tajiks, Shia groups, and secular communist Pashtuns closely associated with the former Soviet regime made these people's refugee status legitimate. Correspondingly, the rise of the Taliban led to the return of many Pashtuns from Pakistan to Afghanistan, as they felt secure with co-ethnics in power. Importantly, most refugees did not return and continued to live in camps, just as they did near the border after 1979. Identified only by their refugee cards, they receive assistance in these camps from UNHCR and other relief agencies. In spite of that, a huge section of Afghans used their ethnic networks to settle in areas all over Pakistan, outside UNHCR-designated areas. Again, except for a small section, these are clearly illegal immigrants seeking economic betterment by their illegal domestic migration within Pakistan (Arif and Irfan 1997: 994).

The Afghans' settlement in Pakistan was considerably helped by their lack of registration. Most did not live in camps; they simply followed historic networks and got absorbed locally in small towns, villages, and big cities. No government effort during a census or registration drive was targeted at Afghans in Pakistan. The last Population and Housing Census of Pakistan, conducted in 1998, too ignored this large population. A confidential survey, also used by the National Aliens Registration Authority (NARA), was based on estimates provided by various police stations on the number of Afghans residing in their policing territories (Shigri 1996). In short, Afghans silently settled down in Pakistan and as a population remained invisible to the state; they were neither identified nor counted. So, when nearly a half million (474,162) Afghans agreed to be voluntarily deported from Sindh province between March 2002 and October 2004, most residing in Karachi, an already muddy picture was further obscured.[46]

Historically, as a result of the India-Pakistan partition, Muslim refugees arriving in Pakistan between 1947 and 1951 were given the right to Pakistani citizenship. However, the 3 million Afghan refugees who came to Pakistan after the Soviet invasion of Afghanistan in 1979 were not given the option of Pakistani citizenship (Arif and Irfan 1997: 993). It was understood that they would return to Afghanistan once the situation stabilized. After the fall of the Taliban after 9/11, there was a renewed focus to count the Afghan population as a result of a tripartite agreement among Pakistan, Afghanistan, and the UNHCR.[47] The resultant census of Afghans in Pakistan, carried out between February 23, 2005, and March 11, 2005, gave us the first estimate of the population. The target population was "all Afghans who arrived in the country after 1 December 1979 and currently residing in different parts of Pakistan." However, "[a]ny person who produced a validly obtained Pakistani identity card (NIC) *was not covered in the exercise*" (emphasis mine).[48] In short, the census left out sections of the Afghan population who have continued to live invisibly in Pakistan. Other Afghans would become visible over time through documents, as they converted their status to full Pakistani citizenship.

Yet, even the imperfect 2005 census produced many surprises. Standard accounts argued that over 2.3 million Afghan refugees had left Pakistan since March 2002, yet the 2005 census revealed over 3 million (3,049,268) individuals who had confessed to being Afghans in Pakistan.[49] This means that, contrary to traditional accounts of 2 million Afghans, over 5 million Afghans were living in Pakistan when the Taliban fell. I would argue that the present figure of 3 million is a further underestimation. Besides missing sections of the Afghan population who lied, hid, or were difficult to reach, there is a large population of Afghans, mainly Pashtuns, who have already acquired proof of Pakistani citizenship and were not included in the census. A population of 5 million underscores the "thick social environment" that allows Afghans to settle invisibly in Pakistan (Sassen 2007).[50] No wonder that a 2006 Pakistan-wide registration program produced only 220,000 Afghans, mostly Uzbeks, Hazaras, and Turkmen, with the majority of Pashtuns staying away from the exercise.

According to the census of Afghans living in Pakistan (UNHCR and Government of Pakistan 2005: 6,7), the majority of the Afghans covered (58 percent) in the registration exercise were found to be living outside camps, mingling and silently being absorbed into Pakistani society. Only 42 percent continued to live in camps and were identifiable as refugees, the tentative boundaries around the camp excluding them from Pakistani citizenship. Nearly 2.5 million, or almost 81.5 percent, of the Afghan refugees are Pashtuns, which means that they can easily be absorbed in the larger co-ethnic Pakistani Pathan and Pashtun communities. Once the Pashtun-led Taliban government fell, the need for Pakistani identity documents among Taliban sympathizers fleeing U.S. forces in Afghanistan increased (they became invisible within the Pashtun areas of Pakistan). Similarly, the 1.7 percent of Baloch Afghans could potentially vanish into the Balochistan region of Pakistan. Other groups, such as the 7.3 percent who are Tajiks, 2.3 percent who are Uzbeks, 2 percent who are Turkmen, and 1.3 percent who are Hazara, would have a harder time acquiring local documents through their significantly smaller networks. But why settle in Pakistan? Political stability, better economic opportunities, and the ease of settlement are all reasons that Afghans prefer to stay in Pakistan. However, when the Taliban was replaced by a minority-friendly government in Kabul, members of minority groups such as the Hazara, Turkmen, and Tajik returned to Afghanistan. The majority of the Afghans (82.6 percent), however, did not want to return despite the regime change.

To underplay the presence of the Afghans in Pakistan, there were claims that large sections of the community had returned to Afghanistan. First, there were reports of almost 1.5 million Afghan refugees returning to Afghanistan as a result of the success of the Taliban in capturing a major portion of Afghanistan (Arif and Irfan 1997: 993). Sensing a clear victory and a possible stable period of rule, some Afghans chose to return. This account, however, ignores the larger settlement of Afghans living outside the camps, those who are living as economic immigrants in big cities such as Peshawar, Quetta, Karachi, and Islamabad (see figure 1.4; Arif and Irfan 1997: 993). The 2005 census made a similar claim about a large-scale refugee return flow to Afghanistan, but again it ignored the hidden populations of Afghans in major cities, especially in Karachi.

"Karachi City is a paradise for illegal immigrants," wrote Azam Ali in 2004. While official figures may provide rough estimates of very visible groups, such as the Afghans and the Bangladeshis, Karachi hides a much larger diversity of migrants. The enormity of the immigrant communities from Africa (Nigeria, Sierra Leone, Somalia, etc.), the Middle East (Iran, Jordan, Syria, etc.), and Asia (Burma, Indonesia, South Korea, etc.) provides an environment of dense ethnic networks (Ali 2004).

FIGURE 1.4. Illegal immigration from Afghanistan to Pakistan. Arrows indicate the direction of illegal immigration. Bangladeshi illegal immigrants enter Pakistan either through the airport or cross over from the western Indian border (southeast section of the map).

It is likely that most of these immigrants are registered. However, there are three groups who are largely unregistered and whose traditional networks facilitate their invisible absorption into Pakistan: Afghans, Bangladeshis, and Myanmarese. Because of historical reasons, claims to Pakistani citizenship are unproblematic for Indian Muslims, but the other three are forced to use their invisible networks, of which there are many. For example, local reports maintain, there are large numbers of Bangladeshi (and Myanmarese) immigrants in over a hundred *katchi abaadis*[51] and slum areas (Ali 2004). Immigrant slums are scattered all over Karachi and can be found in

> 36/G, Landhi, Burmi Colony, Korangi 100 quarters, Noorani Basti, Korangi No. 1, Bilal Colony, Ibrahim Hyderi, Awami Colony, Korangi, Ziaul Haq Colony Korangi, Ali Akbar Shah Goth Korangi, Abbas Nagar Korangi, New Abadi Gulshane Iqbal, Ziaul Haq Colony Gulshane Iqbal, Tin Hatti Liaquatabad, Muslim Colony Azizabad, Yaseen Abad Federal B. Area, Moosa Colony, Rehman Abad, Machchar Colony, Orangi Town Sector 12, Pak Burma Colony Orangi Town, Keamari areas, Clifton Shirin Jinnah Colony, Gizri. (Ali 2004)

The list is a testament to the conspicuous presence of illegal immigrants, even as they are missing from official data. These slums provide a web of networks which make settlement possible. And the density of networks is rising with increasing numbers of illegal immigrants arriving each day in Karachi. According to most accounts, almost 100,000 Afghans lived in Karachi in the mid-1990s (Arif and Irfan 1997: 994). NARA estimated that 400,000–500,000 illegal immigrants from Afghanistan were residing in Karachi by 2001.[52] This figure corroborates the estimate given by director general of NARA, Muhammad Saleem Khan in 2002 (see table 1.7). The 1998 census has a section on migrants, including a conservative estimate of over 600,000 individuals who came to Karachi from outside Pakistan.[53] This figure unfortunately ignores those "foreigners," or children of foreigners, who may have lived elsewhere in Pakistan before arriving in Karachi. Data on "place of last residence" and "birthplace" are important in order to get any reliable estimate of Afghans in Pakistan, given that most illegal immigrants reach big cities like Karachi after moving several times between places within Pakistan. Another illegal immigrant group jostling for space is the estimated quarter to half a million Bengalis who had settled in Karachi by 1989. Their number increased to almost 1.5 million by 1998 (see table 1.7), many of whom have silently settled with the aid of preexisting networks. Current estimates of the Bangladeshi population range between 1 and 1.5 million (Mansoor 2003), while the Afghan population in Karachi is just over a half million (Afghan Research and Evaluation Unit 2005)—a figure quite distant from the 130,746 individuals officially identified in the UNHCR 2005 survey.[54]

TABLE 1.7. Estimates of illegal immigrants in Karachi (by year)

Ethnic/national group	1989	1993	1997	1998	2002
Afghan	96,070	83,823	85,499	200,000	600,000
Bangladeshi	378,125	1,164,793	1,188,089	1,500,000	1,100,000
Burmese	26,725	204,448	208,000	50,000	200,000
Iranian	10,470	2,320	2,366	50,000	200,000
Indian	NA	NA	118,808	NA	
Sri Lankan	445	78	613	NA	
Total	511,835	1,455,462	1,603,375	1,800,000	1,900,000

NA = data not available.

Source: Based on Arif and Irfan (1997: 994). 2002 figures were cited by the previous director general of NARA, Muhammad Saleem Khan; see Pakistan Press International (2002).

The gap between the census figures and estimates (see table 1.7) of the illegal immigrant population is a product of the invisible settlement of this population. Most Afghans and Bangladeshis are happy using their invisible local networks to settle down in Pakistan. For illegal immigrants, it is bothersome to contact the state, be counted, become visible, and be accountable, especially when the entire process of settlement can be taken care of by strong ethnic networks, which are available due to decades of earlier migrations from the same ethnic groups and regions.

Conclusion

I have shown that large illegal immigrant flows into India, Malaysia, and Pakistan are being silently absorbed into the host states. How can 15–20 million Bangladeshis silently settle down in India, with almost no international acknowledgment of the phenomenon? What does such a large concentration of illegal immigrants in India, Malaysia, and Pakistan show? It points to the presence of a strong web of networks that traverse international borders and that have survived the multiple divisions of the South Asian subcontinent into new states after the exit of British colonialism. This thick environment of networks has outlasted the redrawing of borders and any political violence or insurgency that has occurred, including the 1947 partition of India and Pakistan and the creation of Bangladesh from Pakistan in 1971. The networks have outlasted the departure of colonial powers, such as the British and the Dutch, and the creation of modern Malaysia and Indonesia, respectively. Given the millions of illegal immigrants who have settled in India, Malaysia, and Pakistan, it is clear that immigrant communities possess efficient and complex networks to ensure ease of settlement and access to membership. Ethnic networks override the exclusionary power of modern states to restrict illegal immigrants from their territories and political membership.

2

Networks of Complicity

Invisible Muslims, Real Networks

THE PUBLIC PHONE BOOTH IN MANSEHRA DISTRICT WAS LIKE ANY OTHER IN Pakistan (*Dawn* 2002c). Popularly known as a PCO (public call office), the government allocates them to citizens in an effort to generate employment and provide phone service. Often, they also provide a valuable service to foreigners—international phone calls. However, there was something special about this phone booth, which attracted Afghans. Apparently, the staff was providing services beyond phone calls; they were selling Pakistani national identity cards (NICs) to Afghans. For 15,000 Pakistani rupees, an Afghan could acquire Pakistani nationality under an assumed name and address. Since the PCO stood in front of the regional authority responsible for distributing NICs—the district registration office (DRO)—the two illegally shared some of the duties. A few DRO staff distributed Pakistani identity cards to genuine citizen applicants while others worked closely with the PCO outside to extend this service to ineligible foreigners.[1] Employees from the phone booth and the staff from the registration office cooperated in a chain of deception meant to turn illegal Afghans into Pakistanis. In ways like this, illegal immigrant networks fashion a pliable state.

In this chapter, I will reveal the mechanisms by which illegal immigrant networks filter into state agencies, such as the district registration office in Mansehra, thereby ensuring state complicity in the settlement of illegal immigrants. Illegal immigrants may appear invisible to the state, but they possess widespread social networks that seep into state agencies. The continuing arrival and settlement of illegal immigrants in India, Malaysia, and Pakistan further strengthen a community of millions that has extended deep roots into the state as well as the society. Illegal immigrant networks grow and mingle locally. It is the complicity that these networks craft which becomes a critical factor in the lives of illegal immigrants. Complicity ultimately ensures the acquisition of varieties of citizenship documents. I argue that, wherever there is illegal immigration, there are networks of complicity facilitating and encouraging that illegal flow. I begin this section by defining networks of complicity. Following this, I trace the formation of these networks, showing how and in what ways networks produce complicity. Finally, I distinguish between complicity for economic and for political reasons.

By *networks of complicity*, I mean the bending and manipulation of state laws to facilitate the entry, settlement, and socioeconomic and political participation of illegal immigrants by groups (not just individuals) within the political leadership, the bureaucracy, the police and security forces, and the municipal and local administrations. Essentially, networks of complicity corrode the gatekeeping functions of the state. Complicity is possible because all state actors are basically individuals who can perform multiple roles: as a state official in a Malaysian immigration office and as a fellow ethnic of an Indonesian illegal immigrant; as the husband of a Pashtun illegal immigrant and as a Pakistani border guard; as a municipal clerk in Assam during the day and as a slum landlord to Bangladeshi illegal immigrants at night. The duality of these roles not only expands these networks but also keeps them hidden. As a state official, family member, political party member, or nonstate actor, an individual can enforce the law or violate it; in fact, he/she can selectively both enforce and violate it, depending on his/her ethnic/cultural sympathies and self-interest (Nordstrom 2000: 42). Complicity by state officials may range from looking the other way, i.e., pretending that nothing is happening, to actively participating in helping illegal immigrants to enter and settle.[2] For example, border guards in India have been complicit when they allowed the entry of illegal immigrants on orders from superiors. According to an inspector general of police in the border security force of India, in the 1989 national elections, a cabinet-level minister from the Congress Party demanded that an officer "look the other way and allow 50,000 Bangladeshis to come into the constituency, vote and return."[3] Or, to take another example, members of the Malaysian judiciary have come under pressure to throw out any judicial cases that highlight illegal immigration or the role of illegal immigrants in the political life of the state.[4] City officials are complicit when they issue licenses to street hawkers, rickshaw drivers, and hand-cart pullers, or when they illegally license water and electricity connections for illegal squatter settlements. Even National Registration Department officials are complicit when they register the births of illegal immigrant children as those of natives (in contravention of the law) or issue legitimate documents to illegal immigrants in Malaysia (Bernama 2005a, 2005b). In all of these ways, different sections of the state violate or bend laws to accommodate and settle illegal immigrants.

Such networks' role within the state, I believe, deserves further inquiry. The web of networks across the current international borders between India and Bangladesh; among Malaysia, Indonesia, and the southern Philippines; and between Afghanistan and Pakistan are compromising state institutions as they facilitate the acquisition of citizenship-indicating documents, which then allow illegal immigrants access to citizenship.

The Formation of Networks

How are networks of complicity formed? Networks of complicity originate in the web of interrelationships arising from historical migrations across state boundaries. In many colonial states, migration within different parts of the empires in Africa and Asia became international (often illegal) immigration after states became independent, events often associated with the arbitrary drawing of state boundaries. India, Bangladesh, and Pakistan were all part of British India, and migration among those areas was encouraged by the British. Similarly, the southern Philippines and Sabah were part of the ancient Sulu kingdom, whose ties were strengthened by centuries of trade and migration. The modern state and its boundaries were imposed on existing migrating communities, whose dense networks had already begun to spread exponentially.[5] These preexisting ethnic networks filtered into the state, thus explaining how the acquisition of documents has become possible. Because many developing countries only gained political independence within the last fifty or sixty years, there are preexisting internal migration flows that are now construed as international immigrations. These preexisting networks between India and Bangladesh, Malaysia and the southern Philippines, and Afghanistan and Pakistan create cross-border immigrant communities. These communities are resources for poor immigrants who would be unable to facilitate their immigration autonomously. Most notably, these networks facilitate and generate the acquisition of citizenship documents. Ethnic village settlements provide not only shelter and food, but any possible paperwork that may be needed to travel or settle down. Often, these informal networks contain entrepreneurs who manufacture state-acceptable documents. Also, the networks extend into state bureaucracies, which can then provide authentic documents through fraudulent means.

Immigration from present-day Bangladesh to Assam has a long history, since both were part of British India.[6] In colonial times, such immigration was internal migration, because it occurred within the borders of British India (Weiner 1978). Today, the same village-to-village migration is viewed as *international* illegal immigration, since borders are being crossed illegally. With the increased availability of modern communications and affordable means of transportation in modern

India—like Malaysia and Pakistan—it is easy for illegal immigrants from Bangladesh to "disappear" into Assam. Furthermore, family, village, and ethnic ties across international borders supersede national ties, making it possible for illegal immigrants from Bangladesh to feel quite at home in parts of Assam, India. In some villages on the border, the front door of the house opens on the Indian side and the back door on the Bangladeshi side. These Bengali-speaking, fish- and rice-eating ethnic communities with similar customs and racial features create thick, complex, long-term environments that bypass (a) the modern state, and (b) the formal legal features of national citizenship, thus providing a contrast to the modern state in which there are assumed differences between foreigner and citizen.

A similar pattern of historical trade and travel networks undergirded by geographical proximity facilitates the unregulated flows of illegal immigrants from Indonesia and the southern Philippines. The region saw regular migration over the Sulu archipelago, which at one time formed the precolonial Sulu kingdom. Since East Malaysia shares its coastline with the southern Philippines and Sulawesi in Indonesia, these international waters permit easy and unchecked travel across state boundaries.[7] Or, one can always cross the porous land border by walking across the two halves of Borneo shared by Indonesia and Malaysia.

Given the war and recent instability in Afghanistan, it is possible to forget that Afghanistan and Pakistan have a history of migration. War and crisis may have magnified the scale and changed some of the features, but essentially the immigration between Afghanistan and Pakistan has been a continuous process.[8] It is part of a long tradition between the two states. Karachi's status as a migrant city—home to new arrivals as well as those from the second and third generations—has further eased settlement. In sum, Afghans, Bangladeshis, and Myanmarese are likely to find historical settlements that are continually restored by new immigrants.

What network theory does is to explain immigration by drawing on the experiences of migrants as they utilize informal family, community, and ethnic networks to overcome travel costs, employment difficulties, linguistic and ethnic barriers, and housing problems. According to this theory, as these personal networks expand, the process of immigration becomes easier, thus facilitating the settlement of newly arrived immigrants. These familial and kinship networks continue to get wider—a spread of concentric circles encompassing a whole village or immigrant community. However, such a focus on personal and social networks—family and friends—misses another type of network.

Networks can also appear in the role of formal recruiters, such as manpower agencies that facilitate such travel, or the multibillion-dollar human-smuggling industry (Koslowski 2001). Work by Spaan (1994: 93–113), Hugo (2000: 97–126), and Boyd (1989: 638–670) has illuminated the important role that social networks play in enabling immigration. Concurrently, Graeme Hugo has been in the forefront, arguing for greater focus on the role of the "immigration industry" in facilitating migration, especially flows dominated by illegal immigrants, such as those which he has examined between Indonesia and Malaysia (Hugo and Singhanetra-Renard 1991). Further, Hugo has acknowledged that networks filter into state bureaucracies, thus facilitating the workings of an immigration industry.

It is evident that illegal immigrants' ethnic networks—largely personal and social—help them to traverse international state boundaries. Underlying these illegal immigrant communities are their ethnic and religious affiliations. Religious and regional sympathy filters through Bengali-speaking Muslim networks in India. In the case of Pakistan, subsects of Islam, such as within the Sunni Afghan Pashtun or Shia Afghan Hazara networks, generate in-group sympathy. Regional Muslim identity marks the Bugi (from Sulawesi, Indonesia) and Bajau (from the southern Philippines) associations and networks in Malaysia, part of the larger, invisible international flows—financial, human, drugs, medicines—known as "shadow networks."[9] These invisible networks are marked by nonstate sovereignty and are a domain of power and position. As Mazlish (2000: 11, 15) points out, "networks are forms of 'invisible ties' ordering the social system and distributing power and identity."[10] One of the key ways in which current networks provide power and identity is through the distribution of citizenship-indicating documentation. Hence, a critical distinction to note is that immigrant networks "are primarily action-oriented" and are directly linked to recent improvements in communication and transport technologies.[11] Immigrant networks structure social practice (Latham 2000: 3). For example, the web of relations within the Afghan community—further broken down ethnically to Hazaras, Pashtuns, and Tajiks—both shapes and opens possibilities for complicity; their ethnic position as Hazara, Pashtun, and Tajik encourages them to facilitate government documents and resources for other in-group individuals.

Ethnic networks that are present in the community penetrate state institutions. These networks have a corrosive effect on the state, bending, if not bypassing, its regulatory mechanisms. They both utilize state institutions or, when necessary, go around them, bypassing any institutional hurdles. Networks are of two types: personal kinship networks in the informal sense, and networks that seep into official state institutions or other official organizations. Such networks of complicity, which ensure corruption and collusion from state gatekeepers, are facilitating the acquisition of essential documentation for the settlement of illegal immigrants.

Common to most document-producing networks is that they often cater to their co-ethnics before expanding outward. The repeated capture of document-producing syndicates by Malaysian officials during 2005 revealed the pervasiveness of immigrant ethnic networks. The enforcement director of the Immigration Department, Datuk Ishak Mohamed, points out that "[t]hey were set up to target their own countrymen" (Mahidin 2005b). The Pakistani syndicate in Malaysia has largely Pakistani immigrant clients, and the syndicates from Myanmar and Indonesia have mainly clients from their countries. As the document-producing networks expand, they start serving illegal immigrants from beyond their ethnic community, and soon their operations may resemble that of a "mini immigration center," such as the one that was busted by Malaysian officials on April 14, 2005 (Mahidin 2005b; *Malay Mail* 2005c). In this case, state officials nabbed thirty-nine passports belonging to Indonesians, Myanmarese, Pakistanis, Bangladeshis, Nepalese, Indians, Vietnamese, and Chinese. Additional documents captured included fifty-seven Foreign Workers Medical Examination Monitoring Agency (FOMEMA) medical identity cards, thirty foreign workers' identity cards besides immigration forms, and equipment, including a computer and printer used for forging documentation. This was not an isolated incident during 2005; similar raids reported in the daily *Malay Mail* on March 23 and April 20 drew attention to the link between ethnic networks and the complicity of state officials.[12] Networks of complicity are therefore grounded in cultural codes of trust—a system of reciprocal obligations arising from personal and ethnic social ties (Gambetta 1988). The trust and confidence inspired by personal relations or common ethnic backgrounds provide reliability and predictability.

Similarly, long periods of Afghan settlement in Pakistan have nurtured thick ethnic networks to create a favorable social environment in which immigrants utilize networks as tools to reduce uncertainty and risk. There is no better way for lowering risk and uncertainty than to acquire state-authorized identity documents, which gradually enable settlement as citizens. However, this can only occur if the Afghan networks filter into and are continually maintained within the gatekeeping sections of the state: the border checkpoint, the immigration office, the National Registration Department. Immigrant networks seep into state institutions, remain invisible, and ensure complicity by officials to facilitate acquisition of varieties of documents that authenticate citizenship. Networks of complicity coexist with the state though each represents distinct power relations and spheres of accountability. The networks are capable of deploying vast power and moving large numbers of people and large amounts of goods across continents, each time working "through and around" state agents (Nordstrom 2000: 36).

Faith in state power is the basis of our confidence that both territorial borders and the boundaries of citizenship, often managed by the Ministry of Home or Interior, will be secure from illegal immigrants. Yet, when ethnic networks bend state agents and laws, it means the political authority of the state is inferior to the corrosive power of these networks. By creating a parallel web of power and obligation rooted in ethnic ties, networks of complicity call into question the nature and source of state power.[13]

Networks of Profit

Networks of complicity can exist for economic reasons. Facilitating illegal movement between India and Bangladesh are agents known as *dalals*, who charge as much as 400–600 takas on the Bangladeshi side of the border followed by another 400–600 rupees on the Indian side; this includes payments to border guards on both sides.[14] Illegal immigrants are part of a larger informal economy. An Indian Law Commission report asserts, "[C]ross-border [illegal] trade between India and Bangladesh... is estimated at $5 billion. This is three times more than the official trade. The trade has created a network of agents and middlemen working in connivance with the authorities on both sides of the border" (Law Commission of India 2000: 7). A survey of local merchants conducting illegal trade across the international India-Bangladesh border shows that 60 percent of the Bangladeshi traders paid bribes, while 78 percent of the Indian traders paid bribes.[15] Illegal traders on both sides note the increase in bribes in recent years and the pervasiveness of the phenomenon with border guards, local bureaucrats, and politicians involved.[16]

The informal economy among Indonesia, southern Philippines, and Malaysia is characterized by dense networks. For example, it is common for immigrants to use labor operators, or *towkays*, to come to Malaysia. Most of the *towkays* who transport Filipino immigrants to Sabah are paid in Philippine pesos. The boats anchor in the night near the shore, and immigrants carry their modest belongings (only small bags are allowed) on their heads while wading to the shore. Most immigrants already know of friends and relatives in the region; thus, these connections enable recent immigrants to establish themselves in "safe houses," from which they are directed to possible employers. Co-ethnics working as private agents or in the government steer illegal immigrants to shelters and jobs. Later, co-ethnic agents or *towkays* receive part of the initial earnings of new immigrants as payment for their services. Profits from facilitating labor flows are matched by earnings from cross-border trade. Trade across the seas between Malaysia and Indonesia (white garlic, sugar, used clothing, biscuits) and between Malaysia and the Philippines (Champion cigarettes, refined sugar, Aktif soap, washing detergent) has created a dense regional network of state officials and private traders (Vu 1997: 45–46).[17] A High Court judge in Malaysia referred to these lucrative networks of complicity when convicting a police officer for soliciting a bribe to ignore the illegal trade of cigarettes from across the international border (*Hjh Halimah bte Hj Momong v. Public Prosecutor*):

> Only recently the police publicly admitted that foreigners outnumbered the citizens in the Tawau Residency. As I have said before, in all major towns in Sabah, these illegal immigrants could be seen hawking goods of

all descriptions. There *relevant law enforcement agencies have obviously closed their eyes* to these illegal itinerant hawkers who day and night went about selling their wares just about everywhere. (emphasis mine)

Profit underlines the formation of these networks, particularly in the case of Afghanistan and Pakistan. Pathan networks carried arms from Pakistan's intelligence agencies to Afghan Mujahideen (and, later, Taliban) fighters while bringing opium and heroin from Afghanistan to Pakistan. Arms, heroin, and people all went through the same networks with the complicity of Pakistani state officials.[18] Today, Afghan-sympathetic groups have filtered into the Pakistani border police, army units, and intelligence agencies. Collaboration between the Pakistani state and Afghan warlords or Jehadi groups ultimately corroded the state to the point where the regulation of such flows has become impossible.

Political Networks

Networks of complicity can also be present for political reasons. They ensure the maintenance and expansion of political power on behalf of an ethnic, religious, or racial group, a political party, or any other corporate group. Take, for example, the support and encouragement of illegal immigrants by the regional wings of major political parties in India (Congress) and Malaysia (United Malays National Organization). At no time was illegal immigration encouraged as a federal policy; at the national level, illegal immigrants were to be discouraged and deported. Over time, some Congress legislators in Assam and Delhi and some UMNO/Berjaya legislators in Sabah became the "guardians" of specific illegal immigrant groups. Illegal immigrant votes have become so crucial to major political parties that a larger number of groups and political parties is now involved in state complicity in order to strengthen political support. As illegal immigrants have become a political force,[19] state complicity has become pervasive—paving the path to citizenship. For example, a former federal minister and senior BJP leader accused the Congress Party in Assam of issuing land documents and ration cards and placing illegal immigrants on electoral rolls for political benefit (*Assam Tribune* 2005). Similarly, according to court testimony, Malaysia's ruling party in Sabah recruited 43,000 new members, of whom only 14,000 had authentic identity papers; the rest had doubtful citizenship (*Harris Mohd Salleh v. Ismail bin Majin* 1999). Muslim illegal immigrants from the southern Philippines and Indonesia in Malaysia have found political participation rather easy, just as illegal Bangladeshis have in India.

In the same way, reports suggest that the 1.3 million illegal Bangladeshi immigrants in Karachi, Pakistan, have become a viable constituency (Mansoor 2003).

Networks of complicity sympathetic to illegal immigrants permeate critical institutions of the Pakistani state, including political leaders in power. Mehar Bozdar, accused of the preparation of fake national identity cards, has confessed before a judicial magistrate that leading politicians had asked him "to prepare hundreds of fake NICs before [the] election" (*Dawn* 2002a).[20] He later retracted his confession and his accusations against the politicians. The testimony was too damaging against the state, revealing the insidious complicity of state officials in providing proofs of citizenship to illegal immigrants.

Every section of the state which acts as a gatekeeper to territorial or national sovereignty becomes a target of these corrosive networks. And the state is assisted in these activities by the private operators when they send illegal immigrants abroad. Travel agents—either licensed or unlicensed private operators—have contacts (friends, family members, fellow ethnics) in airlines (for appropriate air tickets), embassies (for visas), foreign offices (for passports), the Home Ministry (for clearance), the police (for facilitating background checks), corporations (for employment records), and so on. Travel agents can thus help to acquire the official documents needed for individual identification for travel. Also, once travel or labor-recruiting agents are familiar with the process, they can acquire genuine stamps, seals, and letterheads and are well on their way to creating individual identities in official records with the help of widespread complicity (Ahmad 2006).[21] With similar and sometimes identical stamps, seals, printers, and lamination, it becomes difficult to tell the difference between a fake and a real document. Moreover, with state officials deeply involved, the distinction between fake and real documentation is meaningless.

Complicity by state officials is hard to beat, especially if they are affiliated with the very departments that are supposed to regulate access to national identity cards and to citizenship. After all, state-authorized records are meant to exclude; their purpose is to ensure that national citizenship is safeguarded from noncitizens. While cleaning-up exercises do catch a portion of the illegal immigrants with real NICs, passports, birth certificates, or other identity-indicating documents, widespread complicity is common. The role of networks of complicity has been acknowledged by the Law Commission of India in its *One Hundred Seventy Fifth Report*, where the commission asserts, "[t]here is evidence that many of the illegal migrants have acquired ration cards," and in this process of "suppressing their identities" they were assisted by networks of complicity consisting of local officials and politicians.[22] The Assam governor's report to the president of India is equally revealing, pointing out the "pervasive" corruption and the bribery of officials (Governor of Assam 1998: 9). The governor cites the example of four individuals who were arrested for supplying forged citizenship certificates and other documents to illegal immigrants over a period of fourteen years (ibid.). These networks are instrumental in providing the paperwork for settling down in India.

In Pakistan, the director general of the National Database and Registration Authority (NADRA), Saleem Moin, acknowledges that state officials authenticate the official documents of illegal immigrants, thus paving their way to a computerized national identity card (CNIC; Ali 2004). Officials authenticating documents at the local level include councilors, *nazims*, and other government officials. According to NADRA, about 700 public officials were charged in courts for falsely authenticating documents for illegal immigrants, yet no one has been prosecuted (Shah 2004).[23] However, senior officials of NADRA, too, are complicit in issuing national identity cards to foreigners (*Dawn* 2005d), as are elected politicians holding public office, such as MNAs (members of the national assembly; Tahir 2005). Sindhi politician Makhdoom Jamil-u-Zaman claims, "Nowhere in the world the aliens are issued NIC[s] but in Pakistan it is being done under a well-hatched conspiracy to turn the people of this province into [a] minority."[24] Hence, a leader of the Sindh Taraqi Pasand Party, Dr. Qadir Magsi, accuses another political party, the Muttahida Qaumi Movement (MQM) of encouraging the settlement of "millions of illegal immigrants" in Sindh to demographically overwhelm the natives (*Dawn* 2005e). Is this a political conspiracy?

The collaborative networks among political parties, ethnic groups, illegal immigrants, and the state lend support to accounts of demographic manipulation. These networks of complicity ensure corruption and collusion within critical sections of the state to the advantage of illegal immigrants. All ensure that illegal immigrants remain invisible. In fact, conditions favorable to illegal immigrants have been in place for decades in Pakistan. No one was counting nor had an estimate of the number of illegal immigrants. Such was the neglect that the only record that state agencies have is a report prepared in 1996 by Afzal Shigri, the former inspector general of police in Sindh.[25]

Almost fifty years after independence, the Pakistani state finally acquired a rough estimate of the millions of illegal immigrants within its boundaries through the Shigri report (1996). The report revealed that, between 1974 and 1995, only 11,169 illegal immigrants were prosecuted, resulting in the deportation of the miniscule figure of 1,975 individuals (Shigri 1996).[26] Ironically, the deportation figures resemble India's failed efforts very closely; those concretely identified as illegal immigrants eligible for deportation are fewer than 1,500 in number.[27] A petition in the Delhi High Court in India noted the large "invisible" Bangladeshi population settled in Delhi—as many as 2.8 million—in contrast to the Delhi government's claim of 1.3 million and an even lower figure captured in the official census (*Pioneer* 2004). Accusing sections of the state of complicity in the settlement of illegal immigrants, the petitioner argues, "instead of arranging their deportation, the Delhi Government was conniving with them to establish their citizenship," and "the Government was preparing ration cards and election cards without verifying their address and place of birth" (*Pioneer* 2004). Indeed, the Food and Supplies Department of the Delhi government—the state agency which issues ration cards—is under investigation for producing fake ration cards, duplicate registers, and fraudulent receipts (*Hindu* 2005). Similarly, Bangladeshi illegal immigrants in West Bengal carry fake Indian ration cards and voter identity cards, an outcome possible only with the assistance of networks filtering through sections of the state and the ruling party, the Communist Party of India, Marxist (CPI-M).[28]

Complicity by state officials is quite evident in Malaysia also, and accusations of a political conspiracy are rampant at both the local and federal levels. According to recent reports, networks of complicit officials—all performing gatekeeping functions meant to secure citizenship—include the National Registration Department, the police, and members of the ruling party, UMNO (Thien 2006; Quek 2006). Speaking to the national news agency, Hassnar Ebrahim, a participant in the supply of Malaysian identity cards to illegal immigrants, admitted his role in "Project IC"—a scheme to distribute national identity cards, ostensibly with the cooperation of some members of the state.[29] Ironically, he decried the widespread use of "fake ICs" in contrast to the "legitimate" Malaysian identity cards he was providing to illegal immigrants from the Philippines. Networks of complicity had erased the difference between "legitimate" Malaysian identity cards and fakes. These identity cards were supposedly legal: middlemen filled out forms, charged a 10 ringgit fee for stamp duty, and returned later with ready, authenticated Malaysian identity cards for illegal immigrants. Were sections of the state running a parallel operation, thus providing legitimate yet illegal Malaysian identity cards? These were not fake identity cards; they were real documents acquired fraudulently by illegal immigrants through pliable networks of complicity. Other former illegal immigrants, now citizens of Malaysia, have corroborated this account. For example, Fuad Arif arrived illegally from Tawi-Tawi in the Philippines in the 1970s and finally acquired his Malaysian identity card in 1984. He asserts, "True. Project IC exists. I secured my IC from the project in the early 1980s" (Tibin 2007). Fuad possesses the Malaysian identity card bearing registration number H0504933. A nearby resident, Jamili Bungsu, also confirms the widespread distribution of Malaysian identity cards to illegal immigrants (Tibin 2007):

> Just imagine, in the early 1980s at Kampung Pondo in Pulau Gaya (near Kota Kinabalu), there were only about 10 houses there. But the number soon increased to almost 500 squatter homes whose occupants were immigrants from the Philippines.... It was not their fault that there were locals who were willing to arrange ICs for them. Not many knew who were the masterminds behind the operation. It might have been done by those with high ranks as it was not easy to make an IC.

Yet, another individual, Jaidy Kamlun, from Kampung Pulau Gaya—a prominent settlement of Filipino illegal immigrants—contends, "[i]n Pulau Gaya alone, there are more than 10,000 immigrants from a neighbouring country and most of them were helped by 'locals' to get the ICs."[30] The presence of document-supplying networks is affirmed by yet another member of Project IC—Jabar Khan, a member of UMNO from the Putatan area (*Star* 2007). Jabar Khan asserts that he helped Filipinos and Indonesians obtain Malaysian identity cards. Without a doubt, these networks are instrumental in providing Malaysian identity documents to Filipino illegal immigrants. Illegal immigrants who utilize complicit networks to acquire legitimate Malaysian documents will eventually surface as citizens, just as illegal immigrants in India and Pakistan.

Who then protects citizenship—a frontier of national sovereignty—from noncitizens? The aspiration of the nationalizing state in the post–Second World War era to secure national sovereignty by excluding noncitizens from the citizenship of the nation has failed in developing states. It has failed because the very documents marking the screening process, verifying that a state official has checked, confirmed, and reconfirmed the individual's identity, breaks down due to networks of complicity. A secure citizenship is a myth, a mirage to which India, Malaysia, and Pakistan adhere in an effort to be like other "normal" Westphalian states.

Conclusion

In India, Malaysia, and Pakistan, like in many other developing countries, complicity by sections of the state happens even though the official stance may be opposed to illegal immigration. Developed states too have such networks of complicity, but these states tend to have stronger institutions of accountability, and the issue gets attention from independent media or legislators.[31] In contrast, senior bureaucrats, police force members, immigration officials, passport officers, and border patrol agents in developing countries "toe the line" since their career promotions depend upon complicity. In such situations, there is a failure of regulation because sections of the state guarding the border and its citizenship are actually involved in facilitating the movement and settlement of illegal immigrants. Scholars may ask: what is the deep cause of this complicity? I argue that networks of complicity occur because of a lack of accountability in many developing countries. Further, both illegal immigrants and fellow co-ethnics want to bolster their political influence in the receiving state. In such conditions, networks of complicity are widespread.

Pakistanis in Canada, Arab nationals in Britain, Gujaratis in the United States, Algerians in France, and Turks in Germany—much like the Bangladeshis in India, Indonesians in Malaysia, and Afghans in Pakistan—all can access the necessary set of connections to acquire documentation, which then facilitates illegal immigration. Clearly, while the centralization of data on travel documents, the retraining of immigration and border officials, the introduction of machine-readable passports, and the harmonization of visa-free arrangements are all worthwhile measures for states, they can still be bypassed through the incentive structure built into the invisible networks of illegal immigrants. They are "invisible" when entry and settlement is successful, and "visible" on the rare occasions that they are intercepted by the state. However, a part of their invisibility also comes from the weakly institutionalized citizenship that exists in many developing countries. Citizenship is informal, and native populations may or may not be documented themselves, and into this weak structure of citizenship enters the illegal immigrant.

3

Blurred Membership

J. K. BANTHIA LEANED BACK ON HIS OFFICE SOFA, LOOKED STRAIGHT AT ME, and said, "Both people who have documents and those who are without documents survive in our country."[1] "Huh," I thought to myself, "what does that mean?" In the middle of his gigantic office sat Banthia, a short and unassuming man, who ran the largest identification effort in democratic history. It was his job to count all of the members of the Indian polity, and as he shared with me the findings of the census and outlined the contours of Indian citizenship, I began to understand that, unlike the West, which has a well-established infrastructure for identifying and documenting its citizens, India has had to be flexible enough to accommodate the variety of conditions under which its citizens live.

As the census commissioner, not only was Banthia in charge of the huge survey that counted Indians every decade, but he was intimately familiar with the conditions which make such a task difficult, if not impossible. Counting and identifying Indians is critical to the Indian state. If an individual is counted in the census, then the state can determine if that individual is eligible for the benefits of citizenship. But here we have a problem: if the state cannot determine eligibility for legal membership, even among its own population, the state cannot effectively distribute its resources.[2] With an ill-defined polity, the state cannot determine who owns the resources, who are the recipients of those resources and rights, and on whose behalf those resources and rights are safeguarded. Who is a citizen in developing countries? Who is a foreigner?

It is important to recognize this lack of distinction between citizens and foreigners because part of establishing a coherent, law-based system for the state is its ability to control its population and to determine eligibility criteria for government services.[3] For example, citizenship identification or documents become important and advantageous when the state offers employment through development schemes or social welfare services, which motivates the rural and urban poor to acquire legal identity paperwork. However, conditions of blurred membership imply (a) the absence of proof of citizenship in some regions, and (b) various forms of real or fake documentation that are available in parts of the country. In such conditions, it is impossible for the state to guarantee that those who are receiving benefits deserve them and that those who do not deserve them are not receiving them. Accordingly, it is difficult for authorities in developing countries to monitor and distinguish those who are legal citizens from those who are not based on paperwork alone—making blurred membership the norm.

The benefits of citizenship are compromised by the weakly institutionalized character of membership common to many developing countries. Like India, Malaysia, and Pakistan, many developing countries are predominantly rural, characterized by a lack of social and geographic mobility, and proof of membership in the state (e.g., birth certificates, identification cards, etc.) does not play a significant role in people's daily lives. With the increasing dislocation of traditional rural life, migration to urban areas, and state encroachment into rural regions through development schemes, documents which legally identify the individual become ever more important because the informal recognition process is no longer efficient or effective. Civil, political, and economic rights become contingent on the possession of legal identity documentation as the state becomes the primary distributor of individual entitlements. Such a process of identification from the state creates a condition where many natives are unaccounted for and thus invisible. As states extend their recognition to a wider eligible membership through a developing infrastructure of citizenship, the claims of those left out become more tenuous.

This contingent nature of membership, "blurred membership," is prevalent in many developing countries, which compromises attempts to distinguish between a "citizen" and a "foreigner." By *blurred membership*, I mean the existence of long-time resident members of a polity, citizens by birth who are unrecognized by agents of the state because of their lack of official standardized documentation (Sassen 2002: 282–285).[4] Blurred membership has three features: it does not come from the state; it arises from the kinship networks in which an individual is located in the community; and it is only legible locally, becoming opaque as physical and cultural distances increase. This condition produces ironic results: large numbers of native-born individuals may have no legal paperwork to prove their citizenship status or nationality, especially if they do not often interact with state agencies or rarely rely on state agencies for their survival. Many non-natives, such as illegal immigrants, however, may have multiple documents, often counterfeit, indicating their status as local inhabitants, even though they technically do not have a legal right to reside in the state. The irony is that noncitizens come with the intention of reaping benefits from the host society (hence their documentation) while natives live as they are (hence their lack of documentation).

How does blurred membership arise, and what are its limitations? In theory, as the reach of the state increases, blurred membership should decline, as the role of the state in an individual's life necessitates registering and documenting one's life events. Durkheim (1954) was right to identify ceremony and ritual as essential to binding members of a community together through events marking major transitions in life, such as birth, marriage, divorce, and death, which all become group-affirming occasions.[5] For the modern state, ceremony and ritual represent not only occasions for creating emotional attachments to the nation, but also mark it for identification and render it visible. In effect, providing state-authorized documents is a ritualized entry into nationhood, which is how the state marks the boundaries of the political community. Blurred membership is, therefore, *citizenship from below*, often unchecked and unquestioned by the state. Citizenship from below exerts influence at the enforcement stage—for those who have no voice in the legislature or in the courts. Even when the state wants to check and question citizenship status, it finds it difficult to do so. Many natives, especially the mass of rural poor in developing countries, spend their entire lives with minimal attention from the state. De jure citizenship, offered by the state, is the defining characteristic of modern citizenship, but many in the developing world are de facto citizens only. History supports this notion of citizenship from below; a large part of migratory flows have happened outside the immediate control of any state-like polity, a phenomenon that was true during the colonial era in Asia and Africa (Koslowski 2002: 375–399) and that is clearly present today in many parts of the developing world. The task of identifying people in developing countries is further complicated by endemic poverty and weak institutionalization. This ambiguity in state membership is widespread in many developing countries, including India, Pakistan, Afghanistan, Bangladesh, Sri Lanka, Nepal, Malaysia, Indonesia, Thailand, Ecuador, Honduras, Nicaragua, Nigeria, Ghana, Mozambique, and Angola.

What are the conditions that support blurred membership? First, the inability of some governments to provide reliable documentation results in various types of undocumented natives. The challenges that governments face in the expansion of birth registration is one example. Developing states face another problem: their governments are unable to detect false citizenship documents. The consequences of blurred membership are visible in both immigrant-receiving states, such as India, Malaysia, and Pakistan, and illegal immigrant-sending states, such as Afghanistan, Bangladesh, and Indonesia. While India is a vigorous democracy with an active electoral system, only a section of the population are "formal" citizens.[6] It is problematic that the largest democracy functions without having concretely nailed down its citizenry, especially as it is unable to distinguish its citizens from Bangladeshi illegal immigrants. On the other hand, Malaysia and Pakistan are both Muslim-majority states, but the former is an economically advanced state while the latter is economically poor. The link between Muslim cultural practices and the lack of official sources of identification reveals how Muslim societies, like other poor and traditional societies, pose special challenges to the modern state's requirements of legal identification. Establishing the shape and character of blurred membership in these countries will expose how illegal immigrants take advantage of the phenomenon of blurred membership in facilitating their lives.

Undocumented Natives

The subjects of blurred membership are undocumented natives, that is, long-term residents without citizenship papers. They are native without state recognition of their existence. Most Western scholars think that only immigrants are undocumented; the category of undocumented natives offers a striking contrast.

Are undocumented natives "real" citizens at some normative or conceptual level? They can draw on the discourse of human rights (for example, the 1948 Universal Declaration of Human Rights) since it does protect the individual's right to freedom, liberty, and identity. But does that include the right to claim citizenship? On what grounds, and what will be the acceptable proof of membership in such a political community? According to the Convention on the Rights of the Child (Articles 7 and 8), all children have the right to a nationality, meaning, the child has to belong to some nation and that obligation falls on the system of states to sort out each child's nationality. Unfortunately, this is only a passive declaration because it does not make it incumbent on the state where the child is currently residing or where the child originally came from to proactively take measures to confer nationality on the child. States may register the child of an illegal immigrant, a refugee, a minority, or a single mother in the census—or they may not. As a consequence, both a native and a foreign child without proof of identity risk becoming stateless (Arendt 1968). With a weak infrastructure of citizenship, native children and adults will remain undocumented. If citizenship is viewed as an operational tool to distinguish between citizens and immigrants, then at this operational level, the claims of an undocumented native appear false; she/he is not legible and has no identifiable markers to separate him/her from immigrants.

On the other hand, the *idea* of citizenship only belongs to an individual with legitimate claims to native status. The bundle of rights is rightfully his/hers because she/he is who she/he is—an Indian, Pakistani, or Malaysian. This ideational and legitimate citizenship claim comes close to being a blood- or descent-based citizenship claim. A historical claim to belonging, in the absence of legal proof, is a claim based on descent and/or community recognition. This is like a claim from nature: it is inherent in this individual's personhood to have local cultural codes; and those with local knowledge can endorse each of these cultural referents. The encounters and situations occur in a thick environment of social relations where individuals acknowledge each other's local membership. An individual's fluency in a language, behavior, religious practices, dress, and food habits signal membership to fellow natives. Local community recognition follows, and the vernacular system embraces the native (Scott, Tehranian, and Mathias 2002: 8). In short, there are individuals and groups from the local community who are willing to vouch for the individual's membership claim. Even the state relies on the community in the case of undocumented natives seeking legal citizenship: native claimants are commonly required to produce two or more witnesses to their claim to legal membership. The more witnesses to birth and residence from the local community, the stronger the legal claim. Then again, community recognition can be a fickle thing; recognition is withdrawn or not extended if the individual does not belong to the ethnicity or culture of the community. Hence, ethnic, cultural, linguistic, and religious prejudices can play a role in the inclusion or exclusion of an individual from the community. Blurred membership appears tenuous and arbitrary in this reading.

Testing the limits of blurred membership are its subjects, undocumented natives, some of whom are constantly traveling for their livelihood and hence without a stable address in living memory, while others are living in remote areas untouched by the state (the jungle, mountains, islands, rivers, etc.). I can identify three such groups. The first group consists of victims of dislocation and pauperization in rural areas and of the inefficient government records system in those areas. For example, large development schemes like the Three Gorges Dam in China, the Narmada Dam in India, and the deforestation of large tracts in interior Kalimantan or Sulawesi in Indonesia dislocate entire villages, while globalization skews development in favor of select cities and regions, thereby impoverishing the rest of the countryside. In response to such dislocation, undocumented natives flee to the cities. By 2015, Delhi, Mumbai, and Calcutta will account for over 15 percent of India's overall urban population; Kuala Lumpur will account for about 10 percent in Malaysia; and Karachi and Lahore together will account for over 30 percent of Pakistan's urban population (United Nations Human Settlements Programme 2003: 269–270). In rural areas, natives had an identity, a de facto citizenship based on land possession and networks in the local village community. The local tailor, the cobbler, the farmer, the Hindu priest, the mullah, the midwife, and the local shopkeeper are all relatives or friends who can identify and vouch for each other (UNICEF 1998b: 5–6). Face-to-face contacts and overlapping networks made state identity documents unnecessary for individual identification. There were also traditional records connected to local temples (India), churches (India, the Philippines), and mosques (India, Pakistan, Afghanistan, Malaysia, Indonesia). However, many of these records have no value in cities. Why? Because, among other factors, underlying a city's raison d'être is the relationship between the de jure citizen and the benefits which the city can bestow on that legal citizen. In such circumstances, only state-authenticated records matter. Additionally, in largely Muslim or Hindu societies, religious authorities only distribute documents on the occasion of marriages, if at all. Moreover, the sanctity of such documents may be unquestioned in the local area, but in distant cities such documents are rarely recognized. Increasingly, documents coming from religious heads are unacceptable to city authorities, who demand additional documents authenticated by local authorities. Hence, authentication by a local *nazim* (in Pakistan) or head of a village *panchayat* (in India) on a stamped paper is required in addition to proof provided by a local religious authority. Land records provide legal identification, but the increasing fragmentation and pauperization of small farmers have led many of them to join the larger pool of landless peasants, who are too poor to own land in cities. The rural poor and landless now populate the rising urban slums of cities such as Calcutta and Delhi, Karachi and Lahore, Kuala Lumpur and Kota Kinabalu.

A second group of undocumented natives comes from the dislocated indigenous or tribal groups, which often attach their "identity" to the local environment—its trees, rivers, mountains, and other physical features (e.g., the Orang Asli and Muruts in Malaysia; Bodos, Mishings, and other tribes of Assam and Northeast India). These groups are often dislocated as a result of the state's development projects.

A third group comprises ethnic minorities who are deprived or discriminated against by the majority groups in control of the state. Their pauperization can be a result of a civil war (e.g., Pashtuns or Hazaras at different times in Afghanistan) or an insurgency (e.g., Suluks and Bajaus in the southern Philippines), a war of independence (e.g., Bangladesh after 1971), or ethnic violence (e.g., Chakmas and Hindus from Bangladesh; Bengali Muslims in Assam, India). Their nonpersonhood, and undocumented nativehood, is a result of deliberate state policy. In some cases, such as the Rohingyas in Myanmar or the Hazaras in Afghanistan, their poverty and landlessness are used to deny them legitimate identity documentation.

Very often, groups from the second and third categories become part of the large landless population, migrating to neighboring rural areas or to urban areas for survival (Solinger 1999). These internal migrants are intermixed with international migrants from within the region. Some of these migrants acquire documents, but their citizenship/identity documents are usually deemed to be unacceptable by authorities, or they are accused of being foreigners and threatened with deportation from their own country along with other illegal international migrants. Most, however, do not have any documents to prove their membership in the city or the state. They are continuously exploited, prostituted, beaten, or trafficked. These undocumented natives lose their rural citizenship when they move to the city, but conversely fail to gain any city-based citizenship.

Born with an Identity Crisis?

A birth certificate is a ticket to citizenship. Without one, an individual does not officially exist and therefore lacks legal access to the privileges and protections of a nation.
> —Unity Dow, High Court judge, Botswana[7]

The chronicling of life events associated with members in a polity is the responsibility of the civil registration apparatus of states. A record of a life event has significance both as a legal document (e.g., birth certificate, marriage certificate, death certificate) and as a source of data that are much needed by state policymakers.

Vital to a state's ability to make visible the population in its territory and to separate it from outsiders is the birth registration system. Such a system is inherently designed to obviate any development of blurred membership. The birth record is the most basic of identity documents in the civil registration process of a state. Every child has a right to an identity, to be registered at birth, according to Article 7 of the 1989 United Nations Convention on the Rights of the Child (CRC), which has been ratified by 192 countries (UNICEF 2005a: 1): "The child shall be registered immediately after birth and shall have the right from birth to a name, the right to acquire a nationality."

The United Nations Children's Fund (UNICEF 1998a: 659) has selected "birth registration" as one of the themes needing its attention. One's birth certificate is the basis for the future state identity documents that a resident accumulates, which include a school certificate, a health card, a voter identification card, a national identity card, and a passport. Emphasizing the importance of this basic document to modern states, a High Court judge from Botswana, Unity Dow, contends (UNICEF 1998b: 5):

> Without proof of birth, a child cannot be legally vaccinated in at least 20 countries. More than 30 countries require birth registration before a child can be treated in a health centre. Most countries demand to see a birth certificate before enrolling a child in school. Many require one for supplemental feeding programmes. Such fundamental activities as getting married, opening a bank account, owning land, voting and obtaining a

passport may be denied to a person without a birth certificate, because *it
is the basis on which a country identifies its citizens.* (emphasis mine)

Despite the importance of this document for identification purposes, every year
over 50 million births globally are not registered (UNICEF Innocenti Research
Centre 2002: 2).[8] Overwhelmingly, these low registration rates exist in poor developing countries or in poor parts of developing countries (see figure 3.1); two-thirds
of all unregistered children are Asian (UNICEF and Plan 2003: foreword, ii).

The difference in registration rates between the developed countries, with
98 percent coverage, and the developing regions is immense (see figure 3.1). Sub-
Saharan Africa (71 percent of births not registered annually) and South Asia
(63 percent of births not registered annually) represent some of the largest
populations and lowest registration rates for their child populations. Whereas birth
registration is common in developed states, until recently, Eritrea, Ethiopia, Somalia,
Namibia, Cambodia, and Afghanistan did not have a compulsory birth registration
system (UNICEF 1998a: 663–664). Nigeria, with 5 million births a year, has no
estimate; neither do South Africa, the Congo, Tanzania, and a host of other African
countries. Other states have low registration, which may or may not be reliable.
Sierra Leone has a registration rate of less than 10 percent, while Zimbabwe, one-
third. An estimated 50 percent of children are registered in Bolivia. (ibid).

There is also variation within states. Malaysia has high birth registrations overall, but low coverage in rural parts of the mainland and in Sabah. Turkey's western,
developed part has an 84 percent registration rate, while the less developed, eastern

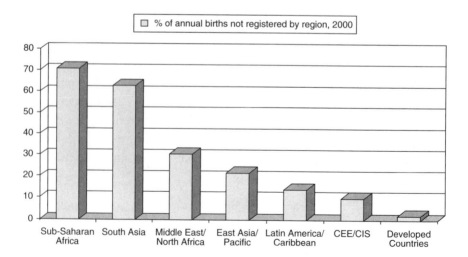

FIGURE 3.1. International birth registration levels. CEE = Central and East Europe;
CIS = Commonwealth of Independent States. *Source*: Based on UNICEF Innocenti
Research Centre (2002: 8).

part has only 56 percent. The Punjab region in Pakistan has 88 percent coverage, but the unruly and poor Northwest Frontier province is estimated to register about half that rate (UNICEF 1998b: 10). The Philippines has high levels of coverage generally, but as one travels farther south (toward Mindanao, etc.), the coverage becomes poor. Indonesia after Suharto, Iraq after Saddam, and Central Asian states after communism have all seen their registration rates decline and their birth and identity cataloging systems come under stress. India, with approximately 350 million poor, has large numbers of people without any birth documents. Consequently, millions of individuals globally are without any basic birth registration documents and, more important, are ineligible for future official identity documents, such as a national identity card or passport. As Judge Dow says, "[A] person who lacks proof of identity is, in the eyes of officials, a non-person" (UNICEF 1998b: 6).

The United Nations Development Program (2000: 75) has shown that South Africa has no data on birth registration, even though citizens are required to have birth certificates for health care and school enrollment. The same UNDP report also estimates that, in Indonesia, between 30 and 50 percent of the births go unregistered, even though birth certificates are a requirement for marriage and school enrollment. Although governments in developing countries are preoccupied with reaching the poor through welfare and employment-generating programs, on average, 35 percent or more of the population is beyond the reach of the state because they lack official documentation, as the World Bank's poverty headcount index shows: 36 percent for Bangladesh, 35 percent for India, 42 percent for Nepal, 34 percent for Pakistan, 54 percent for the Philippines, and 51 percent for Vietnam (Shah 1999: 13). As a result, when the state expands its services, it is forced to relax regulations, to create flexible regulations to reach this section of the population, or to deny them altogether. For example, estimating the birth date of a five-year-old child born in a poor village home with the assistance of a local midwife will require flexibility in state rules. However, once such a child enters the school system, the state will then be able to document his/her growth through paperwork. A variety of easily obtainable documents—some provided by local officials, others acquired illegally through bribery or forgery—become the poor person's identity marker.

Compounding the challenge of weakly institutionalized citizenship is the fact that birth registration is separate from the process of actually acquiring the proof of birth—the birth certificate. Birth registration involves entering into an official record information on the delivery of a child: age, name of parents, sex, location, physical weight or features, etc. As a result of this cataloging of the birth, a state-authorized proof is issued in the form of a birth certificate, which is available on request from the state. This two-stage process is common to India, Malaysia, and Pakistan. The birth certificate is a *feeder document*, which is any document, paper or plastic, real or fake (but seemingly state authorized) that acts as a proof of identity, which then "feeds" into the infrastructure of citizenship by giving access to other identity documents authorized by the state. These documents provide entry into the infrastructure of citizenship. Therefore, a birth certificate is increasingly becoming the basic document needed for entering the school system, accessing health care facilities, obtaining the right to vote, or becoming eligible for licenses (see table 3.1).

For example, in India, Malaysia, and Pakistan, a birth certificate is a critical document for entering school, but it is not mandatory. Only for obtaining an education scholarship in Malaysia is the birth certificate mandatory. However, there are efforts currently under way to make it mandatory to acquire a Malaysian identity card or upon entering the school system in India. In Punjab, India, this requirement has succeeded, but other states are a long way from making birth certificates mandatory. Pakistan, along with India, Kenya, Myanmar, Malaysia, Indonesia, the Philippines, and Uganda, *may* require a birth certificate for school enrollment, but when confronted with widespread blurred membership, these governments do not enforce this rule (UNICEF 1998b: 9). Similarly, while Indonesia and the Philippines *may* require birth certificates for marriage, it is also a common practice among Muslim communities, such as the Bajau and the Sulu[9] in the southern Philippines, or the Bugis in Sulawesi, Indonesia, to have a traditional Islamic wedding without state-sanctioned certification of any kind. Most of these states have also tried to be flexible with their health care programs or immunization efforts by forgoing any birth certificate requirements. The rationale is that it is more important to give access to these services to the members of the polity than to expect them to obtain proof of their membership.

According to section 8 of chapter III of India's Registration of Births and Deaths Act (1969), individuals can "give or cause to be given, either orally or in writing, according to the best of their knowledge and belief," their personal information during a census and other state-sponsored surveys.[10] Censuses and state-authorized

TABLE 3.1. Use of birth registration

Country	Marriage	School enrollment	Health care	Immunization
Afghanistan	No	No	No	No
Bangladesh	No	No	No	No
India	No	Yes	No	No
Indonesia	Yes	Yes	No	No
Malaysia	Yes	Yes	No	No
Pakistan	No	Yes	No	No
Philippines	Yes	Yes	No	No

Source: Based on UNICEF (1998b: 9).

surveys count individuals for the state. For members in a polity, becoming a "person" then depends on two very critical features of the census: its comprehensiveness and timing.[11] However, comprehensiveness faces a challenge in marginalized or rural communities where respondents do not recognize the importance of their dates of birth and marriage. Rural folk or landless poor, often illiterate, are unlikely to be certain about such events in their lives. Additionally, if an event like a birth, marriage, or death were to be recorded at the time of its occurrence rather than later through some interview, the accuracy of the event would be higher and the identity of the individual more precisely known.[12] But the counting of an individual during a census (or other state-mandated surveys) is no guarantee that the state recognizes one's existence. States may count a person without actually recognizing his/her existence. For recognition, a person needs state-authorized paperwork, which usually requires the payment of money or the completion of some bureaucratic procedure. Since both comprehensiveness and accurate timing are lacking in the civil registration process of developing states, and since the distribution of state-authorized paperwork is unreliable, many individuals live anonymous existences.

India: A Democracy without Citizens

The deputy prime minister of India, L. K. Advani, asserts, "Establishing the identity of citizens should start right from the birth" (Office of the Registrar General of India 2003a: 76). As part of an overall effort to develop an identity infrastructure based on documentation, the government of India has outlined the legal importance of birth registration for

1. identifying individuals eligible for inheritance or insurance claims as well as any transfer of property
2. establishing age to enter school; obtaining state employment, including service in the armed forces; acquiring a driver's license and passport; voting; or marrying
3. establishing nationality and citizenship (Office of the Registrar General of India 1998b: 1)

In democratic India, which is approximately 70 percent rural, many citizens are born at home in villages or in remote areas and not in hospitals or maternity clinics, where birth certificates are provided. Obtaining these documents is difficult for many natives living in remote areas of India, such as Assam, Bihar, Uttar Pradesh, Madhya Pradesh, and Chhattisgarh, and for those living in the interior and undeveloped parts of Pakistan, Malaysia, Indonesia, and Bangladesh. Birth registration levels are low in developing countries as compared to the 98 percent and higher rates achieved in developed states.[13] A birth certificate is the first proof of citizenship in India, and it can lead to other documents, such as a ration card, voter ID, or passport. Recent data from an ongoing international program by UNICEF in India show a low overall birth registration rate of 34.7 percent, even though the Registration of Births and Deaths Act of 1969 made it mandatory to report births and deaths in India (table 3.2). There is large regional variation in the birth registration rates of the poor. It is low in rural regional states, such as Assam (29.8 percent), Bihar (1.6 percent), Uttar Pradesh (6.5 percent), Manipur (27.5 percent), Rajasthan (12.4 percent), Madhya Pradesh (29.9 percent), and Orissa (9.7 percent), and higher in economically developed and more literate states, such as Maharashtra (80.4 percent), Haryana (74.7 percent), Punjab (88.9 percent), Tamil Nadu (69.1 percent), and Kerala (89 percent). Big urban centers, such as Delhi, Mumbai, and Calcutta, also have higher birth registration rates than do rural areas. Overall in India, only 28.9 percent of children in rural areas possess this first marker of state identity, and the situation only gets marginally better in urban areas, with 53.7 percent of children below the age of five years registered (table 3.2). Compared to the almost complete coverage in developed states, India has a woefully low overall birth registration rate of 34.7 percent, far behind many states in identifying its citizens.

The standardization of any state-authenticated documentation is vital to any secure citizenship, and yet a government report on birth certificates has this to say (Office of the Registrar General of India 2003a: 9): "there is wide variation in their format and design across the states and even within a state. In many cases, it is not clear from the appearance of the certificate as to whether it has been issued by a Government body or not." Variation in formats is such an endemic problem that in one of the Northeast Indian states, format guidelines from 1918 were still being used in 2002 (Office of the Registrar General of India 2003a: 91). In addition, ignorance of the laws and indifference to their importance are causes for the absence of citizenship-related documents. For example, in Assam, a poor state in India, acquiring documents is a difficult process for natives living in the interior and for the poor living in remote areas or *char* lands (river islands), where official government infrastructure may not be easily accessible or may not exist at all. Very few poor residents of Assam are likely to have school graduation certificates, given the low literacy rates. For example, in 1991, the Dhubri and Barpeta districts had literacy rates of 38.3 percent and 43.2 percent, respectively (Unni 1999: 42).[14] Given that Assam is one of the least developed states of India, there will undoubtedly be a large number of poor natives without any birth, land, or school certificates. Even though such conditions prevail in many parts of India, the burden of providing proof that an individual is not a foreigner lies with the accused, according to section 9 of the Foreigners Act of 1946 (Government of India 2002: 14), which applies to all of India.

TABLE 3.2. Birth registration rates

State	Children below 5 years who are reported to be registered (%)			Children below 5 years who are reported to be unregistered (%)		
	Rural	Urban	Total	Rural	Urban	Total
Andhra Pradesh	27.7	44.1	32.4	8.1	6.8	7.7
Arunachal Pradesh	NC	NC	33.0	NC	NC	1.3
Assam	27.1	59.7	29.8	0.8	0.9	0.8
Bihar	0.9	7.5	1.6	4.5	4.8	4.6
Goa	95.7	95.0	95.3	0.5	0.9	0.7
Gujarat	84.5	93.5	87.5	0.8	0.2	0.6
Haryana	77.3	66.7	74.7	5.7	5.2	5.6
Himachal Pradesh	94.0	89.9	93.6	1.8	2.2	1.8
Jammu & Kashmir	46.7	52.5	47.9	8.5	6.5	8.1
Karnataka	45.2	64.3	51.0	15.6	8.9	13.6
Kerala	88.3	90.4	89.0	4.6	3.0	4.2
Madhya Pradesh	30.1	29.5	29.9	19.4	13.7	18.0
Maharashtra	77.6	85.1	80.4	6.0	1.7	4.4
Manipur	28.5	25.0	27.5	1.7	3.1	2.1
Meghalaya	NC	NC	32.6	NC	NC	1.5
Mizoram	78.1	88.1	84.2	3.6	1.6	2.4
Nagaland	NC	NC	48.8	NC	NC	0.2
Orissa	7.5	24.4	9.7	5.7	6.0	5.7
Punjab	90.3	85.2	88.9	2.1	5.4	3.0
Rajasthan	5.5	40.0	12.4	6.4	8.3	6.8
Sikkim	NC	NC	68.7	NC	NC	1.2
Tamil Nadu	62.7	82.0	69.1	4.7	2.2	3.9
Tripura	NC	NC	47.9	NC	NC	1.6
Uttar Pradesh	3.0	22.2	6.5	8.1	7.5	8.0
West Bengal	48.6	62.1	51.2	0.8	1.5	0.9
Union Territory						
Andaman & Nicobar	NC	NC	92.5	NC	NC	0.7
Chandigarh	NC	NC	71.4	NC	NC	2.4
Dadra & Nagar Haveli	NC	NC	84.6	NC	NC	0.9
Daman & Diu	NC	NC	94.2	NC	NC	0
Delhi	63.3	72.0	70.8	1.6	1.4	1.5
Lakshadweep	NC	NC	92.4	NC	NC	2.4
Pondicherry	NC	NC	93.7	NC	NC	0.6
Total India	**28.9**	**53.7**	**34.7**	**6.9**	**5.3**	**6.6**

Note: Data for Bihar, Madhya Pradesh, and Uttar Pradesh are from before their bifurcation.

NC = Not calculated because of limited sample.

Source: UNICEF (December 2001).

Clearly, this law is biased against the poor. The Foreigners (Production of Proof of Identity) Order of 1991 made it mandatory, though for a short period of time, for any foreigner in Delhi to carry official documents.[15] For the slum-dwelling migrant poor attempting to escape poverty from other states of India (and there are millions of such residents), any accusation by a neighbor could put their entire citizenship under question. This is especially true if one happens to be a Bengali-speaking Muslim migrant from West Bengal or Cooch Behar living in Delhi, Assam, Gujarat, or Mumbai, because they are often confused with illegal Bangladeshis.

Illegal immigrants in India are often poor and settle among the local poor, homeless, rag-picking populations. Bengali-speaking immigrants from Bangladesh and from West Bengal and Cooch Behar in India mingle and struggle to survive together in these urban slum areas. Often, the police raid these neighborhoods to catch and deport "Bangladeshis."[16] In a study of homeless shelters in Delhi by a leading NGO, over 80 percent of homeless people did not possess ration or voting cards (Aashray 2001: 34). Since proof of name and location are critical to being a "citizen," especially in a major city, they face constant harassment from the police. Clearly, blurred membership is not tolerated by the state in big cities to the same degree as it is in remote or rural areas. Since vagrancy is illegal under several urban laws, for the poor, the landless, and the homeless who lack identification, every day becomes a test of their citizenship in a largely indifferent city. In another survey of thirteen night shelters with a collective capacity of managing 2,601 individuals, run by local municipal authorities in Delhi, the lack of an identity card was cited as a common problem faced by the homeless in six of the shelters—Nehru Place, Raja Garden, Old Delhi Railway Station, Fountain Chowk, Delhi Gate, and Shahzada Bagh (Aashray 2002: 8).

Identity cards issued by the state not only give access to state services (subsidized wheat, rice, kerosene, medical facilities, banks) but also protect the poor from harassment by police and other law enforcement officials (Aashray 2002: 18). It therefore becomes imperative for blurred members to acquire some form of state identification, including obtaining an official name and address and being categorized into a recognizable ethnic classification.[17] However, according to an unpublished study of 500 homeless migrants by a leading human rights organization, People's Union of Civil Liberties, 22 percent of the respondents tried but failed to acquire a ration card because they could not afford the bribe demanded (Aashray 2002: 18). The circumstances in which the poor find themselves, landless or homeless, rural or urban, are thus directly the result of the state's neglect and marginalization of them. Blurred membership is informal membership, and wherever state presence is pervasive, it leads to a thin de facto citizenship for native undocumented citizens. It is thin because it is not legally acknowledged. Hence, poor, undocumented citizens risk being deported along with illegal migrants. If rights and the status of citizenship become a function of wealth, the poor have only a tentative claim to citizenship.

Conditions of blurred membership are widespread in India. Yet the law acts as if citizen eligibility is not a major problem. Blurred membership is reinforced by a perceived cultural similarity. The state of West Bengal, yet another major receiver of Bangladeshi illegal immigrants, acknowledged as much in a 1999 affidavit submitted by the West Bengal government to the Supreme Court: "it was quite difficult to identify the Bangladeshi nationals, settled in the state, mainly because of their physical similarity with the population."[18] Police officials who have caught illegal Bangladeshis as far as Punjab recount that the use of fictitious West Bengal addresses and name changes are common tactics adopted by Bangladeshi illegal immigrants (Swami 2003). For instance, a woman will change her Muslim name, such as Khairunnisa, to a generic Hindu name, such as Kalpana, and will list an appropriate West Bengal address (ibid.). Identification becomes doubly difficult with dubious papers. The nonpossession of birth or school certificates or ration cards by many natives, the slow process of acquiring birth certificates, and the multiple indicators of citizenship (such as hand-cart license, rickshaw license, ration card, voter receipt, etc.) have all created the conditions I have characterized as blurred membership in India.

Who Is a Malaysian?

Is blurred membership peculiar to India? Not at all. The infrastructure of citizenship is also weak in Malaysia. Illegal immigrants know that the local population in some parts of these countries have no standardized documents and that settlement will therefore not likely be a major hurdle. Information flowing through networks of family, kin, and/or fellow villagers ensures that illegal immigrants have reliable knowledge about their future host state. Illegal immigrants' confidence in not being detected during residence because the local population itself is in a weakly institutionalized condition further facilitates their settlement.

Malaysia is a model for the region. According to UNICEF, it has 90 percent or higher birth registration rate (1998b: 11) and is continuing efforts to produce a high-security national identity card (NIC). It is certainly ahead of India, Pakistan, the Philippines, Indonesia, and other developing countries in its civil registration system. Such was the enthusiasm of the Malaysian government in documenting its citizens that long-time natives who otherwise face difficulties in accessing citizen rights feel that they become citizens only after acquiring an identity document: "I am very happy today to have registered for an identity card. I am finally a Malaysian citizen," remarked Birang Kasioh, a newly registered individual (*New Straits Times*

2002b). A senior official from Sabah State National Registration Department, Director Datuk Ibrahim Jusoh, proclaimed enthusiastically in 2002, "[a]t least 95 percent of people living in Sabah's interior will have birth certificates and identity cards by 2005" (ibid.).

A closer look at Malaysia's civil registration system reveals, however, that coverage is uneven and that tagging each person with a single identity remains an uphill battle. The use of standard documents is absent or only vaguely present among some native populations. Citizenship is not well institutionalized and defined in Sabah, East Malaysia. In April 1999, an official of the National Registration Department (NRD) in Sabah complained that over 2 million people residing there did not possess birth certificates (*Sun* 1999). A year later, it was reported that a million individuals in Sabah did not have birth certificates, with most of these individuals located in the interior of the region (Bangkuai 2001). This number is significant, considering that the total population of Sabah was about 2.4 million in 2000 (Department of Statistics 2000: 28). In addition, almost 3,000 seafaring Bajau Laut in East Malaysia do not carry any official paperwork; almost 4,000 indigenous Orang Asli in West Malaysia are without any birth certificates; and many poor Indian Tamils are without basic state documents.[19] Another indigenous community, the Penans, had 2,589 birth certificates issued to them between 1988 and 1999 (Bernama 2005a). Yet, as of September 2005, these long-time natives still had over 300 members without any form of identification, and according to the Penans association, most could not afford the fees charged for such paperwork (ibid.).

Along with the inaccessibility of the registration centers and the costs of registration, a critical reason for such inadequate documentation was the lack of awareness of the importance of a birth certificate. As the deputy director of Sabah's NRD, Ali Amat Mohd. Idris, opined, "Many parents in the rural areas could not care less.... They think that a birth certificate is not important" (Bangkuai 2001). However, even with awareness and a desire to acquire documentation associated with civil registration, poverty remains the major hurdle. Unable to acquire a birth certificate, a native complained: "[a] bus trip into Bentong costs 2.50 [ringgits] per person one way. Multiply that by five children and two adults. Multiply that by two for the return trip. We'd rather spend that amount of money on food" (Mahidin 2005a). Given that Birang Kasioh, a sixty-two-year-old native, had to travel three days on foot to apply for his identity card and that many poor farmers cannot afford the 200 ringgits it costs for the journey to a registration center, the conditions for blurred membership continue in Malaysia despite the government's aggressive stance on registering its residents and citizens (*New Straits Times* 2002b).

According to the director general of the NRD, their office must be notified within fourteen days of any birth; however, in case of any complications, the period may be extended to forty-two days (*Borneo Post* 1999e). Beyond the stipulated time

period in which to register the birth, the NRD requires other evidence and interviews parents to determine the child's citizenship. Thus, registration is obviously a
difficult process for natives living in the rural interior and for the poor living in
remote areas or on islands. It has resulted in an estimated 10,000 out of 500,000
babies born each year in Malaysia not being registered within the given period
(Ibid.). Before April 1987, no birth certificates were required for a Malaysian identity card, and the records show that most people did not possess birth certificates.
Since then, however, a birth certificate has become an essential document for
acquiring Malaysian citizenship or an identity card. In fact, it is a legal offense to fail
to obtain a Malaysian identity card after twelve years of age. There were 39,120
applications throughout Sabah for identity cards in 1998 from twelve-year-olds
alone, and it may take as long as two to three years before an identity card is issued
(*Sun* 1999).

Ironically, illegal immigrants can easily obtain a fraudulent Malaysian "blue"
identity card, which is supposedly reserved for citizens only, for as little as 10 ringgits (*Borneo Post* 1999j).[20] The NRD seeks the help of community leaders, village
chiefs, and other agencies to verify or to register people in remote areas who may
not have birth certificates or identity cards. However, this verification process is
susceptible to corruption with the collusion of native chiefs and other local community leaders, who are responsible for verification, resulting in the issuance of
"real" identity cards to illegal immigrants. Village chiefs have the authority to certify the date and place of birth of an individual. The NRD is "worried" about the
possibility of people using other persons' birth certificates to acquire Malaysian
identity cards as well as the problem of "forged" identity cards (*Sun* 1999). Cases of
natives selling the birth certificates of dead relatives to foreigners and foreigners
acquiring a "genuine" declaration form from a village chief to apply for a legitimate
Malaysian identity card have caught the attention of state authorities (Bangkuai
2001). Complicating the issue of identity cards is the problem of unclaimed
Malaysian identity cards. Malaysia shifted to a new "high security" identity card,
and as of February 1999, there were 52,320 unclaimed new identity cards that had
been applied for since the beginning of 1991 (*Sun* 1999). There were 9,344 identity
cards from Kota Kinabalu (capital of Sabah), 7,143 from Sandakan (an east coast
town bordering the Philippines), 8,371 from Tawau (an east coast town bordering
Indonesia), and 4,709 from Lahad Datu (a west coast town).

Despite the fact that Malaysia is being hyped as the model for other developing
countries trying to standardize their citizenship systems, again, the pattern here is
the same. The nonpossession of birth certificates or identity cards by many natives,
the slow process of acquiring birth certificates, the registration for ever-changing
new high security identity cards, the conversion from old identity cards to new
identity cards, the many cases of forged identity cards, and the wrongful acquisition

of identity cards based on others' birth certificates—these conditions have all created blurred membership in parts of Malaysia.

Malaysia, with about 600,000 births annually, has high birth registration rates, but this coverage varies by region and ethnic group. Millions of people are without birth certificates because they cannot afford them or could not travel the long distances from interior rural areas to state registration sites. Importantly, their children face difficulty in gaining access to schooling and hospital treatment because of their lack of official identification documents. In March 2004, well after Malaysian efforts to register citizens and to create a high security identity card had accelerated, the Sabah State Assembly speaker, Datuk Juhar Mahiruddin, regretted that "stateless" natives residing in fishing villages "for generations" were unable to obtain their birth certificates and identity cards (*Daily Express* 2004). They are a classic case of undocumented natives.

Even as the state tries to mark and secure its citizens, many long-time natives continue to face harassment and the threat of deportation because of blurred membership.[21] Hence, it was no surprise that, in a recent registration drive targeting a few rural districts, the NRD managed to register "7,500 of the approximately 8,000 paperless villagers" in Kota Marudu district and a total of 1,229 people in Ranau district (432 birth certificates and 797 identity cards).[22] Even a relatively well-documented state such as Malaysia has evidence of blurred membership in specific regions and among certain ethnic groups. Recall that this is the pattern in India as well. The Malaysian state will continue to find it very difficult to physically distinguish a Malaysian Bajau from a Filipino Bajau or a Malaysian Bugi from an Indonesian Bugi—the language, physical features, and food habits are all the same. Therefore, we may surmise that many illegal Bajaus from the Philippines and Bugi immigrants from Indonesia have settled and been absorbed into the blurred membership of Malaysia.

Pakistan: A Nation of Blurred Muslims

We now consider blurred membership in Pakistan. An illiberal democracy that at times is equally at ease with dictatorship, Pakistan, like many poor developing countries, did not have a good civil registration system until after 9/11. The records of birth registration were poor and often unreliable, and a national database for citizens did not even exist. However, the war on terror made it imperative for Pakistani authorities to identify individuals with certainty. Is the Pashtu-speaking individual from Kabul, or is he a genuine Pakistani of Afghan heritage? Is he a Pathan linked to the Taliban regime who recently migrated to Karachi and has assimilated among the rest of the Pathans?[23] The presence of a Pakistani or Afghan birth certificate could, along with other evidence, locate this individual. It is believed that many Taliban and Al Qaeda–linked individuals are residing in Pakistan and in other parts of the world under assumed identities and forged documents. As a result of the war on terror and militant Islam, Pakistan's birth registration system has come under greater scrutiny, and the government has begun taking steps to create a national database of citizens. Since identity is first established by a birth certificate, an overhaul of the birth registration system in Pakistan was the key to creating a standardized citizenship infrastructure. It was also critical because 50 percent of the population in Pakistan is under eighteen years old. Thus, identification of individuals needs to begin with an efficient birth registration system.

The challenge to creating a national identity database, a recording of every member of the polity, faces many hurdles. Pakistan, like India, is largely a rural society with 66 percent of its population spread over the countryside (UNICEF 2005a: 120). It has low literacy rates; its cycle of life events (birth, death, marriage, divorce) is infused with traditional Islamic practices; and it is a highly corrupt state with pervasive networks of complicity. In Pakistan, marriages require a traditional Islamic mullah, who is usually literate in Islamic teachings but is otherwise an illiterate individual, who can issue a nonstandardized local *nikah-nama*, a marriage document with no state sanction or authority. Divorce is easy with the help of a complicit local mullah; the whole institution of marriage is nonstandardized with little legal protection for women. There is very little documentary proof of a marriage having ever existed.

Today, Pakistan ranks close to Afghanistan as a "failed state," according to a recent ranking by a prominent foreign affairs journal (*Foreign Policy* 2006).[24] Therefore, one would reasonably expect low civil registration rates given the poor conditions in Pakistan. Surprisingly, according to a much-cited UNICEF document of 1998 (1998b: 11),[25] Pakistani birth registration rates are high, ranging between 70 and 89 percent. But this is an absolutely incorrect figure, reflecting both the dependence of international bodies on official state-generated data and the difficulties associated with data collection in these developing countries. A few years later, a government of Pakistan report stated that, for 1998, the overall birth registration was 29.5 percent with coverage being higher in urban areas (39 percent) than in rural areas (20 percent; Government of Pakistan n.d.: 29). Another report cited an even lower overall estimate of a 20 percent birth registration rate (*Daily Times* 2005). These figures are close to the estimates of Plan, an international NGO working closely with UNICEF to improve global birth registration rates. According to Plan, in areas where it has launched campaigns for universal birth registration in conjunction with the rural development minister of Pakistan, birth registration rates have increased from 30 to 80 percent (Plan 2005a: 41). Currently, the government of Pakistan estimates its birth registration rates are between 10 and 30 percent, the rates varying among provinces.[26] What accounts for such poor registration records?

There are two systems of birth registration operating in Pakistan.[27] First, there is a conventional, manual system, which is prevalent in the rural areas, where the Union Council (UC), a system of local governmental entities, is responsible for registering a population of about 12–18,000. The local watchman, parent, or even village elder can report to the UC secretary, who then registers the birth, death, marriage, or divorce. However, a birth certificate is only issued *if it is requested*.[28] Such a request may not be forthcoming if parents do not give any importance to such a document in the life chances of their child—which is the case in Pakistan.[29] Thereafter, the UC, its secretary specifically, becomes responsible for manually entering the event, maintaining the record, and then aggregating, organizing, and transferring these records to the higher district level. This transfer is not guaranteed, and the birth records may remain in a disorganized condition at the local UC level without ever reaching the higher levels of the state to be included in a national database. Moreover, since no accountability mechanism is in place, such a system is amenable to local pressures and networks of complicity.

What are the other reasons for the low birth registration rates, birth registration being symptomatic of the larger civil registration system in Pakistan? According to the Pakistan country report on birth registration:

> Since the system requires that the information be brought to the UC secretary, most of the parents, who have no idea of the importance of registering the birth, do not bother to go to the UC to register their children. On the other hand, if they did want to go to the UC secretary, the UC offices are found to be closed most of the time. When the offices are open, other problems surface: the lack of training, so that the UC secretary may not know how to register the birth, and there may not be any stationary [sic] available at the UC office.[30]

Imagine a developed state unable to register an identity, birth, marriage, or divorce for a lack of pencils or stationery. However, the birth and the broader civil registration system was hampered with nonfunctioning UCs throughout the 1980s and 1990s. Their revival in 2001 only partially alleviated the situation. If parents consider birth registration to be useless, a bothersome exercise that only puts an extra burden on them, and if the state is unable to link birth registration to direct services and benefits provided by the state, the usage of birth certificates will remain an uncommon practice.[31] Additionally, due to networks of complicity, there is a problem of counterfeit birth certificates. According to a local official, a district *nazim* from Lahore, Mian Amer Mahmood, about "80 percent of the birth certificates were found [to be] bogus and fake" (*Business Recorder* 2005a). Since "[e]very union council was issuing birth certificates with different design[s]," there was a clear lack of uniformity, which undermined the "credibility" and "authenticity" of these documents (ibid.). Lahore is the second largest city in Pakistan, and this absence of uniform standards does not bode well for the identification project of the Pakistani state.

The national birth registration effort was further undermined with the introduction at the federal level of the National Database and Registration Authority (NADRA) in 2000.[32] The NADRA registers all individuals over the age of eighteen and is responsible for distributing to them a national identity card. However, to create such a database, it has to register their births as well, thus duplicating the efforts of the local union councils. This redundancy means that Pakistanis have to register themselves twice—once with the local UC, which has a wider presence, and nationally with NADRA. Lack of any cooperation between the two state agencies negatively affects the overall birth registration process.

Clearly, like in India and Malaysia, the cost of registration, the lack of awareness among the population, the absence of uniform standards and formatting, and the lack of effort on the part of state agents are some factors explaining the low levels of birth registration in Pakistan. This results in undocumented natives and thus blurred membership. Such a weak infrastructure for individual identity is further undermined by environmental disasters. Much like the tsunami that struck India, Indonesia, and Malaysia on December 26, 2004, the earthquake of October 8, 2005, destroyed the civil records of individuals in Pakistan. The UC buildings were either in ruins or completely destroyed, and local officials in charge of birth registration were among the 73,000 dead and the million displaced in the country (Pakistan Country Paper 2006: 8). The earthquake damage further highlighted the weak birth and identity infrastructure in these areas as state officials could not plan relief efforts for orphaned or separated children. Since duplicate records are not kept and computerized records are absent, these victims' birth records along with other identity records may be permanently lost. Such a situation presents opportunities for traffickers, human smugglers, and Pakistani parents and their children who desire to access greater prospects nationally and internationally based on counterfeit birth certificates—or genuine birth certificates issued fraudulently. Since birth certificates are feeder documents, they are the entry into the national identification system (passports, national identity cards, etc.) that creates individuals with authorized identities. Such a system is easily accessible by Afghan or Bangladeshi illegal immigrants in Pakistan as well as by Pakistanis seeking to travel abroad under assumed identities.

Sending States: Afghanistan, Bangladesh, and Indonesia

Now I turn to the citizenship-related infrastructures in Indonesia, Bangladesh, and Afghanistan, the three largest senders of illegal immigrants to Malaysia, India, and Pakistan, respectively, to show how these migrants integrate with the populations of the recipient countries, thereby intensifying blurred membership. In the poorer states of Afghanistan, Bangladesh, and Indonesia, documentary legality has very little meaning, and thus paperwork or proof of state authorization is minimal. Although the state may require birth, death, and marriage registrations, it is common for people to ignore such state directives or to be unaware of such requirements.

As a new democratic Indonesia emerged from Suharto's dictatorial clutches, it was under constant pressure from leading NGOs and civil rights groups to take steps to protect individual rights, such as those provided for in the Convention on the Rights of the Child. In Indonesia, approximately 38 million people earn less than US$1 per day, and according to some estimates nearly half of all Indonesians live on earnings of less than US$2 per day (Rosenberg 2005: 119). These numbers exclude a huge population who may be above the poverty line but are unemployed (ibid.). In 2006, a submission to the UN Commission on Human Rights by a gathering of prominent NGOs pointed out that only four of ten Indonesian children have registered births.[33] Assuming that registration also implies possession of a birth certificate, this could mean that only 40 percent of Indonesian children have birth certificates. This statistic may be somewhat exaggerated since we know from the case of India that registration of birth is a process separate from the acquisition of the birth certificate (i.e., the birth of a child may be registered—there is an entry in the official record—but the parents may or may not have started the process to actually collect the birth certificate). This scenario is particularly applicable to countries like Indonesia, where, until 2000, a fee was charged for acquiring a birth certificate.

In Indonesia, a 2000 national survey, the Survei Pendidikan dan Kesehatan Ibu dan Anak (SPKIA)[34] found that only 30.6 percent of children under five had official birth certificates, with similar figures for males (30 percent) and females (31 percent).[35] However, as expected, both the coverage and the need for such a document are higher in urban areas, and so there is a significant difference between urban (48 percent) and rural (20 percent) children possessing birth certificates.[36] Approximately 30 percent of children have local birth records, such as birth notices provided by health care personnel, subdistrict/village authorities, or midwives— but these do not form part of the official state records (ibid.). Many officials are village heads, and as many as 50 percent are not on the permanent payroll of the government, like regular state officials. Instead, these village heads participate in the birth registration process as volunteers.[37] By delegating the authority to certify birth and identity to the local level, the state makes the process arbitrary and open to local pressures.[38] Noting the importance of birth registration, a report on the trafficking of women and children notes how Indonesians without a birth certificate

> could find it difficult to prove their age, receive special protection as a minor, prove their nationality or residency, be admitted to school, obtain a passport, open a bank account, receive health care, be adopted, take exams, marry, hold a driving license, inherit money or property, own a house or land, vote or stand for elected office. (Rosenberg 2005: 121)

With 41.3 percent of the population earning less than $1 a day, and landlessness common as a result of frequent land erosion in the Bay of Bengal basin, Bangladesh is also rife with blurred membership (United Nations Development Program 2007: 239). Bangladesh sends to India millions of poor illegal immigrants from among its reservoir of 63 million people who are surviving below the poverty line (Ibid.). It was no surprise, therefore, when a UNICEF-supported survey in the late 1990s discovered that only 11 percent of the births in Bangladesh were registered (United Nations Development Group 2000: 6.4.1). Another report by Bangladeshi NGOs to the CRC notes that there was an emphasis on the registration of births (via the Birth Registration Act of 1886) since the colonial period, but as a result of subsequent neglect, it is uncommon to be required to show one's birth certificate, and many that exist are fake (Bangladesh Shishu Adhikar Forum 1996: 8).[39] According to most recent estimates, birth registration rates in Bangladesh are a very low 7 percent, and standardized documentation is minimal (UNICEF 2005c: 43).

Like Bangladesh, Afghanistan has had a minimal identity infrastructure. Since the Soviet occupation, civil war, endemic poverty, warlordism, and the harsh anti-women measures of the Taliban have destroyed Afghanistan's civil registration system. A majority of the births, deaths, and marriages take place without state authorization.[40] The last time that birth registration figures were collected was in the 1970s. Recent estimates put birth registration in Afghanistan climbing to 10 percent, which is a reflection of the U.S–backed Karzai government's efforts to regulate the return of the Afghan refugees and to create a modern infrastructure through documentation (UNICEF 2005c: 43). However, this is contingent on there being a liberal, modern, and stable government in Afghanistan. The news that elements of the former Taliban regime are increasing their control over vast swaths of territory in Afghanistan can only mean a setback to civil registration efforts. This untenable situation will create further outflows of Pashtuns, Hazaras, and other groups from Afghanistan to nearby Pakistan and Iran.

Evidence from the field suggests that children go unregistered in developing countries due to (a) a lack of access to the offices responsible for recording births; (b) expensive fees and costs associated with the registration process; (c) corruption among state officials, who demand bribes for registration; and (d) a lack of understanding among the poor on the need to register a birth (Rosenberg 2005: 121). Data available from forty-eight countries cite the cost of registration, ignorance of the need for registration, and distance to the registration center as some of the most common reasons for the absence of birth registrations (UNICEF 2005b: 4). Apprehension that the information may be used against the individual or for military conscription or taxation is among other reasons that the poor in developing countries shy away from state civil registration efforts.[41]

Identification Meets Culture

Cultural factors too inhibit the birth certification system, further complicating efforts at a national identity database and thus adding to blurred membership. In parts of Indonesia, India, Malaysia, Pakistan, Afghanistan, and Bangladesh, a delay in child naming is a common practice. For example, in Indonesia, a child is referred to by a generic nickname or simply called *bayi* (baby), and only after a certain waiting period, usually forty days, is the child given an official name.[42] If the baby fails to survive, the death may not be reported since burial can take place quietly in the house yard or other local compound. Fear of bad luck, the social stigma of an unwanted pregnancy, naming a child without appropriate religious ceremonies, and time-dependent rituals are among some of the cultural factors with which birth registration officials have to contend in rural areas.[43]

Common to Muslim societies and other ethnic groups in the region are naming practices where one name is sufficient. Non-Muslim females in Punjab, India, or Muslim females in Uttar Pradesh, India, can have a single name—showing no naming connection to their parents and only adopting the surname of their husband after marriage.[44] This custom creates inheritance and other legal complexities. Similarly, Mohammad is a sufficient name in Pakistan, Afghanistan, Indonesia, Malaysia, India, the Philippines, and Bangladesh. The former president of Indonesia (Suharto) and the current president (Bambang) are known, like most Indonesians, by one name. Indigenous groups such as the Orang Asli in West Malaysia and the Bajau Laut in East Malaysia do not even remember their legal or proper names—so rare are conventional Western naming practices in these communities (Kaur 2004). The Christian-based practice of having a first name, middle name, and surname is rare among many traditional groups—Muslim and non-Muslim—especially in rural areas. Possessing one name is common to many tribal and lower caste groups in India and to ethnic minority groups in the Philippines,[45] Indonesia, Malaysia, Pakistan, Bangladesh, and Afghanistan. How a civil registration system separates the many Mohammads becomes critical to a system that wants to provide one unique identity per individual. It is common for individuals in these countries to have an "official" name, surname included, which is distinct from their "real" name, which they may use in their daily routine. However, for those untouched by the state in any form, many lead their entire lives with a single name.

Marriage registration is not common in traditional Muslim communities in Afghanistan, Bangladesh, Pakistan, Indonesia, and India. This rarity is due to the fact that Islamic marriages do not require civil certifications of any kind. Marriage registration is a state practice which identifies the person's name, parents' names, age, gender, religion, and other personal identifiers. It also provides legal proof of parentage, nationality, and inheritance. The lack of a registration process harms the rights of the child and the parent, especially the mother. It can deprive them of a legal identity by denying them a nationality. In addition, the Islamic practice of permitting men to have up to four wives—a polygamous practice sanctioned by the Sharia (Islamic law)—makes it difficult to trace the lineages of such a family by any civil registration system. Tracing individuals and their rights is only possible if they are registered with the state at the beginning (i.e., at birth) or at a later stage (like marriage). For example, even though marriage registration is required by law in Bangladesh, the two largest ethnic groups—Muslims (89.7 percent) and Hindus (9.2 percent)—often marry without state verification or authorization. The Muslim Marriages and Divorces (Registration) Act of 1974 requires state confirmation of the "union", but only 40 percent of Muslim marriages are registered, while all Hindu marriages in Bangladesh bypass state authentication.[46] If birth certificates are not widely in use, then the circumvention of age requirements is easy. Hence, incidents of child marriage (under the age of eighteen) are common in these Muslim states; Bangladesh (65 percent), Indonesia (24 percent), and Pakistan (32 percent) have high child marriage rates (UNICEF 2005c: 43).[47] Cultural traditions in marriage or birth are equally responsible for making individuals invisible to the state.

Marriage registration does offer another opportunity for the state to make its members visible to its institutions. Marriage registration seeks to (a) identify an individual not marked at birth, (b) reaffirm the identity of an individual already marked, and (c) trace the socioeconomic pattern of an individual's life. The process of identification during civil registration occurs in two stages, beginning with the entering of the event in records (marriage registration), followed by a distribution of the corresponding registration documents. Civil marriage, when registered, is followed by the distribution of a document which contains unambiguous information on the identity of both of the partners in marriage—address, age, parents' names, religion—and sometimes includes photographs. Such information is necessary for cataloging individual identity. However, most marriages in India, Malaysia, and Pakistan are solemnized under customary or religious law—which often run parallel to the state-sanctioned civil law. In recent years, the Supreme Court of India has insisted that various state authorities at the regional level enforce mandatory marriage registration since it enhances the value of citizenship rights related to property, inheritance, and paternity.[48] Civil marriage is voluntary and barely practiced among the major religious communities in India, Malaysia, and Pakistan. Marriages are common, but their registration is uneven at best; for example, Muslim marriages are to be registered in Malaysia with the State Religious Office, but registration is often subject to the caprice of local imams. Similarly, in India, Malaysia, and Pakistan, individuals may self-report their customary or religious marriage in the census, thus producing information on rates and distribution of marriage without establishing individual identities. Widespread Hindu, Islamic, and other traditional customary marriages in India, Malaysia, and Pakistan do not enhance the infrastructure of citizenship as they fail to add another consistent layer to the civil program that seeks to confirm individual identity.

Gender bias and other cultural factors are accommodated into national laws and play a role in blurred membership. They also trump the liberal features of jus soli citizenship. Patriarchal nationality laws in Pakistan, Afghanistan, Bangladesh, Malaysia, and Indonesia (and India until 1992) mean that nationality can only be passed on through the father, so that children born to native mothers and foreign fathers are not able to procure birth certificates. They also become ineligible for education, health, and other critical rights which are for citizens only (UNICEF 1998b). This is a clear violation of Article 2 of the CRC because that document prohibits any discrimination against children on the basis of nationality or the gender of a parent. It is also a violation of Article 9 of the Convention on the Elimination of All Forms of Discrimination against Women (CEDAW), by which a woman has the right to pass on her nationality to her child (UNICEF 1998b). In practice, many states of Asia and Africa, especially many Muslim-majority states, allow this discrimination to continue.[49] Children of a Malaysian mother and an illegal immigrant father in Malaysia or children of a divorced Indonesian illegal female worker in Malaysia will be without any birth certificate or nationality documentation. According to Malaysian law, immigrants, especially foreign workers, are not allowed to marry during their stay in the country.[50] As a result, immigrants—legal or illegal—do not register their marriages but utilize customary laws or religious rights for their unions. Consequently, their children are ineligible for state documents. If the parents divorce or if the father abandons the mother, the child remains unregistered. This situation creates a mass of poor, paperless children who are invisible to the state: a signature characteristic of blurred membership.

According to Indonesian NGOs,[51] dual nationality is the challenge that the Indonesian and Malaysian governments face in regard to the approximately half million Indonesian children in Malaysia, mostly born to Indonesian illegal immigrants, who are now considered to be "stateless." Malaysia, in an effort to protect its national interest and sovereignty, does not want to distribute Malaysian birth certificates to children born to illegal Indonesian workers (including those with a Malaysian mother and a foreign father) since this will pave the way for their future Malaysian citizenship, which in turn will make millions of Indonesian *parents* eligible for Malaysian citizenship.

Meanwhile, 10,000 of these stateless children who reside in Sabah have no access to education (*Malay Mail* 2005a). Some of them are working odd jobs and earning a meager 200 ringgits (about $62) per month or are whiling their hours away (ibid.). Defending its national interest and sovereignty, Indonesia too resists any deportation of these poor stateless children and their "illegal immigrant" parents from Malaysia. A half million children without birth certificates adds considerably to the blurred membership conditions that overlap both Malaysia and Indonesia. The potential for crisis in this situation was brought to the fore when the December 2004 tsunami struck India, Malaysia, and Indonesia. The tsunami not only orphaned many children, it also wiped out proof of their identities. Fears that children from tsunami-affected areas in India, Malaysia, and Indonesia could be kidnapped and trafficked were well founded. A well-established civil registration system would have eased the process of identifying the children and reuniting them with their families or relatives. However, without proof of identity, it was easier for child traffickers to claim these children as their own, lure them across international borders, and then sell them. The lack of birth registration and possession of identity documentation among rural and poor people fosters an environment of corruption and manipulation where illegal immigration, trafficking, and human smuggling become possible. Agents, traffickers, or potential illegal immigrants can falsify personal details, such as the dates of birth of underage girls, to facilitate their travel abroad (Rosenberg 2005).

Fraudulent documents are commonplace at the local level in societies with blurred membership. For example, in Entikong, West Kalimantan traffickers "facilitate" illegal or legal travel abroad by acquiring fake passports for underage girls from the local immigration office (Rosenberg 2005). The immigration office in West Kalimantan issues passports, ignoring female minors' age, because they cannot question the identity documents issued by the local district office, which in turn must issue an identity card based on a letter verifying the birth date from the appropriate village head (Rosenberg 2005: 121). Village heads and other local community leaders often want to help female minors and other travelers emigrate abroad in order to help poor families back home. The practice of providing a locally authenticated letter that falsifies personal details, such as the birth date or marital status, happens at the local, societal level and is as common to immigrant-sending parts of Indonesia, Bangladesh, and Afghanistan as it is to India, Pakistan, and other developing countries. Pressures from below—the society—create local practices that enable illegal travel.

Blurred membership results from several factors—the inadequate and insufficient collection of data on individual identity and location, the inability to access centers providing legal documentation, and cultural traditions—all of which are interwoven to create from below an indifference and apathy on the part of individual natives to legalize themselves. To "legalize" is to become visible to the state, the sovereign, and hence to become a part of the state-instituted infrastructure of citizenship. By becoming legal, the individual becomes part of the circle of members who form the political community—the nation that forms the state—and eligible for social, political, and economic rights. In short, recognition of the individual is crucial for national sovereignty and for citizenship, yet many states in the developing world can barely confirm the citizenship of individual members.

What is the cumulative effect of such blurred membership? Before 9/11, a centralized, computerized birth registry or nationality database had been absent in India, Pakistan, Bangladesh, Afghanistan, the Philippines, and other developing countries. It was therefore impossible to verify the legitimacy of local documents. Malaysia did have a centralized system, but it was corruptible with many loopholes at the local level. The process of reaching out to a wider poor population implies decentralization—a devolution of authority to the local level with little centralized monitoring. The lack of computerized information on immigrants (tourists, students, etc.) is an indication of weak accountability in the infrastructure of citizenship. It means that one immigration/citizenship center does not know who another center may be allowing into the country. A centralized, computerized database of citizens was nonexistent in Pakistan until recently, even as it sought to identify potential "foreign" terrorists in its territory. The same can be said about India, Bangladesh, Indonesia,[52] the Philippines, and many other developing countries. Such networked computerized databases have been in existence for decades in the developed world, but are only now being planned in the developing world.[53]

Developing countries are thus emphasizing and discussing the use of mobile outreach teams that could expedite the process of birth registration, identity certification, and the distribution of national identity cards. The state is bearing most or all of the costs of making civil registration free as it consolidates identity data. With increasing state management of individual identity, are we entering a new era of more efficient policymaking and smooth international travel, or are we entering an era where centralized identification records can more easily facilitate genocide, ethnic cleansing, human smuggling, and trafficking? Perhaps the existence of blurred membership highlights some of the ways in which the Western, governmental, Westphalian, top-down model of citizenship does not fit the developing world. The anonymity of a blurred existence has an advantage: it frees one from surveillance, by both the state and nearby communities. Even as the state aggressively seeks to eliminate blurred membership globally, societies may pay a price for such an intrusion.[54] On the other hand, an increasing reliance on standard documentation to identify individuals may have unintended consequences that undermine state sovereignty further. To better understand this, in the next chapter, we will turn to analyzing the emergence of a documentary citizenship over the last fifty years.

4

Documentary Citizenship

Write me down, make me real.
—Slogan for a global campaign on birth registration (Plan 2005b).[1]

WHO IS ABU HANIF? IS HE AN INDIAN OR A BANGLADESHI ILLEGALLY LIVING IN India? Abu Hanif was arrested in the Bengali *basti* (slum) of Delhi on June 20, 2000, in a midnight raid. Hanif claimed that he came to Delhi from a small village in West Bengal (the Indian Bengal). The police accused him and other Bengali-speaking Muslims of being Bangladeshi illegal immigrants. Abu Hanif lived among Bengalis—some from the Indian side, others from Bangladesh. They looked like him, ate similar food, spoke the same language, and were all extremely poor. As Bengali Muslims, they were all under suspicion for being illegal immigrants. In a letter dated June 29, 2000, a senior Delhi police official accused Abu Hanif of being a foreigner and insisted that he prove his citizenship with valid documents. In response, Abu Hanif produced a ration card, a voter identity card, a Delhi administration card, and a passport (Y037960)—all seemingly issued by the Indian state (*Abu Hanif alias Millan Master v. Police Commissioner of Delhi & Others*).[2] The difficulty is that many illegal Bangladeshis also possess such state documents—either fake or real but fraudulently acquired. Is Abu Hanif an Indian who can stay in his country, or is he a Bangladeshi who must be deported? The answer lies in his documents.

What is the link between documents and illegal immigrants' access to citizenship?

International immigration scholars may insist that network theory accounts for the role of documents in immigration. But the acquisition of citizenship documents is not central to most network analysis, which seeks to uncover the connections and relationships that explain illegal flows (i.e., trafficking of drugs, arms, women, etc.). Current scholars will be hard pressed to identify any major work that focuses on the role of *fraudulent* documents in the acquisition of citizenship. True, scholars have recently examined the *revolution identificatoire*, especially the passport and its impact on the Western nation-state (Noiriel 1996; Salter 2003; Torpey 2000).[3] The passport is one of many documents used by people to migrate and settle. Yet, how relevant is passport travel to illegal immigrants from developing countries? They are not always crossing borders via airports. A few scholars have examined the use of fake documents in illegal crossings of borders and employment (Koslowski 2000b; Caplan and Torpey 2001; Andreas 2000). However, scholars have paid insufficient attention to—actually, not even entertained the possibility of—fraudulent documents giving illegal immigrants access to citizenship. The ability to use illegally acquired identity documents to bypass state regulations is omnipresent in developing countries. An independent analysis of the process by which documents enable people to travel and gain access to citizenship is, therefore, urgently needed, but is yet to be done. I contend that documents are vital to illegal immigration. Documents such as birth certificates and identity cards are the path to membership in a political community—the state citizenry.

Documents have come to embody individual identity in developing countries. The documentation of individual identity is part of a larger infrastructure of citizenship meant to identify members of the polity, thus creating a "citizenship from above"—from the state. The increasing dependence of modern states on documentation to identify their members is a major reason that illegal immigrants seek to acquire citizenship-indicating documents. Illegal citizenship depends on two conditions: the existence of immigrant networks which subvert gatekeeping sections of the state and the existence of blurred membership. When these two conditions are met, immigrants can and will illegally acquire citizenship-signifying documents, instantaneously becoming full members of the polity. This is the phenomenon known as "documentary citizenship"—the process by which illegal immigrants gain citizenship through the acquisition of fraudulent documents. The state's dependence on an infrastructure of citizenship is increasingly creating a nation of document-wielding individuals—citizens and illegal immigrants alike. Organizing the world according to levels of documentation reveals the global rise in documented nations. By transforming illegal immigrants into citizens, documents challenge the traditional view of the relationship between immigrants and the state.

Overlapping Identities and Sovereignties

The evolution of documentary citizenship can be traced to historical efforts at forming national boundaries, one of which is by using documents. Imperial powers were at a loss in their colonies, the developing states, where they encountered a bewildering array of natives with different ethnic, religious, racial, cultural, and culinary traditions. The British Empire encountered a huge diversity of ethnic groups in Afghanistan, Pakistan, India, Bangladesh, Burma, Malaysia, Singapore, and Brunei. The Dutch Empire had to contend with the diversity of the Dutch East Indies stretching over modern Indonesia. Precolonial polities in South and Southeast Asia were aware of the need for enumeration of their inhabitants, but only for taxation or conscription purposes; the identification and surveillance of the general population was of little interest.[4] Cultural identities were fluid and did not imply any national exclusivity; their recording was of little concern to the ruling monarchies, sultanates, and kingships (Kertzer and Arel 2002: 2). In the precolonial period, the family, dynasty, or ruler was the locus of individual identity and sovereignty (Rudolph and Rudolph 1985). Overlapping or multiple sovereignties marked such societies,[5] with imperial formations and regional kingdoms in tension, and small polities paying tribute to one, two, or more overlords while remaining sovereign. Exclusive territorial sovereignty simply did not exist; boundaries between sovereign units often consisted of mountains, forests, and rivers, which created a thick geographical border.[6] The kingdom was "a patchy territory full of hierarchically sovereign units. As its limits were marked by the frontier towns, the realm of a kingdom was usually not bounded either" (Winichakul 1996a: 73). Since exclusive territorial sovereignty did not exist, it did not contain exclusive subjects; overlapping identities marked the era.

During the precolonial and colonial periods, immigration flows took place between weakly institutionalized political entities, such as kingdoms, city-states, empires, and other nonstate entities (also see chapter 1; Koslowski 2002: 375–399). Fluid boundaries with minimal control over populations and the lack of a centralized citizenship structure marked the historical period in developing countries. In such circumstances, exiting a polity required paperwork signed by the local priest, the local temple, or other religious institutions recognized in neighboring political entities; these documents were the initial mark of an identity. Documents authenticated by religious and monarchical authority were used by both local/regional travelers and long-distance immigrants. At the highest level, official ambassadors or other couriers carried documents identifying them as royal messengers when carrying royal letters and gifts between rulers. This was as common to the kingdoms in the Indian subcontinent as it was to the rulers in Java, Indonesia. Hence, in the period up to the nineteenth century, much like in Europe, documents such as safe conduct passes and letters of marque were often used by travelers (Salter 2003: 19, 150). The documents were meant to regulate "troublemakers," such as the gypsies, vagrants, political agitators—in general, migrants from the lower classes—who were always the focus of surveillance and policing due to public safety concerns (Lucassen 2001: 253). However, until the nineteenth century, the state's need for the surveillance of troublemakers required only basic monitoring. Similarly, state enumeration efforts were aimed at registering and identifying segments of the population targeted for taxation or conscription; comprehensive enumeration, such as a census, to identify social identities was of no interest to the state (Kertzer and Arel 2002: 7). Precolonial identification schemes in the European, the Ottoman, or the Mughal periods were not standardized.

Citizenship from Above: The Desire for Order

When did developing states begin to push for documentation to support citizenship claims? How and when did developing states begin to keep track of their "official" members, and therefore deny or grant rights based on that status? In Western countries before the seventeenth and eighteenth centuries, passage within the country required documentation, i.e., it was an internal state issue (see Polanyi 1944).[7] Lifting these internal restrictions was a great emancipation, as it created a right to travel and gave access to national markets within the state (ibid.). In the international realm, however, restrictions on travel between states remained. Systematic documentation of individuals appeared in the nineteenth century as part of an infrastructure of citizenship meant to secure the state from foreigners. It was in the nineteenth century that "the rationalization of administrative surveillance" began; it was established as a distinguishing feature of some states by the First World War (Noiriel 1996: 72).[8] The state expanded and intruded into socioeconomic affairs via taxation and poor relief. This created incentives to provide paperwork to individuals (Lucassen 2001: 254–255). The Netherlands, Belgium, and Italy initiated population registration. Prussia began individual surveillance at the start of the nineteenth century, systematized it in 1842, and introduced identity papers in 1846 (ibid.: 250–251). About the same time, censuses were conducted in British India between 1868 and 1872, in 1881, and thereafter once every decade (Guha 2003: 148).[9]

For the imperial powers in developing countries—the British (South Asia), the Dutch (Southeast Asia), and the French (North Africa)—keeping political order and stability promoted their drive to document membership in Asia and Africa. However, in parts of Asia and Africa, making society legible (Scott 1998) through identification schemes was also the culmination of indigenous efforts at state making (Guha 2003). For example, Todar Mal, a senior administrator of the Mughal Empire in South Asia, created land surveys, settlement records, and a revenue management structure before colonial efforts to mark individuals for the purpose of extracting resources and maintaining order (Habib 2001). Another systematized attempt to identify individuals began during colonial times when Indian civil servants collaborated with their British officers to introduce fingerprinting in South Asia (Sengoopta 2003). Fingerprinting was born in the Indian subcontinent due to the administrative needs of an insecure empire. Among other uses, it was a means of monitoring individuals, especially the empire's political opponents, of which there were many, and groups characterized as criminal. Prior practices of using ink for fingerprints had existed in ancient China and India, but their systematic use for bureaucratic purposes was a colonial effort. Order and stability in the colonies required the introduction of new technologies to create a "classificatory" grid of exclusive individuals (Anderson 1991). Therefore, colonial governments collaborated with knowledgeable native bureaucrats of the imperial civil service to implement the censuses, surveys, and mapping to regulate the boundaries of the political community, to safeguard the territory, and to efficiently extract resources.

Welfare and public safety concerns drove the identification system (Cole 2001: 63–65).[10] There was the administrative need to guard against impersonation and fraud in the disbursement of pensions, and a public order need "to strengthen administrative control over the country-side" or to be the "eyes" and "ears" of the policing system (ibid.).[11] With only a few individual identities marked and cataloged, the difference between citizen and noncitizen was impossible to tell.

The attempt to identify citizens only became an urgent task with the formation of newly independent states, such as India, Pakistan, Bangladesh, Afghanistan, Malaysia, and Indonesia. Independence for these states marked a shift from monarchical sovereignty to popular sovereignty. There was a democratic push from below that drove the various movements for independence in the developing world. Finally, the "native" Indian, Bangladeshi, Pakistani, Malaysian, and Indonesian would have a say in the political affairs of the state via adult suffrage. It was the emergence of universal suffrage which gave citizenship a concrete foundation by creating a circle of individuals who could legitimately claim the right to political expression in the affairs of the state (Noiriel 1996: 78–79). Suddenly, citizenship began to have specific meaning, like access to welfare services and voting rights. As developing states expanded their functions and began to extend into socioeconomic affairs via taxation and poverty alleviation programs, more incentives were created to provide paperwork to individuals. The state suddenly began to have meaning in the everyday life of residents. Population registration became a priority in all of these newly independent states as welfare and other public services were

implemented for the benefit of the poor. It was soon necessary to show identification documents in order to utilize hospitals, dispensaries, schools, public distribution systems, banks, and electricity and water services. With the expansion of the
services provided by the state, residents began to carry multiple documents.
Standardized paperwork, issued by the state, marked individual identity at the
national level. Documents such as ration cards, high school matriculation certificates, national identity cards, and passports are all markers of what I call "citizenship from above."

Such documentation, however, still does not exist for millions of people in
India, Malaysia, and Pakistan. In developing countries, the limited resources and
capacity of the state constrain the expansion of documentary requirements.
Citizenship from above is therefore bounded by the economic development of the
state. The greater the degree of economic development, the more resources a state
can devote to its democratic, welfare, and distributive functions, and the greater its
need for policing and surveillance through documentation.

The trend toward documenting identity was further strengthened when many
states imposed passport controls during the First World War (Torpey 2000: 121).
Adherence to international travel norms, especially the passport, was essential to
quickly integrating these newly independent states into the international system.
Importantly, as John Torpey (2001: 270) points out, identity cards became a "cur-
rency of domestic administration, marking out eligibles from ineligibles in the
areas of voting [and] social services." This occurred even as nationalist forces sought
to distinguish the membership of the nation-state, so that the welfare state provided benefits to only those deemed eligible. Citizenship and democratic practices
combine via the issue of eligibility—who is a participant in a democracy—making
documentation indispensable to modern states. Naturally, members of these newly
independent nations developed a close relationship with the state; they became
preoccupied with who was "in" and who was "out"—something only a bureaucratic
system of identification could determine (Torpey 2000: 121). Modern India,
Malaysia, and Pakistan followed a Weberian path as democratization led to increasing bureaucratization (ibid.; Weber 1978).[12] Thus arose an infrastructure of
citizenship.

But how did documents come to embody membership identity and, therefore,
allow the state to distinguish between citizen and noncitizen? Since the Second
World War, population registers, national censuses, national databases, identity
documents, and passports were all developed by the state to distinguish citizens
from noncitizens. This was possible because, from the middle of the twentieth century, documents came to embody individual identity. As Gerard Noiriel (1996: 76)
effectively argues, the legal identity connecting the individual to the state "material-
ized" through "the Card and the Code." Connecting individual identification

accurately and reliably to the physical body was the task of this infrastructure of citizenship. Over time, this meant the "turning of real lives into writing," as Foucault has argued (1977: 192; 1991). The infrastructure of application forms, photographs, signatures, corporeal attributes, and legal histories seeks to depict the civic community in an easily communicable way. However, creating an infrastructure of citizenship does not occur in a linear fashion; it has its bumps. Of the statistics collected and documents registered, many are not in a shape or form that allows them to be used effectively for control, identification, or surveillance. One could argue that, in many cases, they are of no more use than if they had never been collected, issued, or registered. The processes that have to be completed to make such records a reliable instrument of governance are not simple. Converting heaps of files with information on individual identities into a form easily communicable, such as a central database, is a major goal of institution building.

In theory, of course, agents of the state should be able to reliably identify any individual citizen. Documentation has become fused with individual identity to create a distinctive feature of modern developing states: your document is your identity. Citizenship from above has made it easier for the state to monitor the identity and mobility of individuals. Meanwhile, the state has increased its list of "troublemakers" from the nineteenth century (criminals, vagrants, political opponents, the unfamiliar traveler) to include newer groups (traffickers, terrorists, smugglers, and illegal immigrants).

The bureaucratic exercise of identifying members of the political community also has influenced social practices. Post-independence India, like Pakistan, Afghanistan, Bangladesh, Malaysia, and Indonesia, began to celebrate "birthdays" and to organize life events chronologically. Older generations were baffled by these new celebrations since the only birthdays that were celebrated in pre-independence India, Malaysia, and Pakistan were those of deities, prophets, and saints. According to Islam—at least the versions practiced in this region—the celebration of the birthdays of individuals was not encouraged, and may have been forbidden; only prophets and saints are worthy of such celebration. The same was true for the Hindus, Sikhs, Jews, and Zoroastrians in the region. Even today, people in rural areas have no tradition of celebrating birthdays. The practice of documenting numerical markers of identity, such as age at entrance to school, high school graduation, dates of vaccination, marriageable age, and other markers of life events, is a post-independence phenomenon—after a Westphalian state came into existence. Traditional religious schools, madrassas, monasteries, and temples did not require identification documents, least of all a birth certificate. In fact, only in the 1980s, with economic liberalization and the rise of cable television, did big cities in these countries start celebrating anniversaries or Father's Day, Mother's Day, and Valentine's Day. As numerical markers inscribed on paperwork institutionalized the demarcation of the lifespans of individuals in developing states, the emergence of documented individuals became inevitable.

As citizenship from above came to be established, the desire to control populations, including their movement and access to benefits, was a preoccupation of new leaders trying to build successful nation-states in the developing world. The identity infrastructure was critical to drawing the lines around the community and the territory. The borders drawn by the colonial empires, sometimes dividing large settlements of ethnic groups into two or more territorial states, were to be preserved. Colonial India was divided into the Republic of India and the Republic of Pakistan (and later the Republics of Pakistan and Bangladesh). Large colonies in Africa were fragmented into new states with overlapping ethnic groups, and the colonies in Southeast Asia were sharply divided into distinct states, such as Malaysia, Singapore, the Philippines, Indonesia, and Brunei. Newly independent states sought to emulate the practices of their counterparts in the developed world by creating institutions to monitor and control ethnic groups within their boundaries, to regulate the flow across them, and to maintain and protect their sanctity. After all, demonstrating control over borders, determining who is allowed entry and who is excluded, are defining features of sovereignty in the international system.

Governments want their populations to remain within their boundaries and to move to other territorial states only with their permission. They seek to protect their borders from any unauthorized entry by peoples belonging to other states. As a result, citizenship from above involves making judgments on the eligibility of an individual to enter and participate in the decisions of a polity. Judging the citizenship of an individual is first and foremost a cultural phenomenon. The state may find it difficult then to make this judgment if illegal immigrants and other outsiders appear to look and behave like most citizens. The perception of sameness is then no guarantee of legal membership in a multiethnic state. The very foundations of the documentary system, therefore, seek to determine the identity of the individual, including background and travel history, in order for a judgment on citizenship to be made. Fingerprinting, birth certificates, death certificates, marriage certificates, identity cards, passports, visas, and other identity markers became valuable in such an enterprise of control and regulation. Border checkpoints, border fences, special border police, and border identity papers became important markers that divided domestic populations from foreign ones. With documents, we can tell that you do not belong here, even if you look like some of us. ID, please? Passport, please?

Preoccupied with the orderly expansion of state functions and the maintenance of law and order, the only entry into the community of citizens that was acceptable to the modern state was the process of naturalization. The state desired that only certain individuals enter its community, and the state wanted control over that decision. It allowed them entry through naturalization only after verifying their background and local standing—in other words, their eligibility. Verification involves vouching for individual identity and location claims by two or three witnesses, with agents of the state authenticating the process of verification. Verification of local claims by local people or agents of the state underlines the citizenship-identifying document system in most developing countries. Local verification also allows the crossing of citizenship's final frontier, the naturalization process. The conditions for noncitizens, legal immigrants, and eligible refugees are even tougher since they have to prove to the state their irrefutable and permanent local residency, familiarity with local culture, and loyalty. Citizenship is closely monitored by the agencies of the government responsible for internal security; after all, the control of entry into a body politic is viewed as the most precious indicator of state sovereignty. The Home Ministry in India and the Interior ministries in Pakistan and Malaysia control access to citizenship. Their ultimate function is to monitor and regulate a citizenship from above. Indeed, this has been the norm since World War II and has been strongly reaffirmed globally since 9/11.

Given that the state now monitors the citizenship of the individual in such a way, does it achieve its goals of making state membership secure? Recall that the birth certificate is the first document identifying the individual and that its absence in circulation and use indicates blurred membership (see chapter 3).[13] Recall also that *blurred membership* refers to the residence of an individual within the state without recognition from any of the state agencies above. Even as blurred membership occurs from below—from the society—increased state involvement in identifying its members creates a citizenship from above. Recall that networks of complicity make it difficult to tell the difference between real and fake documentation, so anything that looks legitimate will enable citizenship. The acquisition and possession of seemingly legal documents by illegal immigrants that "prove" juridical membership in a state, a process through which citizenship status can be ascribed to a noncitizen, is what I call "documentary citizenship." Documentary citizenship, then, is a response from below to citizenship from above. Documentary citizenship is an informal device, a back channel, to many of the benefits associated with the narrower and more difficult path to legal citizenship. It expands and accelerates the incorporation of illegal immigrants into the citizenry of a state. More important, it allows many illegal immigrants access to safeguarded citizenship rights, including political suffrage. Political suffrage, as we know it, is closely linked to legal citizenship since it opens the door to many protected domains of state decision making and citizenship rights, such as the legislature and public offices involved in defense, foreign, and security policymaking. Through documentary citizenship, illegal immigrants have a say in governance—who rules—a matter critical to all democratic states.

Inasmuch as paperwork determines an individual's legitimate membership in a state, documentary citizenship has become the sine qua non of citizenship. For example, a fake or fraudulently acquired ration card in India, a national identity card (NIC) in Pakistan, or an identity card (IC) in Malaysia transforms illegal immigrants into citizens instantly, thus challenging the standard model of the relationship between immigrants and the state. Documentary citizenship allows illegal immigrants to enter, settle, and most important, gain full citizenship rights, all the while bypassing official naturalization. Because the state relies on multiple items of paperwork to identify an individual, there are varieties of documents indicating different gradations of citizenship for an immigrant. As long as local government agencies cannot tell the difference between legal and fake paperwork, fake documents ensure incorporation into a host society just as well as do legal documents. Therefore, it does not matter whether individuals possess legal or fake paperwork. For an immigrant, access to a country and its benefits (food, shelter, employment, school, health services)—citizenship rights—are more important than compliance with its laws or regulations or any obligations that may come with membership. Hence, a fake or fraudulently acquired but real driver's license, bank account, child's birth certificate, health certificate, *patta* document (land deed), electricity bill, water bill, state identity card, passport, electoral roll slip, street vendor municipal permit, and school diploma are all documents that ensure an immigrant's incorporation until the immigrant is suitably settled and can get legitimate paperwork.

In many ways, fake documents are preferred by illegal immigrants because they are cheaper, since they avoid bribes and higher state fees; faster, since they do not get delayed or mired in bureaucratic procedures; locally available, since state agencies often are absent in rural or difficult to reach areas; and allow for the avoidance of responsibilities and duties, which come when states legally tag or register you (for example, the obligation to pay taxes occurs only after you become legally "visible" to the state). What is more, the illegal immigrant can always use initial fake paperwork to later acquire authorized state documents, if necessary. Fake documents are therefore as real as legal documents in the way they create a pathway to membership. Moreover, state-authorized paperwork is distributed so arbitrarily, often via bribery and networks of complicity, that the authenticity of standard paperwork in many developing countries is thin. Widespread complicity by state officials implies that the line separating de facto and de jure is either nonexistent or thin. Fake paperwork authenticated by legitimate state officials transforms it into a legal document, creating an environment where it is difficult to distinguish between genuine and fraudulent documentation, hence the common acquisition and use of illegal paperwork. Since documents are the ultimate signifier of citizenship, and the state increasingly relies on them as it increases its distributive and regulatory role, they are critical to the widespread incorporation of illegal immigrants. It is my argument that today, citizenship everywhere is acquired and expressed through documents, either real or fake.

As the developing state increasingly emphasizes documentation for the detection and regulation of individuals, one can observe a rise in documentary citizenship. Understanding the relationship between documentation and citizenship is crucial. However, this does not reveal how and to what extent documents play a role in illegal immigrants' access to citizenship.

Two to Tango: Networks of Complicity and Blurred Membership

As we have seen, in some areas of the developing world, especially where the state has a presence—such as in towns and cities—blurred membership (chapter 3) begins to decline and paper documentation becomes more prevalent. But even today, the homeless and other poor lead blurred lives in urban centers. Delhi and Calcutta, Kuala Lumpur and Kota Kinabalu, Karachi and Lahore teem with blurred residents. As large rural to urban migratory flows create mega-cities in developing states, many urban poor remain blurred members and thus de facto citizens[14]— unable to prove their national membership to the police and never able to establish their citizenship and rights. Into this blurred condition of rural and urban areas enters the illegal immigrant.

The presence of blurred membership alone in urban or rural areas does not guarantee the illegal immigrant's acquisition of identity-signifying documents. For an illegal immigrant to acquire citizenship documents that legitimize her/his stay, there must be co-ethnic immigrant networks that have infiltrated the state institutions, thus creating a web of complicit state officials (chapter 2). In short, there are two critical factors by which documentary citizenship is acquired by illegal immigrants: the existence of networks of complicity (chapter 2) and the existence of blurred membership (chapter 3). So, while blurred membership and complicit networks are vital on their own, only the simultaneous presence of both factors enables the acquisition of citizenship documents. The gradual accumulation of identity documents, fake or real, then gives illegal immigrants access to citizenship. Each of these documents, at various times and in a variety of ways, permits the illegal immigrant to claim local legitimacy. Figure 4.1 provides a visual representation of my argument on documentary citizenship.

In short, any changes in the level of networks of complicity and in the level of blurred membership produce changes in the level of documentary citizenship.

My analysis, however, raises a fundamental question: why should illegal immigrants acquire documents for citizenship? Citizenship-indicating documents provide a stability of access to everyday rights—a citizenship from above—and confer

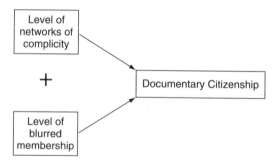

FIGURE 4.1. A model of illegal immigrant citizenship

tangible benefits without questions or harassment from state authorities. They effectively allow illegal immigrants to meet the requirements of a citizenship from above through means generated largely from below. As illegal immigrants in a foreign country, they are often subject to harassment while entering, while traveling, while seeking employment, while on the job, and so forth. Therefore, the search for documents is always a primary task for illegal immigrants. And what does this acquisition of paperwork tell us about citizenship? Recall that Hannah Arendt (1968) recognized that losing legal citizenship—and legal citizenship always means one authenticated by the state with a document—amounts to losing individual rights. Illegal immigrants require documents to exercise citizenship rights and to protect themselves from any violation of such rights. As we have seen, educating one's kids at school, seeing a doctor, participating in a cultural program, or exercising any other civic right typically involves showing identity documents to some local authority. To sell vegetables, one needs a permit; to drive a rickshaw, one needs a rickshaw driver's license; to beg at a street corner, one needs a document to avoid deportation—in short, these activities all involve the exercise of economic and civic rights conferred through documentation. Similarly, identity documents are required in order to take part in a political demonstration, to hold a meeting of union members or other political organizations, or to vote. The more benefits there are, the greater the amount of paperwork needed in developing countries.

At some stage in the practice of social, civic, economic, or political citizenship, one always needs to offer a proof of citizenship. Due to an initial lack of local networks and a history of local membership, illegal immigrants are at risk of being deported or jailed. In weakly institutionalized states, many natives will not carry any documents, but, unlike illegal immigrants, they have local networks, neighbors, and contacts to save them from state harassment. Illegal immigrants may use family and kinship networks to facilitate adjustment into the local community. However, the neighbors and local community members are aware that the immigrant is a newcomer to their area, which poses limitations on the illegal immigrant's wider acceptance into the local community. Therefore, illegal immigrants cannot depend on local support as much as a native can. So, the practices of citizenship, which involve sociopolitical and economic rights and duties, can only be accessed by illegal immigrants through the varieties of identity documents.

The theory and practice of citizenship are fused together through illegal immigrants' possession and use of illegally acquired citizenship documents in their daily lives. Are some markers of citizenship more standardized and immutable than others? Yes. In most developing countries, the passport is the ultimate marker of citizenship. Possession of a passport is an indication that the individual has overcome multiple verification exercises from a variety of state agencies as represented in the range of documents required to apply for a passport. The final round of verifications of the identity and location of the individual ensures that the state has certified the membership of the individual to the highest degree of confirmation, and now he/she can be allowed to travel abroad as a passport-holding member of the state. But, as we shall see in India, Malaysia, and Pakistan (chapter 6), even a passport is not a foolproof indicator of citizenship.

The Process of Acquiring Documents

How does the process of citizenship through documentation work? For illegal immigrants, confronting the problems associated with illegality begins after entry, specifically during residence and settlement. Many illegal immigrants travel regularly between their home country and host state, thus making mobility a crucial part of illegal immigration. *Legal* immigrants are unlikely to confront illegal status during entry, residence, and subsequent settlement; they therefore pose a qualitatively different challenge to the state. By contrast, for *illegal* immigrants, the illegal nature of their entry and residence are central security concerns.

For legal immigrants, entry occurs *after* the acquisition of legal documents; for illegal immigrants, entry most often occurs *prior* to the acquisition of legal documents.[15] In contrast to legal immigrants, illegal immigrants are invisible to the state precisely because they lack legal documentation.[16] Since political invisibility deprives one of social, economic, and political rights, illegal immigrants strive to acquire seemingly legal documentation. Therefore, as soon as an illegal immigrant enters a developing country,[17] he/she starts seeking some form of citizenship documentation to legitimize his/her entry and stay. This is a cumulative process. Illegal immigrants accumulate varieties of documentation over time, as they ease their way into citizenship. Each piece of documentation—plastic or paper—brings an additional layer of legitimacy until, finally, the illegal immigrant becomes "visible" as a citizen. Both the state's distributive and regulatory institutions recognize the legitimacy of an individual "citizen" through his/her display of documentation. It is the state's role in fusing one's identity with a document which makes this possible.

Although the acquisition of documents is the process through which an illegal immigrant finally accesses legal membership or citizenship, one must not conflate the desire to seek documentation with the *legal* acquisition of *legal* documents, such as work permits, local licenses for business, local identity cards, driver's licenses, or rickshaw licenses. Many illegal immigrants will make do with fraudulent documents in their everyday lives as long as they are indistinguishable from legal ones. Illegal immigrants also rely on networks of complicity to access legal and legitimate state documents by using fake paperwork in their applications. The blurred nature of this membership allows both illegal immigrants and criminal natives to gain access to citizenship rights and benefits.

Figure 4.2 captures the stages of documentation as an individual accumulates various documents during the process of procuring proofs of citizenship. Figure 4.2 is the right side of the overall model portrayed in figure 4.1. As modeled in figure 4.2, there are two well-known paths to citizenship for an immigrant: path X and path Y. The path of legal entry (X) involves documents given by state authorities at every stage of legal residency; the route to citizenship involves accumulating degrees of state-authenticated documents—each ensuring increased safety and stability in the immigrant's stay in the host state. Arriving with a work permit or as a visa-holding visitor, a legal immigrant over the years seeks legalized residence either through her/his employment or through marriage. Thereafter, the legal resident can apply for naturalization. At each stage, the permission and acknowledgment of the state is sought, which results in more legal paperwork and authorization.

Contrast this with the other path (Y) modeled in figure 4.2. Illegal entry may involve somehow getting employment illegally and then trying to get regularized through government amnesty programs. A history of amnesty programs creates an expectation of more such regularization schemes, thus opening another path through which illegal immigrants acquire legitimate paperwork and gain access to citizenship.[18] Yet another route is to enter illegally, then find employment, and then get the employer to help you acquire legal work permits. Finally, one can enter illegally, work illegally for years, and yet become eligible for citizenship through marriage to a local citizen, as often happens in the case of illegal immigrants. At some point, illegal immigrants can access citizenship by legalizing their residence through work, marriage, or the sponsorship of their own children. Legal residence makes one eligible for naturalization and citizenship.

However, the third route, path Z, often ignored by most scholars, is the one that I find so common among illegal immigrants. Illegal immigrants may enter illegally, but with fake documents they can open bank accounts, send kids to school, get a local license for a petty business, or gain entry to a local hospital. Over time,

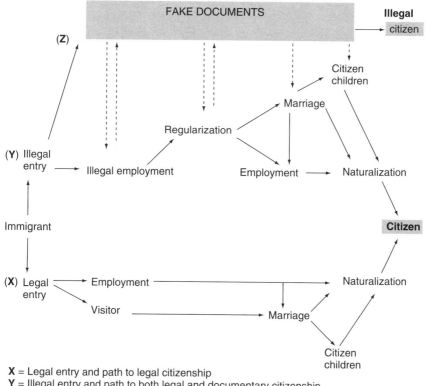

FIGURE 4.2. The documented path to citizenship

different fraudulent documents give them access to legitimate employment and residence—all legal citizen rights. Eventually, they acquire real documents by building a history of local residence based on fraudulent documents that appear real. One can use either local documents or national-level documents for acquiring citizen's rights. Local documents work when one does not possess national-level identity documents, such as a birth certificate, national identity card, or passport. Creating a history of local legitimacy is important before an individual embarks on the more ambitious acquisition of national documentation. Gradually, one builds a record of local membership, acceptance, and familiarity. The goal is to access national-level documentation, which may or may not precede this process.

In figure 4.2, there are arrows pointing toward access to legal or authorized membership involving legalized paperwork. However, one may continue to hold fake citizenship documents and live as an illegal "citizen" with the same benefits as genuine citizens (see shaded "citizen" in figure 4.2). For example, illegal immigrants can easily enter the electoral rolls because of the weakly institutionalized nature of citizenship in Malaysia (Sadiq 2005a). Fake documents or one's illegal presence on the electoral rolls ensures eventual access to legal citizenship. But what path Z indicates is that, in the practice of citizenship, illegal immigrants have become "citizens" through the use of fake documentation, or of real documentation acquired through fraudulent means. In multiethnic countries receiving large illegal flows of immigration, one's identity or membership is increasingly dependent on the paperwork one holds. That is precisely why there are cases of people losing their identity, of mistaken identity, and of forged identity. *Legal identity could not be lost, mixed up, or forged if it were not based on documentation.* If there is an absence of standardized paperwork, it is possible for illegal immigrants to become members. They can forge, buy, or otherwise obtain an identity as members of a state, i.e., as citizens. In this way, citizenship in developing countries may be easier to access than in developed states.

We have seen the process by which illegal immigrants gain access to documentary citizenship in developing countries (through networks of complicity and the existence of blurred membership). However, we still need a framework to locate the role of documentation in the larger effort to regulate individual mobility. A global classificatory grid that shows the role of documents in the settlement of illegal immigrants would be valuable.

A World of Documents

We have seen that the distinctions made by developed states between citizens and immigrants may not hold for developing states. The wall around the polity for developing states is blurred. The availability or absence of standardized documentation is a measure of the development of the state and its institutions for the purpose of monitoring its citizens and foreigners. Being developed or less developed reflects a state of economic progress. These characterizations provide us with means to analyze the political world of immigrants—both legal and illegal.

In figure 4.3, column II and row B represent developed states that have a range of institutions to mark their citizens with standardized paperwork. In such states, there is a widespread use of legal documents, officially standardized and regulated, that designate a person's identity as a citizen. In such states, borders are reasonably well-guarded, and mechanisms to regulate and monitor immigrants are well-established. And yet, despite a well-developed infrastructure of citizenship with common use of standardized documentation, these states have copious numbers of illegal immigrants. The presence of an established infrastructure is no guarantor against the tide of illegal immigrants seeking entry. However, the common presence of such an infrastructure in states like Germany, Japan, France, and Australia can

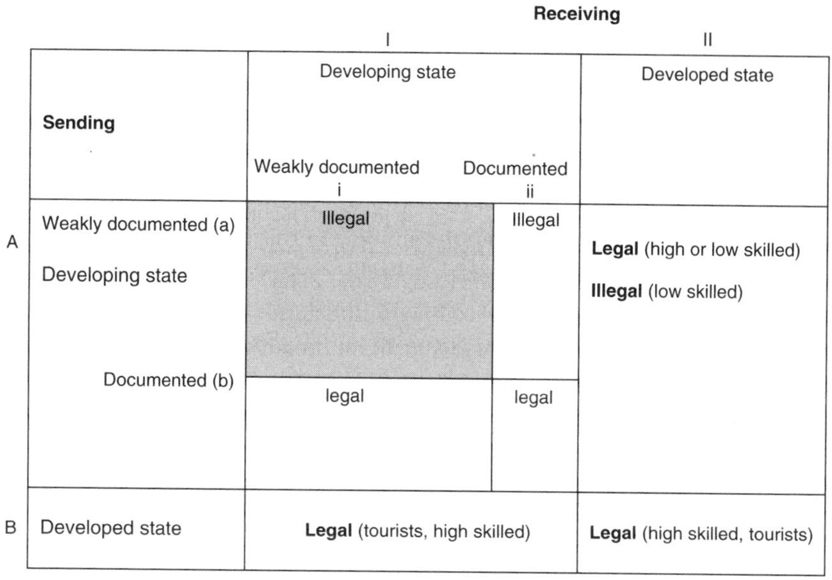

FIGURE 4.3. A world of documentary citizenship

have a deterrent effect on a prospective illegal immigrant. This category also includes rich but authoritarian states, such as Singapore, Saudi Arabia, Bahrain, and Brunei. The documentation of citizens and strict guarding of borders are also features of some developing countries with authoritarian (or communist) regimes. I classify such states as "developing states with documented populations"(aii and bii): Cuba, China, Libya, North Korea, Myanmar, and Vietnam. Finally, there are developing states with limited resources, poor populations, and a lack of standardized paperwork to identify people (ai). Paperwork may be more visible in urban locations than in rural populations or in remote areas where state authority is weakly felt. Another marker of developing, weakly documented states is the range of documents used to identify a person in the absence of a standardized system. So, in developing, weakly documented countries, paperwork is neither widespread nor standardized. Examples of such states are Indonesia, Pakistan, Thailand, Ghana, the Ivory Coast, Malaysia, India, Nepal, Sri Lanka, the Philippines, Guatemala, and Ecuador. I disaggregate immigration flows into four types in order to show this generally neglected aspect of immigration (see figure 4.3).

- Flows between developed states (B-II), such as those of highly skilled labor, tourists, retirees, and sometimes low-skilled labor are characterized by documented immigrants entering through legal means. These are immigration flows between developed states, such as France, Germany, the United States, and Japan. This category also includes rich but authoritarian states, such as Singapore, Saudi Arabia, Bahrain, or Brunei.

- Flows from developed states to developing states (including authoritarian and communist regimes; B-I), such as the immigration of highly skilled labor in the form of experts, advisors, technical personnel, and tourists, are characterized by holders of legal documents arriving through legal channels.

- Flows from developing states to developed states (A-II) are characterized by the legal immigration of students, highly skilled and low-skilled workers, and by legal spousal reunification, with official sanction and legal documents. This category also includes illegal immigration through the use of fraudulent documents, especially by low-skilled labor. Immigration from developing democratic states (India, Bangladesh), authoritarian states (Myanmar, Zimbabwe), and communist states (China, North Korea) to developed states are all included here. Most studies of immigration focus on this quadrant.

- Flows between developing states (A-I) include immigration that is mostly illegal (a-i and a-ii), sometimes without any documents and sometimes using fraudulent documents. Most immigration in this quadrant involves the movement of illegal migrants without official authorization and/or without documents, or with fraudulent documents (a-i). This quadrant does not inform most immigration theories (see shaded area in figure 4.3).

Documented, legal immigration (b-i and b-ii) comprises a negligible portion of the migration found in most developing countries. There is some legal immigration from developing but authoritarian/communist states (with documented populations) to weakly institutionalized developing countries, including educational or business trips by Vietnamese, Cubans, Myanmarese, or Libyan nationals to India, Pakistan, or some other poor developing country (b-i). Similarly, educational and business exchanges between communist/authoritarian states may dominate their immigration flows. Since the use of standardized documents and identity papers is widespread in both receiving and sending communist states, such immigration is mostly legal (b-ii).[19]

It is important to understand that weakly documented illegal immigrants commonly originate in developing countries where the process of acquiring standard documentation may be costly or not easily accessible. This is a feature of sending states. Very few persons who come from a developed state or a documented but developing state (e.g., authoritarian states) will enter a developing country illegally even if there is a lack of standardized documentation in the receiving state. The fact that these migrants carry proof of identity is a mark of the high surveillance capacities of these states.

Categorizing states by documentation levels reveals a relationship between immigration and the infrastructure of citizenship. States with a weak infrastructure of citizenship permit easier settlement of illegal immigrants. A significant part of the world's migratory flows are illegal (chapter 1), with fraudulent documents, and many migrate between developing countries to access the rights of full membership. This provokes an important question: what kind of documents are acceptable indicators of citizenship, and how many such documents are required? The prevalence of documentary citizenship makes it impossible to tell a citizen from an illegal immigrant as both possess the same documents.

The Rise of Documentary Nations

The first task of state bureaucratization is to make the subjects in the territory visible in order to separate them from foreigners. This task is assigned to the civil registration system, beginning with birth registration. This is followed by a range of other documents. Today, document use has spread from state-controlled activities to the private economy. From being merely document-requiring states, we have become document-requiring societies. Today, economic transactions, education, mobility (travel by car, plane, train), entertainment (for instance, ID cards at bars), and even our health care all depend on documents.[20] The exercise of a range of citizenship rights is contingent on the possession of an appropriate document. This vision of a document-bearing society is promoted by an infrastructure of citizenship fixated on circumscribing and controlling the political membership of the state. In short, the rise of the documentary nation has gone unnoticed even as it

TABLE 4.1. Varieties of citizenship-indicating documents in India, Malaysia, and Pakistan

	First national ID	Second national ID	Final national ID	Other acceptable IDs
India	Birth certificate	None	Passport	ration card, high school certificate, voter ID, voting receipt, land title, university ID, caste certificate
Pakistan	Birth certificate	New national ID	Passport	high school certificate, old national IC, manual birth certificate, *nikah-nama* (Islamic marriage certificate)
Malaysia	Birth certificate	MyKad, MyKid, MyPR	e-Passport	voting receipt, old blue national IC, old red national IC, certificate by village head

Note: ID = identity document; IC = identity card.

permeates every feature of the modern state. Using documentary citizenship, illegal immigrants enter the documentary nation with ease. This phenomenon can be seen in more detail by examining documentation in India, Malaysia, and Pakistan, summarized in table 4.1.

Documentary Citizenship in India

In India, a de facto national identity card, which reaches more people than any other identity document, is the ration card; it is widely available, it is cheap, and it reaches some of the very poor who are otherwise outside the reach of the state. India has instituted a widespread public distribution system that provides basic commodities (grains, rice) at government-subsidized prices for the poor. To make this scheme work, the government supplies an official document—the ration card—that has become a major marker of identity in India. Since the 1990s, the ration card has been used to prove domicile status in the various Indian states and is accepted as one of the standard documents to verify identity by the passport office, banks for opening an account, and hospitals for medical treatment. Because the target population lives in blurred membership, eligibility for the ration card is very flexible, often arbitrary, and easily corruptible. Therefore, a ration card is easily forged or fraudulently acquired. In fact, recent data show that more ration cards were distributed than the estimated number of people living below the poverty line. There are allegedly over 218 million ration cards *officially* circulating in different states of India. They are distributed by almost 476,000 ration shops and outlets spread over the most underdeveloped parts of the country (table 4.2).

There is also the challenge of bogus ration cards, which blurred membership facilitates and the existence of which the government of India is well aware. Although the Indian government seeks to remove holders of these bogus ration cards from its decentralized database, it is virtually impossible, given the numbers and breadth of circulation, to repossess or collect all of the bogus ration cards throughout the country that continue to be used by individuals as national identity documents.[21] For example, in West Bengal in a period of less than a month, about 1 million bogus ration cards were detected, in addition to the 1.9 million that had been detected earlier in 2005. Many are allegedly in the hands of illegal Bangladeshi immigrants who have crossed the border (Ghosh 2006). Bogus ration cards are held by people of several types: (a) ineligible individuals above the poverty line in possession of legitimate documents; (b) noncitizens such as refugees; (c) illegal immigrants in possession of legitimate documents acquired using fake identities; (d) individuals possessing deleted or expired cards who continue to use them for identity purposes; and (e) individuals holding counterfeit ration cards. Illegal immigrants from Bangladesh in Delhi, West Bengal, and Assam are likely to have a

TABLE 4.2. Distribution of ration cards in India

State	Projected population in 2000 (in 100,000s)	% population below BPL	BPL households in 2000 (in 100,000s)	No. of shops distributing ration cards	Ration cards (in 100,000s)	Data reported
Andhra Pradesh	754.66	25.68	40.63	40,688	159.02	6/30/03
Arunachal Pradesh	11.92	40.86	0.99	1,284	3.64	3/26/03
Assam	261.96	40.86	18.36	33,229	53.37	9/30/03
Bihar	731.11	54.96	65.23	41,818	123.84	2/28/03
Chhattisgarh	249.25	42.52	18.75	7,869	45.11	11/13/03
Delhi	139.64	14.69	4.09	3,121	35.11	12/31/03
Goa	15.95	14.92	0.48	528	3.30	1/31/04
Gujarat	482.52	24.21	21.20	14,284	109.67	5/31/03
Haryana	198.31	25.05	7.89	7,228	44.89	1/31/04
Himachal Pradesh	67.11	40.86	5.14	4,043	13.44	9/30/03
Jammu & Kashmir	99.45	40.86	7.36	3,927	18.30	4/1/03
Jharkhand	268.31	54.96	23.94	14,395	29.09	9/19/02
Karnataka	520.91	33.16	31.29	20,575	116.49	1/31/04
Kerala	322.62	25.43	15.54	14,135	63.74	11/30/03
Madhya Pradesh	548.22	42.52	41.25	18,688	134.31	4/22/02
Maharashtra	911.15	36.86	65.34	49,921	220.99	8/31/03
Manipur	25.18	40.86	1.66	2,551	3.17	1/31/04
Meghalaya	24.34	40.86	1.83	4,297	2.90	3/19/03
Mizoram	9.52	40.86	0.68	1,011	2.29	10/31/03
Nagaland	16.84	40.86	1.24	290	1.99	4/1/03
Orissa	358.57	48.56	32.98	23,579	79.01	8/31/02
Punjab	235.36	11.77	4.68	13,874	54.71	9/30/03
Rajasthan	535.59	27.41	24.31	20,391	124.02	10/31/03
Sikkim	5.59	41.43	0.43	1,071	1.32	3/23/04
Tamil Nadu	617.74	35.03	48.63	27,995	168.30	1/31/03
Tripura	37.82	40.86	2.95	1,432	7.25	12/31/03
Uttar Pradesh	1626.04	40.85	106.79	74,788	380.79	10/16/03
Uttaranchal	75.84	40.85	4.98	7,332	21.97	7/31/02
West Bengal	790.06	35.66	51.79	20,441	160.11	6/30/03
Union Territory						
Andaman & Nicobar	3.86	34.47	0.28	483	0.87	12/31/03
Chandigarh	8.88	11.35	0.23	56	2.23	1/31/04
Dadra & Nagar Haveli	1.90	50.84	0.18	78	0.33	5/13/03
Daman & Diu	1.40	15.80	0.04	51	0.29	3/31/03
Lakshadweep	0.71	25.04	0.03	35	0.14	8/31/02
Pondicherry	11.11	37.40	0.84	408	2.78	2/28/04
Total India	**9969.44**		**652.03**	**475,896**	**2188.78**	

BPL = below poverty line.

Source: Government of India (2004a: 93).

higher incentive to acquire these documents, which prove their citizenship, than long-time inhabitants residing in difficult-to-reach areas, such as the interior of Assam or Northeast India.

As the Indian state gradually intervened on behalf of its poor and illiterate, identification became crucial to the disbursement of another welfare right—the right to education. The infrastructure of citizenship became embedded in the right to education as the state sought to distinguish between those who were eligible and those who were not. It was yet another opportunity for the state to make legible its population at a crucial point in their life cycle—having completed a decade of schooling, the transition (graduation) to higher stages of education and opportunities. Hence, high school graduation became another life event, much like birth or marriage, generating an opportunity for the state to confirm an individual's age, gender, name, and parentage (usually the father's name). Two kinds of documents are issued at the high school level: one confirms mere enrollment or eligibility for the exam while the second is distributed after graduation. The high school graduation certificate (along with the birth certificate and the ration card) is another identity-confirming document. Since the high school certificate is de jure accepted as a birth certificate in court, it can lead to other identity-affirming documents, such as a passport. High school graduation, the culmination of a decade of education—a fundamental right ensured by the state—which is normally associated with a celebration of educational achievement, has become a crucial component in the infrastructure of citizenship. A total of about 117 million individuals (76 million males and 41 million females) can confirm their Indian identity through this document, according to the latest census.[22] It is possible that some of those people may never have collected this document, while others may have lost it, but when the practice of any citizenship right requires confirmation of identity, the individual should be able to produce this document to confirm his/her claim. Assuming that every high school graduate possesses this document, there are still only 117 million people with this identity document in a population of over a billion. In Assam, the regional state that receives most of the Bangladeshi illegal immigrants, about 3 million people can produce this document out of a total Assamese population of 26.6 million.[23] Like the ration card, the high school graduation certificate serves a particular section of the Indian population—in this instance, mostly, the literate middle class and elites in their smooth exercise of citizenship rights in India. If, later, some of them travel abroad and require a passport, this graduation certificate will be "fed" into the infrastructure of citizenship to confirm their membership in India's polity.

The entire citizenship-identifying documentation system in India is weak, and the government is deeply interested in creating a centralized and standardized documentary infrastructure. According to the deputy prime minister of India, L. K. Advani:

[The a]bility to establish personal identity is the most basic requirement of an individual right from birth. Every individual is asked to prove his identity several times during his life. In our country we do not have an organized system of providing identification papers to the citizens. This has resulted in several types of documents like ration cards, election identity cards, driving licenses, etc., being used for identification. Government has now decided to establish a National Register of Indian Citizens and issue Multipurpose National Identity Cards to the citizens of the country. This would help the people and the various Government and non-Government organizations in establishing the identity of the citizens wherever required. (Office of the Registrar General of India 2003a: 76)

The Indian government believes that documents are the best embodiment of citizen identity. Hence, an initial survey, a pilot project, was launched to introduce the multipurpose national identity card (MNIC) in India.[24] So far, over 3 million records have been entered, and biometric measures, such as photographs and the fingerprints of 1.7 million out of 2 million individuals (fifteen years and above), are now part of the record.[25] The background checks and verification of 2.8 million individuals, out of a total of 3 million records, is complete.[26] Since only 0.3 percent Indians out of a total population of over a billion have been identified and recorded, the process of completely sealing Indian citizenship through an MNIC, if ever implemented, is going to be an institutional nightmare, its effectiveness in weeding out noncitizens doomed like its predecessors the ration card, the birth certificate, and the high school graduation certificate, among others. With illegal immigrants from Bangladesh in possession of Indian documents, a recent survey in Delhi by a leading NGO points to a number of individuals being deported to Bangladesh despite possessing common markers of Indian nationality and citizenship: an election card, a ration card, a village land title, a *gram panchayat* (village council) certificate, etc.[27] These documents are commonly used to establish locality, address, and identity. In fact, so indeterminate is Indian citizenship, and so common the use of a range of documents to legitimize citizenship, that there are many judicial cases challenging the arrest, identification, and deportation of illegal immigrants from India.[28] Abu Hanif, mentioned earlier, is one of them.

In India, a range of documents is needed for a passport, but all of these documents—ration cards, birth certificates, high school certificates, marriage certificates, and others—can easily be forged or fraudulently acquired by individuals or through networks of complicity (Garari 2003). Given that it is hard to tell an Indian Bengali from a Bangladeshi—the ethnic features, height, language, costume, and diet are all the same—we may surmise that many illegal immigrants possess one or more of these documents, which makes them eligible to settle in India. Or, they can use fake identity documents since state agencies often cannot distinguish genuine identity documents from forged ones. At each level—neighborhood, municipality, town, city, region, state, and nation—the gradual accumulation of paperwork leads to the ultimate prize: a genuine Indian passport.[29]

After 9/11, two Indian citizens were arrested in the United States (Jha 2001). Each had multiple Indian passports with different personal details. When questioned about this case, officials in India pointed out that there was no way to check whether the same individual had been issued multiple passports. One of the suspects had two passports issued to him from the passport center of Hyderabad (a southern city) and one from the passport center of Karnataka, a neighboring Indian state. India has a total of twenty-eight passport offices, and not all have been computerized or linked with each other. According to an official, "[I]f the same man applies for a passport at two different centers and can successfully defraud the verification system, there is no link between centers to detect this" (Jha 2001).[30] Although seemingly a problem of modern India, this has been a challenge since colonial times. As one official in colonial India grumbled, it was "almost ludicrous to observe...*how often the same things are called by different names, and different things by the same names*" (emphasis mine; Cole 2001: 63–65).

An Indian passport also can be acquired through an "agent" outside any passport office for about 1500 rupees (approximately $34).[31] In fact, until the early 1990s, a passport could be acquired through a travel agent without the applicant's physically going to any passport office (Jha 2001). However, even with all of these leaks in the infrastructure of citizenship, there is a required verification of each passport application by the police that could stop the fraud. As S. R. Tayal, a senior official in the Ministry of External Affairs, said, "[T]he critical element in the issuance of a passport is the police verification of a person. If that is compromised there is nothing we can do" (Jha 2001). Given the widespread accusations of rampant police bribery, it would not be hard for people determined to acquire a passport to overcome this check.

An Indian passport is the marker of Indian citizenship with the highest level of monitoring, control, and, most important, acceptability. Once one has an Indian passport, one's citizenship is conclusive. Therefore, even if the 15–20 million illegal immigrants from Bangladesh may not plan to go abroad on Indian identity documents, acquiring various Indian documents, especially a passport, gives them more stable Indian citizenship. No one questions your citizenship once you possess a passport.

Documentary Citizenship in Malaysia

Does the more centralized and economically developed Malaysia have a more secure citizenship than India? Given the millions of illegal immigrants over the decades who have quietly settled down in Malaysia from Indonesia and the southern Philippines, how many have been naturalized through the official, legal channels acceptable to the Malaysian state? Between 1962 and 2004, the National Registration Department (NRD) received 530,328 applications for citizenship and approved 479,433 of them.[32] In forty-two years, close to a half million foreigners were officially made Malaysian citizens, having cleared the strict citizenship requirements of the NRD (*New Straits Times* 2004). This would suggest a migration rate of about 11,000 individuals a year, which does not explain how most of the over 2 million illegal immigrants settled in Malaysia. Those arriving as illegal immigrants in the 1970s could claim local citizenship, depending on their access to documentary proof, and reappear as "citizens" in the censuses of the 1980s, while those arriving later could follow the same path to invisible absorption, showing up as legitimate citizens in subsequent censuses of the 1990s and 2000s.

It is well known that foreign individuals in Sabah, East Malaysia, hold multiple Malaysian national identity cards. According to Francis Loh Kok Wah, a leading social scientist studying Malaysia, it is clear that "tens of thousands of illegal immigrants have been issued with ICs illegally" (Loh 1999: 35). He cites how the opposition party, Parti Bersatu Sabah (PBS), provided documentary proof of 49,270 people who had acquired identity cards by merely submitting declaration certificates that they were citizens (*surat akuans*; ibid.). The PBS report had four volumes, the first of which contained the names of 15,366 people who were issued KPT (Kad Pengenalan Bermutu Tinggi) identity cards, while three other volumes contained the names of 11,855 individuals, 10,925 individuals, and 11,124 individuals—each of whom was issued a non-KPT blue identity card (ibid.). In this documentary circuit, it was immaterial at what point the identity serial number was legitimate, or when it was removed by the authorities.[33] At some point, de facto citizenship transformed into de jure citizenship, and it became possible to add the person to a larger history of legitimate membership.

One of the rare (and confidential) surveys of illegal immigrants in East Malaysia was conducted in Sabah by the Resettlement Division of the Chief Minister's Department in 1988 and was aimed at Filipino illegal immigrants.[34] Filipino Muslim refugees, mainly Bajau, Suluks, and Samals from the southern Philippines, numbered 71,224 according to a 1977 "refugee census"; 69,508 according to a 1984–1985 census by the NRD; and 70,000 according to a government survey by 1986.[35] The survey sought to cover eighty-one Filipino settlements in the state, but due to the obvious noncooperation of the illegal immigrants, only 20–30 percent of the "settlers" in fifty-eight Filipino sites could be included.[36] Even then, the results were astounding: as of August 1, 1988, the survey had registered 107,136 illegal immigrants, out of a total of 215,357 individuals covered in the sample.[37] According to the report, illegal immigrants tried their best to hide their true identities, and "many settlers were already in possession of blue ICs, either genuine or fake ones."[38]

Documents were found all over the Filipino settlements. For example, in the Sandakan district, close to 50 percent claimed their place of origin as the Philippines (Tawi-Tawi, Jolo, and Mindanao) while 20 percent reported coming from Indonesia.[39] Close to a quarter of the population was found to be in possession of the blue identity card, even though only 19 percent declared their nationality as Malaysian.[40] About 22 percent of the respondents were recent arrivals and had been in Sabah for less than a year, and an overwhelming majority—88 percent of the immigrant households—were Muslim.[41] In the Kunak district, also, most immigrant households were Muslim (88.9 percent), the majority of which were from the Philippines, and 13 percent of the households actually acknowledged owning a blue citizenship IC.[42]

In the Sandakan district, surveyors noted the widespread presence of fake or real but fraudulently acquired ICs in the following immigrant settlements covered by the survey: Kampung Istimeva (population 2,701), Kampung Lupak Meluas (population 3,166),[43] Kampung BDC (population 7,378), Kampung Baru (population 1,554), and Kampung Muhibbah (population 5,271).[44] There was enough evidence in this confidential survey by the Chief Minister's Department to indicate a steady stream of illegal immigrants, the majority of whom were from the southern Philippines and, to a lesser degree, from Indonesia. All were Muslim, and most possessed some identity card, if not outright citizenship papers—making documentary citizenship the norm.

Let me illustrate documentary citizenship with individual cases.[45] Table 4.3 contains information on two individuals, both of whom are members of the Malaysian ruling party, United Malays National Organization (UMNO), and both of whom are also holders of multiple identities—some Malaysian and some Indonesian, depending on the paperwork. Individuals are supposed to possess only one Malaysian IC number and a single national passport. However, Amirullah Paraba, a member of the ruling political party, UMNO, is registered under two different Malaysian identities according to the records of the NRD: (a) Amirullah **B** Pareba (H 0557065), and (b) Amirullah **DG** Parabba (H 0666952).[46] Also, Sarif Saidi Sarip Alawi is a member of UMNO under two Malaysian identity numbers: (a) Sarif Saidi Sarip Alawi (H 0535499), and (b) Sari**p** Saidi Sarip Alawi (H 0535199).[47] Variations on names allow for multiple identity card numbers. So, "Abd Wahid Ahmad" can also be "Abdul Wahid B Ahmad," who can also be "Abdul Wahid Bin Ahmad," who is also "Abdul Wahid Bin Hj Ahmad Saloko," who is…and so on.

If an individual immigrant from Indonesia or the Philippines has access to two national identity numbers from Malaysia, he/she can acquire two Malaysian passports, travel abroad under those two identities, and vote under each of those identities. Clearly, this is a common practice for illegal immigrants from Indonesia and

TABLE 4.3. Multiple names, multiple identities in Malaysia

	UMNO	Malaysian IC number (A)	Malaysian IC number (B)	Indonesian passport (C)
1. Name	Abd Wahid Ahmad	Abdul Wahid B Ahmad	Abdul Wahid Bin Ahmad	Abdul Wahid Bin Hj Ahmad Saloko
Identity number	H 0512745	H 0540086	H 0021561	39522
2. Name	Marang Bin Laupa	Marang B. Laupa	Marang Laupa	Marang Bin Laupa
Identity number	H 0557513	H 0557513	H 0506760	31203

Note: UMNO = United Malays National Organization; IC = Identity Card.

Source: Mutalib (1999: 193–194 and 208–210).

the southern Philippines in Sabah, East Malaysia, and West Malaysia. According to a leading political personality of Sabah, natives feel threatened by this "process of 'citizeni[z]ation' of Filipinos from Mindanao" (Kitingan 1997: 33).[48] The Malaysian government at the federal level is accused of "condoning" the easy access to citizenship by providing blue ICs to illegal immigrants (ibid.: 22–23). However, as we know, complicity is only one of the two factors explaining why documentary citizenship flourishes in Malaysia; the other is blurred membership.

According to one of the first surveys of the informal sector in Kota Kinabalu—the area around the capital region of Sabah, which is characterized by the widespread presence of illegal immigrant settlements—local hawkers faced serious business competition from the illegal Filipino and Indonesian businesses (Johari 1992: 45). In this informal economy, out of a total of 168 respondents, a majority (64.3 percent, or 108) claimed that they were operating without any license or permits. This includes even the daily temporary hawker receipts issued by the Kota Kinabalu Municipal Council at the low rate of 3 ringgits, which just about anyone can procure (ibid.). Significantly, most respondents conducting informal businesses felt that it was (a) not necessary to have a license/permit (31 percent, or 52 respondents), while others (b) purposely did not apply for it (23.8 percent, or 40 respondents; ibid.: 46). Proofs of authorization such as licenses and permits help local state officials to exclude ineligibles such as illegal immigrants who do not have the permission to trade in local areas. On the other hand, as the survey reveals, many natives fail to obtain documentation from municipal authorities. How is the state to protect native commercial interests when it cannot distinguish between the eligibles (natives) and ineligibles (illegal immigrants)? The illegal nature of hawking and informal trading in these bazaars also brought to light the "Ali Baba" business, where native entrepreneurs acquired the license/permit while the actual business was run by foreigners (ibid.). In an environment of informal residence and economic activity, the conditions of blurred membership prevail even in a highly documented state such as Malaysia.

Unlike India and Pakistan, Malaysia has a more advanced infrastructure of citizenship that does not rely on education for identification. However, educational certificates and transcripts do produce a record of local membership. For the national infrastructure of citizenship, a birth certificate and the national identity card suffice. Sometimes, a marriage certificate is taken to judge the eligibility for citizenship of those under eighteen who are married. The seed of Malaysian citizenship begins with a birth certificate, followed by a national identity card for everyone at age twelve and above, and culminates in a passport for all Malaysians traveling abroad. If there are gaps in the first two, as I have shown there are, the identification system is not secure.

Perhaps technology will overcome a weak identity documentation system. What is the recent Malaysian record in this regard? Does a high-tech national identity card system ensure the inviolability of Malaysian citizenship? The recent switch to a biometric identity card, MyKad, as a replacement for the earlier system of national ICs of various colors (the blue IC indicating Malaysian citizenship, the red IC indicating permanent resident status, etc.),[49] is supposed to make Malaysian citizenship more secure and tightly regulated. By 2003, some 5.4 million MyKads had been issued out of a total 18 million Malaysian identity card holders.[50] Yet, 12.4 million eligible individuals had yet to apply for the chip-embedded smart card. From December 2005, when 1 million individuals had yet to apply for a MyKad,[51] to March 2006, the number had been reduced to 700,000 individuals.[52] Meanwhile some 724,097 applicants had not collected MyKads.[53] This is a source of worry since on earlier occasions unclaimed and lost ICs of various colors were utilized by illegal immigrants.

Additionally, between 2001 and 2005, as a result of changes in religious affiliation, there were 9,788 applications for a change in the applicant's name on the MyKad.[54] It is such loopholes—changes in name, lost documents, unclaimed documents—that provide opportunities for fraudulent identity cards to be created. As a result, Malaysia's high-tech MyKad has already been found in the possession of illegal immigrants.[55] In one instance, police seized more than 150 MyKads from illegal immigrants.[56] Were they fake MyKads sold to unsuspecting illegal immigrants, or were they genuine MyKads based on the information from uncollected but legitimate MyKads? An answer to this question almost seems superfluous. Meanwhile, another change is taking place: MyKads will no longer be issued to permanent residents. A new card called MyPR will be issued for about 300,000 permanent residents.[57]

Do these technological upgrades matter? To answer that question, we have to first answer another: do the local municipal hospitals, schools, night markets, plantations, and banks have the personnel and machinery to check the authenticity of each and every MyKad? Technology cannot overcome pervasive public and private sector corruption. The ability of the state to enforce its own measures, its reach, is at stake here. With every upgrade, there is an assumption that all Malaysian citizens are being covered, that everyone is quickly going to change to the new card and has the resources to do this, and that those issuing and monitoring the process will be unsympathetic to the foreigners seeking Malaysian citizenship. In practice, however, the MyKad could become another blue IC—present everywhere due to uncollected documents, lost documents, or conversions from one category to another, giving easy access to determined illegal immigrants. Meanwhile, for those residents of Malaysia who are still not possessors of any form of identification, the chances are that they have yet to notice the change from the colored IC to the new biometric MyKad.

Unimpressed by the high-tech measures of the Malaysian state, prominent Malaysian NGO activists are calling for a royal commission of inquiry to probe the easy settlement of many illegal immigrants and the role of identity cards in that settlement (Thien 2006). Leading NGO activists Patrick Sindu (president of the Consumer Association of Malaysia) and Joshua Kong contend that there are about 2 million illegal immigrants in Sabah alone with many, about a million, possessing "original" Malaysian identity cards.[58] Joshua Kong is no longer concerned about foreign workers with work permits (domestic maids, plantation workers, contract professionals). He is also not too worried about the illegal immigrants who possess fake ICs for a limited period. But he is deeply concerned about the "overnight *bumiputeras*"—illegal immigrants who acquire citizenship documents and, because they are Muslims, instantly become indigenous/*bumiputera*. *Bumiputera* status opens the door to affirmative action policies. It is the documented (but illegal) immigrants from Indonesia and the Philippines posing as indigenous natives who can "destroy" Sabah, he claims (Thien 2006).

Illegal immigrants from Indonesia and Malaysia with documentary citizenship have been the focus of the opposition PBS too (*Daily Express* 2003). While there were an estimated 1.2 million Indonesian workers in Malaysia by 2004, Indonesian authorities acknowledge that about 650,000 of them entered Malaysia without proper documentation, many with Indonesian passports secured from passport brokers of dubious quality (Salmi 2004). In Indonesia, data from the national Ministry of Women's Empowerment show that 63.8 percent of Indonesian workers have fake ICs (Naommy 2004). On entering Malaysia, Indonesians contact local Malaysian community leaders, such as the village security and development committee chairpersons or village heads, who then issue supporting documents that confirm the local roots of illegal immigrants (*Daily Express* 2005). Many illegal immigrants who are caught produce these documents, claiming they are from village so-and-so in Semporna or Kudat (ibid.). Forged statutory declarations (*surat akuans*) or forged supporting documents, backdated to create a long local history of nativity, often lead to the acquisition of legitimate national identity cards (*Daily Express* 2003). Meanwhile, it is common for women trafficked from Indonesia to have their passports and other travel documents altered to change their names, addresses, and, most important for underage girls, their ages, according to interviews conducted by Human Rights Watch (2004: 29).

But why don't illegal immigrants register and acquire legitimate documentation in Malaysia? According to a Malaysian scholar, this could be because

> some migrants prefer to remain illegal to avoid what they may perceive as all the bureaucratic hassles of registering. Some may not see the necessity to register for the simple reason that they are satisfied with their present arrangement. But whatever the reasons for their lack of documentation, or willingness to be properly registered in the State, the continuing presence of undocumented foreign nationals in Sabah remains as a major concern for the government and Malaysians in Sabah. (Kurus et al. 1998: 175)

In this context, being "properly" documented refers to the official registration and documentation process, i.e., legally authorized paperwork. However, for the illegal immigrants, such state documentation has the disadvantage of being more costly and slower, even as it opens the path to a slow, bureaucratic, legal naturalization process. On the other hand, one can buy a cheap fraudulent IC and acquire citizenship instantly. The choice for a poor illegal immigrant is clear: the latter is a more efficient path.

Documentary Citizenship in Pakistan

Pakistan, too, has an infrastructure of citizenship built on regular verification of critical life events, such as birth, education, and marriage. Therefore, education in Pakistan, like in India, is an opportunity for the state to unambiguously locate individuals within its political community. The accumulated individual information in the primary, middle, or high school record, such as age, sex, parentage, and address, is cataloged in a standardized, easily communicable shape. This results in paper identity markers, such as certificates and transcripts. For example, high school is a critical point in the life cycle of a Pakistani, and graduation substantially improves the life chances of such an individual. As in India, a high school graduation certificate is a common identity document which feeds into a larger infrastructure of citizenship. A variety of identity markers, some overlapping, some particular to a life event (high school graduation, marriage), accumulate to form a record of identity and local membership that is verifiable at different periods in an individual's life. For example, the computerized national identity card (CNIC) of Pakistan requires a birth certificate, educational certificates (including transcripts), and the corroborating identity cards of the parents, among other proofs of identity. Both birth certificate and school certificates enable an individual to build a record of local membership, which feeds into a larger national identity infrastructure, resulting in a CNIC or a passport. This edifice allows the Pakistani state to include some people and exclude others.

Two organizations form the backbone of the infrastructure of citizenship in Pakistan: the National Database and Registration Authority (NADRA) and the National Aliens Registration Authority (NARA). The NADRA was created in 2000 and is responsible for issuing CNICs to Pakistani citizens. Its twin organization, NARA, was established in August 2001 under the Ministry of Interior to register noncitizens, such as illegal immigrants and refugees, and it initially focused on the Afghans in Karachi (Afghan Research and Evaluation Unit 2005: 2). As of 2005, the NADRA had distributed registration numbers to about 16 million children and overall had registered over 65 million people out of a total population of 165 million (*Daily Times* 2005). The new CNICs are for a limited period and are replacing the older national identity cards (Masood 2003). They can be renewed with updated information. Since NADRA is responsible for the identification of Pakistani citizens, its registration of 65 million individuals in so short a time is an impressive effort, on the surface. The directorate of Passport and Immigration (P&I) of Pakistan distributed 1.3 million machine-readable passports (MRPs) in about two months by the end of January 2006, even as 7 million old Pakistani passports were still in circulation. Authorities acknowledged that replacing the old passports will take additional time (*Pakistan Observer* 2006). Given that military dictator General Zia ul-Haq first required Pakistanis to obtain national identity cards in the 1980s, this is progress. But the state is far from the stage where every Pakistani national has been identified with a secure national identity card or a passport (Wines 2002: A4). With a population of 165 million, Pakistan may not have the resources to provide a secure NIC to everyone, especially considering that many native Pakistanis have yet to receive any documentation since independence. With regard to Pakistan, recall the question raised earlier in our discussion on Malaysia: will technology overcome a weak identity documentation system?

The integrity of a system to protect Pakistani identity is not in new technology but in the hands of the individuals who manage it. The NADRA's integrity is critical since it has to maintain a registry of citizens, a database which acts as a warehouse of personal information on Pakistani citizens, and networks with other government agencies that are responsible for monitoring Pakistani individuals for distributive and travel purposes.[59] While it is common for Pakistanis to carry fraudulent IDs or multiple IDs locally, increasing pressure has been exerted internationally, since Pakistan was put on the watch list of the U.S. and European governments due to increasing incidents of trafficking (Masood 2003).

Here is an indication of how widespread documentary citizenship is in Pakistan. In response to a question as to whether a person without a national identity card could obtain a passport, obtain a university degree, or operate a business, leading human rights activist and founding member of the Human Rights Commission of Pakistan Asma Jahangir (2002) replied, "yes, anything is possible in Pakistan." As the scheme for a new computerized high-tech card was being launched, senior officials of the NADRA noted the difficulty in detecting fake documents and also noted the widespread use of official attestation of fake documents.[60] If an agent of the state authenticates a fake document, does it make it legal? It matters very little; since there are no consistent formats and standards, no one can tell the difference. No wonder the same report estimates that 10 million fraudulent NICs were in circulation by September 2001.[61]

So unreliable is the identification system in Pakistan that over 700,000 cell phone sets were reportedly issued to those using fake identity cards (*Business Recorder* 2006).[62] Meanwhile, news reports on fake NICs appear regularly in the national media.[63] For example, in a raid in May 2006, government agents in Lahore seized four sacks of fake and/or illegal documents, including blank degrees and certificates for medical and commerce colleges and other educational institutions, blank driving licenses, genuine Afghan and Pakistani manual passports, Pakistani and Afghani identity cards, fake visa stickers of Oman and the United Arab Emirates (UAE), driving licenses for these countries, revenue stamps of the Northwest Frontier province and Balochistan governments, *nikah* (marriage) certificates, fake stamps of Pakistan consulates in Jalalabad (Afghanistan), and motor and vehicle registration documents, among other forms of identification (Ahmad 2006). With these documents, any illegal immigrant could show proof of local employment, vehicular ownership, educational background, marriage, and Pakistani identity. The individual could even travel abroad with the visas, passports, and foreign licenses available.

During election time, when NICs are mandatory for voting, there is a sudden rise in reports about fraudulent identity cards. According to a report in 2002, in Peshawar, 24,798 bogus cards were found (Wines 2002: A4). In Larkana, in south-central Pakistan, a group that had produced 29,000 fake identity cards was caught. In Quetta, there were claims of widespread IC fraud, while in Landi Kotal, a tribal area, identity cards were available for a bribe of 300 rupees, or about US$6. It is interesting to see that the incidents of fraudulent identity cards rose when state-mandated use was necessary; otherwise, Pakistanis could carry on their daily civic lives with little monitoring of their identities.

Asma Jahangir, founding member of the Human Rights Commission of Pakistan, notes in her interview that many Pakistanis do not have NICs or birth certificates and that most medical certificates are false and easy to obtain (Jahangir

2002). She believes that people do not make fake passports in Pakistan; instead, they acquire *"legitimate* documents *fraudulently"* (emphasis mine). Importantly, she believes many Afghans living in Pakistan have fraudulently acquired NICs and passports in Pakistan (ibid.). The minister for state and frontier regions, Sardar Yar Muhammad Rind, concurs with this assessment, telling the National Assembly in Pakistan that "some Afghan nationals have secured Pakistani identity cards and passports, which are illegal," while another state minister stated during the same debate that "Afghan refugees had acquired manual identity cards in large numbers" (*Pakistan Tribune* 2005). According to a survey of Afghans in Karachi, the largest city in Pakistan, "many of the Afghans have acquired Pakistani identity documents and claim to be migrants of long standing, or indeed, natives of Pakistan."[64]

For example, near the Al-Asif Square, Sohrab Goth, Karachi, about a quarter of the Afghans possessed documents of varying types, including Pakistani identity cards, passports, and/or gun licenses.[65] Since they possessed Pakistani ICs, many now owned apartments in the Al-Asif area.[66] Locally elected councilors have supported several foreigners—mostly Afghans—who have applied for Pakistani NICs, thus defeating the purpose of creating a secure high-tech Pakistani national identity card (*Dawn* 2004c). Ultimately, any NIC relies on verification, and if local officials are complicit in fraud, both Afghani and Bengali illegal immigrants can acquire Pakistani national identity cards. What's more, the post–9/11 rush to create a national database and to distribute high-tech identity cards to many Pakistanis overrode the need for careful background checks (Qaiser 2004). Hence, in December 2003, sixty-seven CNICs were discovered to be in the hands of illegal immigrants in Karachi (ibid.). A month later, in January 2004, seven Afghans and many others were detected with CNICs in the Khaar area. The next month, February 2004, forty-three foreigners were discovered to be in possession of CNICs in the Northwest Frontier province (NWFP), and so on. The issue of illegal immigrants with Pakistani ICs has become a topic for debate in the National Assembly and in the national media.[67]

Some 26,000 illegal Bangladeshis registered themselves in a post–9/11 registration drive, most in the hope that legalizing would pave their way to naturalization (*Khaleej Times* 2004). Most Bangladeshi Muslim illegal immigrants live in the Machhar (mosquito) colony of Karachi, and many have acquired Pakistani identity cards (ibid.). They do not view the more expensive path to legal work permits or naturalization as necessary; as one Bangladeshi migrant from Karachi said, "We often spend much less than this [the official fees] to get [forged] Pakistani documents" (Mansoor 2003).[68] Large-scale documentary citizenship could not exist without the extensive complicity of Pakistani state officials, and therefore, legal countermeasures are all but impossible (*Dawn* 2002b).[69] In fact, the Bangladeshi deputy high commissioner in Karachi has refused to accept the deportation of

Bangladeshis, since many possess Pakistani ICs and passports (Khan 2004). Again, securing the sovereignty of the state presents the same fundamental problem as in previous case studies: who is a Pakistani of Bangladeshi origin, and who is a Bangladeshi illegal immigrant? This is the same challenge that the Indian government faces when it tries to deport Bangladeshi illegal immigrants back to Bangladesh; most do not have Bangladeshi documents while many have Indian identity documents.

The fake identity card or passport racket is a thriving business in all major cities in India, Malaysia, and Pakistan. Given the decentralized nature of the document-issuing apparatus in these states, it is no surprise that even the most secure of the state identity documents—the passport—has been at the center of serious security breaches in recent years. In response, the governments of India, Malaysia, and Pakistan are trying or considering high-tech methods. In the Indian case, officials argue for machine-written and machine-readable passports. Scanned passports, it is thought, will control tampering with photographs. Accordingly, a national identity card project is under consideration in India (Office of the Registrar General of India 2003b).[70] The same is the case for Pakistan. Malaysia has already implemented such a scheme, but this has done little to stabilize and secure national identity. From the examples of the United States, Germany, France, and other countries, we already know that groups specializing in fraudulent documents will adapt and upgrade their technology as well. And there is another problem: since the delivery of a national identity card or passport may take place by standard mail (which will continue as long as there are people living in widespread areas), a determined move to intercept a document before delivery can easily succeed (*Times of India* 2000).

Conclusion

Attempts to control peoples and to maintain borders are being challenged from above (i.e., by globalization) and below (i.e., by civil society). From above, globalization processes and institutions compromise state sovereignty with respect to trade, finance, communication, crime, terrorism, and health. From below, illegal immigration and refugee flows weaken the territorial sovereignty of the state.[71] A powerful bastion of state control is sovereignty over territory and persons—that is, including citizens and excluding noncitizens. Domestically, the weak institutionalization of citizenship results in sections of the population being invisible and outside state control. Documents facilitate the daily life and settlement of residents while bypassing state regulations. That is, multiple levels of documentation, complicit officials, and helpful co-ethnic immigrants enable individuals to circumvent the surveillance and control exercised by state officials. When people migrate across international borders, these very documents enable their movement and incorporation into a new polity. Thus, states are constantly trying to regain control of their sovereignty by implementing compulsory birth registration, marriage registration, national identity cards, and high-tech cards with biometric measures. Moving to ever more advanced levels of documentation technology to monitor people is the response of states to this challenge from below. According to David Lyon:

> New ID cards are part of a large-scale trend towards "social sorting"—classifying and profiling groups of people in order to provide different services, conditions or treatment. Specifically, new ID cards are intended to include those designated as "eligible members" of nation-states and to exclude undesirable others. (Lyon 2004: 2)[72]

Today, movement without identification and state-authorized authentication is increasingly difficult. I would argue that some document, passport, or national ID (fake or real) is critical to the movement and settlement of individuals. All documents, whether passports or national IDs, are a means for social and political control—which involves control over movement, especially across international boundaries, and control over settlement. That is their purpose: to create order. The key issue is how this mechanism for order gets undermined by pressures from below, as individuals unwelcome by the state utilize it to gain documentary citizenship. Recall that this is a separate pathway to citizenship based on documentation achieved through networks of complicity and the prevalence of blurred membership. A world of documents is ironically enabling illegal immigrant incorporation while neglecting native citizens. Documents are essential to citizenship rights, so as long as states are not able to distinguish between real and fake identification, illegal immigrants, criminal natives, and international organized crime lords all have their golden ticket to being invisible or visible to the state as they choose. In short, documents give states power for social and political sorting and thereby order, and yet it is the documents themselves that undermine this fig leaf of order and security.

PART II

The Proof

HAVING CONCEPTUALIZED DOCUMENTARY CITIZENSHIP AND DEMONSTRATED ITS mechanisms, in the second part of the book I empirically demonstrate the widespread prevalence of documentary citizenship among illegal immigrants in India, Malaysia, and Pakistan. To prove that illegal immigrants are indeed acquiring full citizenship through the acquisition of fake or real state documents, I show that illegal immigrants in India, Malaysia, and Pakistan are (a) exercising national and state-level franchise (chapter 5), and (b) traveling abroad under their assumed identities (chapter 6). As a result, documentary citizenship threatens national sovereignty by giving illegal immigrants access to secure citizenship rights, such as national voting and public office. Moreover, territorial sovereignty is violated since illegal immigrants adopt assumed identities to travel abroad. Clearly, documentary citizenship has major implications for our understanding of the immigration process (chapter 7). Indeed, illegal immigration between document-based polities—a characteristic of the modern state—poses new challenges and requires us to rethink our understanding of citizenship.

5

Voters across Borders

We vote not to elect our representative but to ensure our citizenship of India.
—Afzalur Ali, a rickshaw puller of Bangladeshi immigrant background in India.[1]

THERE WAS AN EERIE SILENCE IN MY NEIGHBORHOOD IN SABAH, MALAYSIA, ONE DAY in March 1999. My upscale apartment was surrounded by two large illegal immigrant settlements, slum houses made of cardboard and scrap material. On occasion, I would play soccer with young boys from the settlements. However, this day was different; it was election day. To my surprise, I noticed an almost empty settlement to my right as I passed. But for a few small children, the place seemed deserted. I thought to myself, "Ah, perhaps they were caught by the authorities in a deportation sweep," but that was not the case. As it turned out, early that morning, a majority of the community had left to catch buses ferrying them to various polling booths to exercise their suffrage.[2] Illegal immigrants were participating in a very colorful and democratic exercise—voting. These illegal immigrants were voting much like citizens. How could this be possible?

A political community is often defined in terms of "universal suffrage"—a condition in which all adult citizens can vote and stand for elective office, regardless of race, ethnicity, religion, gender, or socioeconomic status. Elections and suffrage rights are at the very heart of the functioning and legitimacy of the democratic state (Dahl 1989, 2005; Huntington 1991). For democratic states, defining the boundaries of democratic citizenship is critical because citizenship determines suffrage, which in turn shapes the process of political representation (Smith 1997). Most comparative political analyses of democracy assume that the polity is bounded by a sharp line of citizenship, but some immigration scholars have challenged this assumption.

They point out that, due to strict naturalization requirements and jus sanguinis rules for the attribution of citizenship, large numbers of immigrants who become permanent resident aliens and their children who are born in those democratic states have been denied the right to vote (e.g., Germany, Japan).[3] This fact, they argue, calls into question just how democratic such states actually are in practice. By focusing on the mechanics of citizenship acquisition through documentation, this chapter turns on its head the problem posed by immigration to maintaining the boundaries of the polity. In liberal democracies, such as India, and illiberal democracies, such as Pakistan and Malaysia, the legitimacy of democratic citizenship is challenged not by the exclusion of long-term legal immigrants and their children, but rather by the easy inclusion of illegal immigrants.

This chapter asks the following questions: why and how are illegal immigrants exercising the franchise in developing countries? What are the implications for national democratic politics? There is compelling evidence that *millions* of illegal immigrants use either fake documents or real but fraudulently acquired documents to access the national franchise in their host states. Data gathered on illegal immigrants from Bangladesh in India, from Indonesia and the Philippines in Malaysia, and from Afghanistan and Bangladesh in Pakistan, show that documentary citizenship opens the door not only to the exercise of suffrage by illegal immigrants, but also to public office, thus directly challenging the boundaries that scholars typically draw between immigrant and citizen. The recruitment of illegal immigrants as voters also advantages certain political parties, giving insight into why the manipulation of migratory flows takes place. Contrary to our expectations, illegal immigrant voters are redefining democratic practices and citizenship.

In light of the experience of developing countries, mapping the complexities of citizenship in a time of globalization is urgently needed. This fact presents major problems for democracies and democratizing states that seek to delimit their *demos*. Weak documentation systems leave states open not only to the illegal entry of economic migrants, terrorists, and criminals via document fraud, but to massive electoral fraud as well, which has serious implications for the conduct of democratic politics. By acquiring and possessing seemingly legal documents that "prove" juridical membership in a state, a noncitizen[4] can easily acquire citizenship status. Once this status is achieved, unquestioned political suffrage is gained.

Given the weak and varying state capacities in the developing world, an analysis of illegal immigration to India, Malaysia, and Pakistan brings to light the contradictions that exist in our understanding of democratic citizenship and democratic practice and their real-world political implications. Not only does documentary citizenship enfranchise illegal immigrants, but the political participation of these individuals can alter political outcomes in favor of governments that enable illegal immigrants to acquire proof of citizenship and the ability to vote.[5] In effect, illegal immigrants may vote in order to secure their identity and citizenship status. While the act of voting may not be of particular significance to them, it may have serious political consequences for the host country.

It is true, as some scholars have observed, that there has recently been a dramatic increase in the rights and privileges granted by many developed states to immigrants,[6] but at no time have these states opened national- and state-level voting or high public offices to noncitizens. Public office is considered a matter of state security, since access to it allows entry into the guarded domains of foreign, defense, and domestic security policy. States make their fundamental foreign and security policies based on recommendations by elected officials, who are accountable to the voting citizenry and are assumed to represent the demos, which the state both represents and regulates.[7] In short, citizenship continues to be—and is assumed by the conventional wisdom to be—the highest and most protected form of membership in a state because it ensures legal, political, and social rights and duties that are not (in theory) accessible to noncitizens. This assumption is fundamental to most of the literature on immigration which, not surprisingly, is overwhelmingly dominated by cases from Western Europe and North America.[8]

Traditionally, scholars view the expansion of political rights, especially immigrants' right to vote in local and/or national elections, as a sign of liberal citizenship (Bauböck 2005: 683–687; Brysk and Shafir 2004: 209–215). Legalized or naturalized citizens who acquire dual citizenship through state-authorized mechanisms in developed countries are viewed as part of a liberalizing citizenship regime and rising immigrant transnationalism (Bauböck 2003; Carens 1987:). The extension of voting rights to immigrants in local elections (as in the Nordic countries and Japan), to citizen diasporas (as in Mexico, Italy, Spain, France), and to *legal* immigrants in national elections (as in New Zealand and Chile) is viewed by many scholars as a sign of expanding citizenship norms.[9] Yet, according to traditional theories of immigration and citizenship, these rights are conditional on legal status and residency.[10] For instance, the introduction of the concept of *denizenship* by Tomas Hammar is meant to capture immigrants' status with *almost* full citizenship in a liberalizing Europe (Hammar 1990). Yet, as a status, documentary citizenship is distinguished from the expansive denizenship by the fact that documentary citizens can acquire national-level suffrage and public office—in short, even the most secure citizenship rights are available to them—whereas denizens can neither vote in national elections nor hold national office (ibid.).

Immigrants' access to the most secure citizenship rights calls attention to the post–Second World War international system of "crustacean" borders and citizenship (Ngai 2005: 9–11). Buffeted by the nationalism of postcolonial states, the protection and boundary making around citizenship became an act of securing national sovereignty—of displaying independent nationhood and a distinct identity.[11] National sovereignty is, therefore, directly linked to the creation and maintenance of a national identity, a unique nation-state unto itself. Since national identity is about securing the political realm, i.e., drawing boundaries around the community of individuals who make up the citizenry, preserving the nation is fundamentally about the nation's right to determine its own membership.[12] By permitting unauthorized members to enter the body politic, documentary citizenship assaults national sovereignty.

To capture the contradiction of noncitizen voting, I use the term suffraged noncitizen. A *suffraged noncitizen* is an outcome of documentary citizenship, a phenomenon common to India, Malaysia, and Pakistan. For example, suffraged noncitizens are known in Malaysia as "phantom voters," of which there are three types (*Daily Express* 1999c):

1. foreigners who were illegally issued identification cards/receipts and were registered as voters;
2. foreigners who were issued fake identity cards or receipts bearing the names of others who appear on the electoral rolls; and
3. foreigners who were illegally issued fake identification cards/receipts bearing the names of dead voters whose names are still on the electoral rolls.

States are grappling with the social reality of documented illegal immigrants behaving as citizens.

Here it may be asked: what motivates these illegal immigrants to vote? Do they have rational, self-interested reasons to exercise the franchise? While certain political parties in India, Malaysia, and Pakistan benefit from illegal immigrants' votes, what is the benefit for the suffraged noncitizen? Besides gaining material benefits from political parties during elections, such as the distribution of water tanks, rice, money, and fishing nets of various sizes (many Indonesian and Filipino immigrants are excellent at fishing), there is the additional lure of access to better living conditions if one can secure Indian, Malaysian, or Pakistani identity cards from political parties in exchange for votes—an issue well covered by various local dailies during elections (*Daily Express* 1999d). The local IC comes with the expectation that these immigrants will vote for their benefactors, the powerful political parties in Assam, India; in Sabah, Malaysia; and in Karachi, Pakistan. Some of these illegal voters earn lucrative pay by working for the ruling party during elections, making billboards, mounting posters, and distributing pamphlets.[13] Also, connections with powerful members of the ruling or opposition party and other officials bring privileges for these illegal immigrants.

Bangladeshis in Indian Elections?

India is a vigorous democracy with high electoral participation and a thriving party system.[14] The fact that illegal immigrants are exercising citizenship rights in India has broad implications for both domestic and international politics. For example, it has caused widespread anti-immigrant sentiment, which often breaks out into ethnic riots, violence, and regional tensions in areas such as Assam—a case we shall explore in detail below.[15] These tensions result, in part, from the weaknesses of the developing Indian state, which is characterized by weakly institutionalized citizenship norms and multiple forms of identity-authenticating documentation. Struggling to control the entry and access to Indian citizenship of illegal Bangladeshi immigrants, the Indian state is like a paper tiger; it is weak and porous (Rudolph and Rudolph 1987).[16]

Blurred membership in a weakly institutionalized state creates problems with electoral politics, as only full citizens are allowed the right to vote. Both as a conceptual goal and a constitutional safeguard, this is correct: only citizens can vote and contribute to the outcome of an election in India, while legal and illegal immigrants have to sit out this affirmation of citizenship.[17] A look at the legal rules regarding electoral politics in India confirms this theoretical distinction. According to the Election Commission (EC) of India, "a non-citizen cannot be a contesting candidate in the elections," and, according to Article 84(a) of the Constitution of India, only a citizen of India is eligible to contest a parliamentary election.[18] Similarly, Article 173(a) of the constitution makes citizenship a prerequisite for contesting a seat in the state's legislative assembly.[19] Moreover, according to the Representation of the People Act of 1951, section 4(d), only an individual registered as a voter can stand for parliamentary elections; the same rule holds true for a state assembly seat, according to section 5(c). No individual can impersonate another person to vote, and no individual can vote twice (even if his/her name is included in the electoral rolls at two places); both are considered cases of impersonation and are punishable by law under the Indian Penal Code, section 171D.[20]

Here we might notice a curious paradox: in a state that is not even able to provide basic documents like a birth certificate or marriage certificate (chapter 3), how does India believe it can identify and control its electorate by having individuals prove their citizenship using documentary evidence? For example, on August 28, 1993, an order was issued by the EC to introduce electoral identity cards in an effort to mitigate the effects of bogus voting and voter impersonation.[21] The purpose of electoral ICs was to establish an elector's identity at the time of polling. Aware that the right to vote comes from the existence of an individual's name in the electoral rolls, the EC was encouraging the practice of using electoral ICs as a means to determine an individual's right to vote. However, the task of providing electoral ICs to well over 600 million voters, and monitoring and regulating their misuse seemed to be too ambitious, if not impossible. The EC is well aware of the weakly institutionalized nature of citizenship in India, asserting in 2000 that since "it is for the first time in the country that the production of Electoral Identity Cards for the purpose of voting is being insisted upon," it would permit voters to exercise their franchise provided they could establish their identity (to the presiding officer or to any other polling officer authorized by the presiding officer) by using "some documentary evidence."[22] The multiplicity of documents is a significant problem. For example, in the state of Assam by 2006, twenty-one alternate documents could be used to exercise suffrage, ranging from student identity cards to disability certificates:

> 1. Passport; 2. Driving license; 3. Income Tax Identity Card; 4. Identity card for employees of State/Central Government, Public Sector Units, Local Bodies or Public Limited Companies; 5. Passbook issued by Public Sector Banks/Post Offices/Kisan (farmer) passbook; 6. Ration Card; 7. Caste Certificate; 8. Student Identity Card; 9. Land Document; 10. Arms License; 11. Transport Conductors' License; 12. Pension Document (for dependent of ex-servicemen); 13. Railway Identity Card; 14. Freedom Fighters' Identity Card; 15. Physically-Handicapped Certificate; 16. Permanent Resident Certificate; 17. Tea Gardens Association Certificate; 18. Panchayati Raj (Local Councils) Certificate; 19. School Certificate; 20. Revenue Certificate; and, 21. Domicile Certificate.[23]

Further, the EC currently asserts that "all members of a family are entitled to use any of the above-mentioned documents even if it is issued in the name of the head of the family or any other member of the family" (*Assam Tribune* 2006). Examining the list of eligible documents, one is persuaded that almost any "document" would prove one's eligibility to vote as long as it is acceptable to the state officer concerned.[24] It just needs to display some semblance of conformity with state rules. Officials are not going to look any further than that. Curiously, the EC even allows individuals with a record of electoral IC possession the ability to vote using the variety of above-mentioned documents, even if they are unable to produce them at the time of the election. By acknowledging the use of a variety of documents for identification, and their use even in cases in which an electoral IC had previously been issued, the EC admitted that nailing down the nationality and identity of the country's electorate was a difficult if not impossible task—possible in some circumstances, but impossible in many others. Circumscribing and marking the boundaries of Indian nationality, building a wall around the polity along with its attendant voting rights appears neither final nor definite in India.

The chief election commissioner of India, M. S. Gill, wrote that "a clean and accurate electoral roll is the basis of good elections" (Election Commission of India 2000a: vii). However, in the conditions of blurred membership prevalent in developing countries such as India, the electoral roll is sometimes compromised by ethnic and religious politics. The sanctity of national citizenship is trumped by local sympathies. For example, the Constitution of India gives all citizens the right to vote irrespective of their caste, religion, or race. Yet it is common to hear of minorities, scheduled castes, scheduled tribes,[25] and other marginalized groups being arbitrarily removed from the electoral rolls. In one blatant case, 15,800 Muslims were illegally removed from the electoral rolls even as 21,000 Hindu names were arbitrarily included in Uttar Pradesh.[26] While this violates the strict procedures and rules laid down by the EC and the Supreme Court[27] regarding the deletion or the inclusion of individuals on the electoral rolls, it also points to the ease with which local ethnic and religious politics can enable the exclusion of a citizen or the inclusion of a noncitizen on the electoral rolls. Citizenship is no longer a privilege, even in the largest democracy in the world; it is now a tool which arbitrarily excludes or includes individuals who have particular ethnic or religious sympathies. If national elections are an exercise in national sovereignty, then an indeterminate electoral roll is a sign of an ambiguously defined nation.

Assam—an Indian state with one of the largest concentration of illegal immigrants—has been recognized as a particularly difficult case, since, according to the EC, the "citizenship status of some of the residents in the State [Assam] has been a matter of contention amongst various groups."[28] The EC has been increasingly embroiled in questions of determining the citizenship of individuals on its electoral rolls: are they or are they not citizens of India? Since matters of citizenship rights and illegal Bangladeshi immigrants obtaining suffrage rights reached the High Court of Assam as well as the Supreme Court, the EC decided to defer to these judicial bodies and use their judgments as guidelines. For example, in the case of *H. R. A. Chaudhury v. Election Commission of India and Others*, the Gauhati High Court held (in a ruling later upheld by the Supreme Court):

> [The] rolls are to be prepared on the basis of the statements submitted by the Heads of the Households in a constituency in Form 4 under Rule 8 of Registration of Electoral Rules, 1960....The statement made by a Head of the Household has its own value and cannot be lightly brushed aside. *Rules do not contemplate any inquiry into the question of citizenship at the stage of preparation of draft roll.*[29] (emphasis mine)

Hence, self-statements made by heads of households, taken during a survey, determine who is on the draft electoral rolls. Naturally, the head of an illegal Bangladeshi immigrant family is likely to provide the "right" Indian domicile statements regarding his/her family's location and residence. This process of self-identification, a "confession" taken at face value, is not just peculiar to India. Many other developing countries, such as Malaysia and Pakistan, prepare their electoral rolls on the basis of self-statements. If, however, the conductor of the inquiry, while preparing the draft electoral rolls, is a person with nativist Assam Gana Parishad (AGP) or Hindu right-wing Bharatiya Janata Party (BJP) sympathies, it may well be possible that not only could he/she appropriately exclude an illegal Bangladeshi household member, but could exclude native-born legal Muslim voters not to his/her liking as well. The same High Court judgment allowed for an objection to the presence of noncitizens on a draft roll to be raised only *after* the draft roll was published. This means that, once a person is on the draft rolls, his/her citizenship and eligibility to vote can only be questioned after the publication of such a record. So, one's presence on an electoral draft roll becomes critical to proving citizenship status, instead of vice versa. Proving that an individual is a noncitizen after the publication of an electoral draft roll is difficult. How can you question an individual's citizenship after he/she has already been included as a citizen?

The EC recognized that determining an individual's citizenship was a political matter beyond its responsibilities (which was to conduct free and fair elections), and so it deferred to the federal government on such matters:

> [T]he question of whether a person is a foreigner is a *question of fact* which would require careful scrutiny of evidence since the enquiry is quasi-judicial in character. This question has to be determined by the *Central Government*.[30] (emphases mine)

The EC of India, while directing registration officers in Assam to seek local verification in cases where citizenship was doubtful, allowed the process for further inquiry to be referred to appropriate state authorities under the Foreigners Act of 1946 and/or the tribunals set up under the Illegal Migrants (Determination by Tribunal) Act (IMDT) of 1983. Such doubtful citizenship cases were then to be placed on the electoral rolls with the letter *D* (doubtful/disputed) added at the bottom of the appropriate page. These D-category "citizens" were not allowed to exercise their franchise while their cases were pending before the appropriate authorities or tribunals. There were approximately 375,000 voters in the D category on the 1997 electoral rolls of Assam—most of whom were suspected to be illegal Muslim immigrants from Bangladesh (*Hindustan Times* 1999c). However, a curious problem arises from putting individuals in a moratorium, one that is every bit as political as using self-statements to prove citizenship authenticity. If the D-category cases are found to be citizens at a later point,[31] they would have unjustly been disenfranchised. Accordingly, the EC is being challenged on this matter before the Supreme Court.[32] Moreover, the fact that the Indian government has created a particular category to designate

individuals who have questionable citizenship *and* who have been able to successfully insert their names on national electoral rolls is indicative of the pervasiveness
of illegal immigrant voting. Clearly, documentary citizenship is challenging democratic politics by extending citizenship rights to illegal immigrants, and when the
EC confronts questions surrounding the determination of citizenship, it is forced to
defer to other institutions of the state, such as the judiciary and the federal
government.

The exercise of suffrage by illegal immigrants is proving to be consequential to
the regions receiving large numbers of illegal immigrants. The increasing realiza-
tion among natives—both documented and undocumented—that illegal immigrants exercising documentary citizenship are changing the political outcomes in
the state is leading to anti-immigrant xenophobia. Affected regions such as Assam
are marked by high anti-immigrant nativism (Weiner 1978).[33] Additionally, being
pro–illegal immigrant or anti–illegal immigrant has become the fulcrum around
which state and national politics is being organized.

"Save Assam to Save India"

Illegal immigration has changed the evolution of politics and the interplay of India's
political parties in Assam. According to Asamiyas (nationalists, mainly high-caste
Hindu Assamese) and other natives of Assam in Northeast India, illegal immigration is actually supported to some extent by the ruling Congress Party (both at the
federal and state levels) as a way to demographically overwhelm them. In Assam, we
see a political motivation driving the phenomenon of illegal immigration and its
documentation. While regional nativism is hostile toward illegal immigration, the
response is different at the federal level (Baruah 1999). At both levels, plural host
societies have priorities about who can be absorbed or integrated, priorities colored
by race, religion, degree of competitive advantage, and so on.

With the slogan "Save Assam to Save India," the anti-illegal immigrant movement in Assam launched one of the great awakenings of regional identity in the
history of India, threatening the tenuous balance between federal and regional
authority (Hazarika 2000: 64). The Assam movement began with a parliamentary
by-election for the Mangaldoi constituency in March 1979 in which objections were
raised regarding 70,000 names on the electoral rolls, 45,000 of which turned out to
be Bengali illegal immigrants. Voting and behaving as full citizens, these illegal
immigrants had clearly breached the conceptual wall separating immigrants and
citizens. Without naturalization or authentication from the state, illegal Bangladeshi
immigrants had gained Indian citizenship.

The ensuing furor snowballed into the anti-immigrant movement led by the
All Assam Students Union (AASU), members of which later formed the regional

nativist party, the Assam Gana Parishad (AGP). They were supported by Assamese cultural organizations, such as the Assam Sahitya Sabah (Assam Literature Society), and many famous Assamese literary figures (Baruah 1999: 122–123). During the period between 1979 and 1985, ethnic and religious riots, demonstrations, and general civil disorder resulted in as many as 5,000 deaths and the dislocation of over half a million persons. The anti-immigrant movement also took on an anti-Muslim tone. Two large massacres of immigrant Muslims in Nellie[34] and Chaolkhowa Chapori gave the anti-immigrant forces an increasingly xenophobic tenor, with more interest in protecting high-caste Asamiya Hindu dominance. The massacre was a critical moment in the politics of Assam, demonstrating the extreme anti-immigrant sentiment and support for regional nativist organizations.

What grievances did these Assamese have, and why did the anti-immigrant movement become so violent? First, the increasing role of Bengali culture had relegated the native Assamese culture, especially the language, to secondary status.[35] Second, immigrant settlers from outside viewed Assam as a land frontier, to be filled with immigrant labor. The historic settlers were domestic migrants from neighboring states in India, such as tea plantation laborers (usually tribal members from the Bihar and Orissa states of India), Marwaris (traders from Rajasthan), and Bengali Hindus, who came during colonial times as administrators. The historic settlers were also international immigrants; some were part of the internal migration within the British Empire, others came from newly independent states in the area as international immigrants: Bengali Muslims and Bengali Hindus from Bangladesh and Nepali Hindus. In short, these settlers were now being replaced by predominately illegal Muslim Bangladeshi migrants, who were encroaching upon native land, often dispossessing the local Assamese, especially tribal members. Bengali speakers were overwhelming Assamese-language speakers, and as a result of the successful illegal immigration of Bengali Muslims, they were influencing regional elections in modern Assam, an indication of their full membership as suffraged noncitizens. Overwhelmed culturally, numerically threatened, and having lost large tracts of native land, the Assamese felt that they were now about to lose political power as well. They were in a corner in their own homeland (Dasgupta 1997: 351).

The anti-immigrant violence was a response from below—from local native members of the community who resented the failure of state institutions and political leadership to protect *their* national sovereignty from the intrusion of documented illegal immigrants. Violence became a symbolic reassertion of a prior claim to the territorial land—as a native and as a citizen. While there are multiple narratives of the Nellie massacre, they all center on the long-standing and currently illegal role of encroaching Bangladeshi Muslims.[36] The political provocation for the Nellie massacre of 1983 came from the centrally imposed state election in Assam, which leaders of the Assam movement sought to boycott, as it contained illegal immigrants on the electoral rolls who were ready to utilize their documentary power—and vote. Since the election became a referendum on illegal immigration, the news that a few immigrant Bengali Muslims sought to exercise their franchise created a furor in the anti-immigrant movement. The documentary citizenship of Bangladeshi illegal immigrants was resented by a marginalized native community. The Tiwas, along with other plains tribal members and anti-immigrant Assamese, went on a rampage against the Bengali Muslims, killing about 1,600. Other narratives argue that the Nellie massacre was a result of deep-rooted animosity generated by years of encroachment of traditional tribal land by immigrant peasants, largely illegal Bengali Muslims, who had slowly acquired the rights to these lands from tenants. Finally, there was the immediate provocation: a narrative of the abduction and rape of four Tiwa girls by immigrant Bengali Muslims. Each account criminalized the illegal immigrants for gaining the franchise, for gaining access to land, and for predatory sexual behavior.

The political turmoil over illegal immigration could only be resolved by intervention from the highest political leadership, at both the federal and regional levels. The anti-immigrant movement tentatively ended with the Assam Accord in 1985 between the federal government, led by Prime Minister Rajiv Gandhi in Delhi, and the regional anti-immigrant groups, led by student leader Prafulla Kumar Mahanta of the AASU.[37] The Assam Accord focused on disenfranchising the suffraged noncitizens from Bangladesh who had arrived in Assam between 1966 and 1971, while detecting and deporting all those who came after 1971.[38] Those who came to Assam prior to January 1, 1966, were to be regularized, while those who came between January 2, 1966, and March 24, 1971, were to be deleted from the electoral rolls for a period of ten years, after which they were to be reinstated (Baruah 1999: 140). The Assam Accord resulted in the passage of the Illegal Migrants (Determination by Tribunal) Act of 1983 (IMDT). What did the act accomplish? If an individual were a genuine citizen who was falsely accused of being an illegal immigrant (due to blurred membership; see chapter 3), then she/he would be unjustly disenfranchised for ten years. On the other hand, if an individual were an illegal immigrant, then citizenship would be acquired by he/she being "reinstated" after the ten-year moratorium. Ultimately, the illegal immigrant would achieve citizenship solely based on documentary evidence.

The pervasiveness of illegal immigrants in Assam proved too powerful for state government. Only strong intervention by the federal government could contend with their eventual access to Indian citizenship. Initial documents, such as names on electoral rolls, in the end resulted in the acquisition of genuine Indian citizenship through legalization.

Party Politics

The anti-immigration Assam movement mobilized many sections of the society and resulted in the formation of several political groups, the first of which was the nativist political party, the AGP. The more radical fringe, which had less faith in the democratic process and more in violence, created the militant group United Liberation Front of Assam (ULFA). Both of these anti-immigrant forces relied on the Assamese base, typified by the AASU. The accession to power of the AGP in the election following the Assam Accord resulted in high expectations among its anti-immigrant constituents, who believed that the accord would be implemented completely and that the IMDT would expel the illegal immigrants from Assam. However, the IMDT failed as an immigration regulation mechanism.

According to news sources (Bhushan 1996), prior to June 1995, only 25,000 of the 289,767 cases taken up for scrutiny were referred to sixteen tribunals, as a result of which 9,170 persons were declared illegal migrants. The tribunals served deportation orders on 5,421 individuals found to be illegal immigrants; however, only 1,305 migrants were deported. The process of identifying and legally deporting Bangladeshis to Bangladesh (which, by the way, does not recognize that there are any illegal Bangladeshi immigrants in India)[39] via a judicial system known for its slowness therefore created disenchantment with the AGP. It also led to the popularity of the violent militant organization, the ULFA. The ULFA emerged as a result of disillusionment with the political process, specifically, the failure to achieve the long-term goals of the Assamese movement. Not surprisingly, the more radical elements in the Assamese movement ended up taking arms and joining the ULFA. Slowly, ordinary Assamese began to get disenchanted with the AGP. It was neither able to deport a substantial number of illegal immigrants, nor could it control the violence. Furthermore, the AGP began to be intimidated by the ULFA, with which it shared a common Assamese base.

Correspondingly, Muslims in Assam—both the immigrant Bengali Muslims and the local Asamiya Muslims—were increasingly alienated from their political guardians, the Congress Party, because of (a) the violence toward and massacre of immigrant Muslims (Misra 1999)[40] during the Assam agitation; and (b) the focus on immigrant Bengali Muslims for detection and deportation as a result of the Assam Accord, which marked the entire Muslim community for harassment. This resulted in the formation of the United Minorities Front (UMF) after the Assam Accord in 1985. Since then, regional parties such as the UMF have relied on the same electoral base as the Congress Party: Muslims, especially immigrant Bengali Muslims, tribal members, and domestic migrant communities that worked on tea plantations. The Congress Party had always been vulnerable to the popularity of any regional minority party during election time, which resulted in its 1985 loss to the AGP (sixty-four seats with 35 percent of the vote) when many minorities drifted to the UMF (seventeen seats with 11 percent of the vote), effectively undercutting the Congress Party's vote bank (twenty-five seats and 23 percent of the vote; Baruah 1999: 139). From then on, the state was hopelessly divided into pro- and anti-immigrant political parties, some diluting their agenda to broaden their base, only to risk mass exodus from their ranks to rival political organizations. Illegal immigrants, especially their direct political role as documentary citizens, became the fulcrum of Assamese politics and a national political issue.[41]

In 1991, the AGP, the state's anti-immigrant party, lost power to the pro-immigrant Congress Party. Why? Clearly, illegal immigrants as a voting bloc are a source of conflict for political parties, both locally and nationally. At stake was the definition of national sovereignty, of how thick a wall to build around the nation-state. One political opinion wanted to absorb the illegal immigrants due to their documentary status and not to view them as threats to an expansive, liberal, if not self-serving, conception of the nation. This view recognized the pressure from below exerted by illegal immigration and sought to harness it politically. On the other side were natives who felt that the boundaries of the nation were being redrawn by the entry and settlement of illegal Bangladeshi Muslims, and they feared that their vision of national sovereignty was under threat. Both visions provided political capital for electoral mobilization. This led to a change in position, a reluctant admission that illegal immigrants had become a political force due to their exercise of the national franchise. Accepting the power of documentary citizenship, the AGP, the anti-immigrant party, now sought to cultivate sections of the pro-immigrant constituency in the state.

Since the 1985 Assam Accord, realizing the increasing importance of the Muslim and immigrant vote in Assam, the AGP entered into an alliance with other pro-Muslim, pro-immigrant parties, such as the Communist Party of India (CPI) and the Communist Party of India, Marxist (CPI-M). These political compromises meant a dilution of the AGP's strong anti-immigrant stance. Eventually, the AGP began to lose its charm for the increasingly restless Asamiya middle class and the elite in Assam. The AGP, unable to deliver on the promises of the Assam Accord, with its youthful leaders facing corruption charges, and losing Assamese support to a rising militant ULFA, was doomed to lose the election in 1991 (Baruah 1999: 142, 156). The Congress Party was back in power in 1991, increasing its vote share to over 29 percent (see Table 5.2). However, the pro-immigrant Congress Party was always looking over its shoulder for any emerging minority coalition, such as the UMF, as was the anti-immigrant AGP, which was facing the dual threat of a militant ULFA and a Hindu nationalist BJP.

The Assamese middle class and elite were increasingly alarmed at the rising influence of Muslims in Assam politics, and they directly linked this phenomenon to the settlement of a large number of Muslim illegal immigrants from Bangladesh (see table 1.6, chapter 1). Table 5.1 shows that Muslim representation in the Assam legislative assembly remained well below the percentage of Muslims in the Assam population until the late 1970s. The highest percentage of Muslim legislators was achieved in the 1983 elections. This occurred during the tumultuous period of the anti-immigrant Assam agitation during which most Asamiya Hindu–dominated areas boycotted elections, while the Muslim and Bangladeshi illegal immigrant–dominated areas saw strong electoral participation, which was achieved through their documentary status. It is important to take note of the decline of Muslim representation in the Assam assembly in the 1985–1991 period as a result of the anti-immigrant and anti-Muslim sentiment sweeping the state. The pro-immigrant Congress Party was ousted from power. However, the Congress made a comeback in 1991 with substantial Muslim support, and with its return the percentage of Muslim legislators remains at a significant level.

Despite the six-year civil disobedience movement and large-scale violence, the resultant Assam Accord did not lead to the large-scale deportation of immigrants that anti-immigrant groups such as the AGP expected. Ironically, it may have raised awareness among illegal immigrants from Bangladesh that more trustworthy types of paperwork would have to be collected, either illegally or legally through networks of complicity. In a sense, the illegal immigrant networks after the anti-immigrant Assam agitation gave cues to future illegal immigrants to prepare to invest in the documentary evidence of their citizenship. With an increasing Muslim

TABLE 5.1. Muslim legislators in the Assam Legislative Assembly (1952–2001)

Year	Total Muslim legislators	Total seats	Muslim share of legislators %	% of Muslims in population
1952–56	15	108	14%	22.60
1957–62	15	108	14%	22.60
1962–67	14	108	13%	23.29
1967–72	20	126	16%	23.29
1972–78	21	126	17%	24.03
1978–83	28	126	22%	24.03
1983–85	32	126	25%	24.03
1985–91	25	126	20%	24.03
1991–96	24	126	19%	28.43
1996–2001	27	126	21%	28.43
2001 to present	24	126	20%	30.90

Source: Adapted from Dasgupta (2000); Election Commission of India, Statistical Report on General Election [Year] to the Legislative Assembly of Assam (1951–2001). Census figures for 1951, 1961, 1971, 1991, and 2001 are used as close approximations for the appropriate period overlapping with the state elections. Term wise list of members to the Assam Legislative Assembly since 1937 can be viewed at http://assamassembly.gov.in/ala-since-1937.html.

population in the electorate as many former illegal immigrants became citizens, and with some of the new illegal immigrants gaining access to the vote, there was an accompanying rise in Muslim legislators. The percentage of Muslims in Assam increased from 22.6 percent in the 1950s to 28.43 percent in the 1990s, and the corresponding proportion of Muslim legislators rose from 14 percent in the early 1950s to a high figure of about 21 percent in the late 1990s. In addition, as the percentage of Muslims increased in Assam due to the illegal immigration of Bangladeshis, the assertive Bengali-speaking Muslim electorate was no longer satisfied with having just any pro-immigrant, pro-Muslim representative; they increasingly wanted other Muslims as representatives. Therefore, the percentage of Muslim legislators in the state assembly increased over time, which, in turn, alarmed the Asamiya Hindus even more.

The Hindu nationalist BJP's increasing popularity in Assam has to be understood in the context of the political and electoral impact of illegal immigration. Initially, the Assamese Hindus were wary of the BJP because, unlike the AGP, which was opposed to all immigrants from Bangladesh (irrespective of their religion), the BJP's Hindu nationalist view distinguished between Bangladeshi Hindu immigrants, who were seen as refugees, and the Bangladeshi Muslim immigrants, who were seen as "infiltrators" (Nandy 2001).[42] This stance made the BJP very popular among immigrant Bengali Hindus of the Barak valley, where it won parliamentary seats in Silchar and Karimganj in 1991. Distinguishing between Hindu illegal immigrants, who were welcomed as refugees escaping Muslim persecution in Bangladesh, and Muslim illegal immigrants, who were to be deported back to Bangladesh, the BJP slowly started winning over some sections of the Asamiya high-caste population. The BJP positioned itself as a Hindu nationalist party capable of protecting both the high-caste Hindus and the anti-immigrant interests. As a result, the BJP increased its popularity and vote share as it expanded its influence from the Bengali-dominant Barak valley to the Asamiya heartland in the Brahmaputra valley.

The BJP's manifesto opposing Bangladeshi illegal immigrants sounded more credible than the AGP's position because the BJP was in power at the federal level and could push through some of the policy measures needed to manage and control illegal immigration from Bangladesh. For example, during the 1998 parliamentary elections, the BJP platform spoke of the threat of illegal immigration, promising to delete the names of noncitizens from the electoral rolls, to repeal the IMDT, and to strengthen the current immigration laws to detect and deport all illegal immigrants. The platform talked about introducing a national register and identity cards for all citizens (Srikanth 1999). Furthermore, leading BJP leaders, such as the former BJP president, Kushabhau Thakre, raised the issue aggressively, describing the illegal immigration as a "demographic *akraman* [attack]" in which "Bangladesh has officially decided to part with its large population and send them to India" (*Hindustan Times* 1999a). This strengthened the belief that only the BJP in power at the federal level could do something about the Bangladeshi immigrants at the local level and caused the Asamiya Hindu middle class and elites to shift their votes to the BJP. The result: the AGP failed to win even a single seat in the 1998 and 1999 parliamentary elections, while the BJP won one parliamentary seat in 1996 and in 1998 and two in 1999.

On the other hand, there has been a rising consolidation of the minority and immigrant vote behind the Congress Party (see table 5.2), although, on occasion, immigrant Muslims have shifted their votes to regional minority organizations, such as the UMF or the Assam United Democratic Front (AUDF). Most of the time, such rebellion against the Congress is led by local Muslim leaders, disenchanted with the capacity of the Congress Party to protect Muslim immigrants. If such parties succeed, and the Muslim vote is divided between the Congress and another regional party, the Congress loses the election to an anti-immigrant party, such as the AGP. However, more often than not, there has been an upward trend, with the Congress Party increasingly getting the support of Muslims, both immigrants and natives. Notice the steady increase in the votes secured in 1991 (29.35 percent), 1996 (30.56 percent), and 2001 (39.75 percent), all indicating the consolidation of the minority and immigrant vote behind the Congress.[43] What has further helped the Congress Party is its electoral alliance with the Muslim-led UMF or AUDF, which has been especially strong in the immigrant Muslim strongholds of Dhubri, Nagaon, and Barpeta. The Congress Party's increasing dependence on the immigrant Muslim vote also has to be seen in the context of its shrinking electoral base among tea-growing laborer and tribal communities. The Congress dominated such areas

TABLE 5.2. Congress party's performance in Assam assembly elections, 1951–2001

Year	Seats contested	Seats won	Votes (%)
1951	92	76	43.48
1957	101	71	52.35
1962	103	79	48.25
1967	120	73	43.60
1972	114	95	52.20
1978	126	26	23.62
1983	109	91	52.53
1985	125	25	23.23
1991	125	66	29.35
1996	122	34	30.56
2001	126	71	39.75

Source: Based on Election Commission of India, Statistical Report on General Election [Year] to the Legislative Assembly of Assam (1951–2001). Assembly election results for Assam since independence are available at: http://www.eci.gov.in/StatisticalReports/ElectionStatistics.asp

(e.g., Kokrajhar) until 1985, but has been losing support either to independent tribal leaders or to the increasing influence of the BJP. The Congress's shrinking support among tribal members, high-caste Hindu Asamiyas, Bengali-speaking Hindus, and tea laborers is turning it into a party overwhelmingly supported by only one group: immigrant and native Muslims. And the more it is viewed as such, the more anti-Muslim and anti-immigrant voters will shift their votes to the BJP.

The BJP continues to make inroads into the state based on its dual strategy of (a) preferential treatment for all Hindus (high-caste Asamiyas, tribal members, non-Assamese labor, and most crucially, Hindu illegal immigrants from Bangladesh); and (b) a firm anti–Muslim immigrant stance. Public disenchantment with the AGP has helped the BJP to increase its vote share from a low of 9.6 percent in 1991 to 15.9 percent in 1996, to 24.4 percent in 1998, and close to 30 percent in the 1999 elections (Goswami 2001: 1585). The BJP has spread its influence from the Bengali Hindu immigrant community in the Barak valley, which first welcomed it, to the high-caste Asamiya Hindu–dominated Brahmaputra valley, and is now the main rival to the Congress Party in most areas. Having tripled its vote share since 1991, the BJP continues to use the heady mix of Hindu nationalism and anti–Muslim immigrant sentiment to strengthen its electoral base.

Can the BJP replace the AGP as the main anti-immigrant party in Assam? This depends entirely on the degree to which the AGP can hold on to its anti-immigrant Asamiya base. If the AGP seeks to expand its political constituency to the Muslims, it risks losing some sections of the native Assamese electorate. Anti-immigrant parties such as the AGP have an impossible task ahead of them: to gain the pro-immigrant Muslim vote without alienating the nativist Asamiya constituency. Otherwise, they will be swamped by an increasing Muslim electorate in coalition with other minority groups. This explains the continuing dominance of the Congress Party in Assam.

Document-wielding illegal immigrants make for an active and loyal electorate, which incites both nativism and party politics. For pro–illegal immigrant groups in India, electoral participation is enhanced through documentary citizenship, while those opposed to illegal immigrants decry the devaluation of a secure citizenship.

Indonesians and Filipinos in Malaysian Elections

In India, as we have seen, political parties are discovering illegal immigrants to be a useful voting bloc in order to gain and maintain political power. On the other hand, from below, illegal immigrants are discovering that voting is useful to strengthen their citizenship claims and to acquire a voice in the political process. Similarly, Malaysian politics too is witnessing the direct political influence of Indonesian and Filipino illegal immigrants.

When discussing Malaysia, I will explore the motives that drive state actors to adopt policies that encourage illegal immigrant voting. One motive for such practices is to use illegal immigrants as voters to assure political control by a Malay Muslim party, such as the United Malays National Organization (UMNO). The beneficiaries of such manipulation of ethnicity and migration at the subnational level are the parties that get the votes of these illegal immigrants; the officials and local illegal entrepreneurs who sell citizenship documents; and, finally, the illegal immigrants who not only become citizens with voting rights but also have access to affirmative action policies with their status as *bumiputera*, or "sons of the soil." The opposition to illegal immigrants' voting in Malaysian elections is led by native-born, non-Muslim groups that feel political power slipping away from them into the hands of a coalition of indigenous Malay and illegal immigrant groups.

Illegal immigration is changing the ethnic makeup of Sabah in significant ways (see table 5.3). At the beginning of the twentieth century, Kadazandusuns were the dominant ethnic group, comprising about 42 percent of the state population (Tomiyuki 2000: 37). They fell to 32 percent by the 1960 census, 28.1 percent by 1970, and then by 2000, to their alarm, they had fallen to 18.1 percent (see table 5.3). Similarly, Muruts have seen their share decline from 4.9 percent in 1960 to 3.2 percent in 2000. Both of these non-Muslim groups overwhelmingly support the non-Muslim, non-Malay regional party, Parti Bersatu Sabah (PBS), which opposes the migration and settlement of illegal immigrants in Sabah.

TABLE 5.3. Political affiliation and ethnic group representation in Sabah (%)

Political party	Ethnic group	1960	1970	Census 1980*	1991	2000
PBS (regional)	Kadazandusun	32.0	28.1		18.4	18.1
	Murut	4.9	4.7		2.9	3.2
UMNO (national)	Malay	0.4	2.8		6.6	12.4
	Bajau	13.1	11.9		11.4	13.0
	Filipino	1.6	3.1		8.2	NA
	Indonesian	5.5	6.0		7.6	NA
	Other	1.3	2.2		1.9	4.8
MCA (national)	Chinese	23.0	21.3		11.7	10.1

NA = not available.

*The 1980 census collapsed all those who were not Chinese or Indians into a single category called Pribumi, thus making it impossible to obtain data for individual ethnic groups.

Note: Muslim illegal immigrants from the southern Philippines and Indonesia filter into many categories such as Malay, Bajau, and Other.

Source: Adapted from Leete (2007: 62) and Tomiyuki (2000: 37).

In contrast, the UMNO, which derives its support from Muslim groups, has seen the ethnic makeup of Sabah change in its favor. The Muslim Malays have risen from just 0.4 percent of the population in 1960 to 12.4 percent of the population in 2000; the Indonesians have risen from only 5.5 percent of the population in 1960 to 7.6 percent in 1991—with many posing as Malays, Bugis, or members of other indigenous groups (see table 5.3). The Filipinos were a negligible presence in the 1960 census (1.6 percent), but increased to 8.2 percent of Sabah's total population by the 1991 census even as they filtered into native categories such as "others" and Malays (Tomiyuki 2000: 37). Continuing Filipino and Indonesian illegal immigration is further increasing the stock of various Muslim ethnic groups (Bajaus, Bugis, Suluks, etc.) while non-Muslim groups such as the Kadazandusun, Muruts, and Chinese, are declining into demographic and political insignificance. The incorporation of illegal immigrants as citizens is critical to the changing political demography of Sabah. This would not be possible without documentary citizenship.

Article 119(1) of the Malaysian Constitution, like the Constitution of India, accords the right to vote in any state or parliamentary (national) election *only* to citizens.[44] Furthermore, recent constitutional jurisprudence holds that noncitizens or those who have been convicted of possessing fraudulent citizenship documents are *ineligible* to vote (see *Harris Mohd Salleh v. Ismail bin Majin*). In practice though, illegal immigrants are enjoying political suffrage, i.e., they are suffraged noncitizens. For example, a female illegal immigrant confessed to having voted in the last five elections in Sabah, the first three times from Sembulan and the fourth and fifth times in Kuala Penyu (*Borneo Post* 1999a: A1).[45] We can therefore assume that there are cases of Indonesian immigrants who have voted both in Sabah and in the national elections in Indonesia if we consider that an estimated 1.4 million Indonesian immigrants voted in the 1996 Indonesian elections while still living in Malaysia (Kassim 1998: 285).

Confronted with the reality of documentary citizenship, a leading political figure of Sabah remarked:

> The transient population in Sabah, comprising [*sic*] mostly of Filipinos and Indonesians, now number more than 500,000. And it is projected that by the year 2008, the transients will overtake the locals....More than two-thirds are adults and more than 100,000 have been given blue identity cards and are now appearing as voters in the electoral rolls. (Kitingan 1997: 22)

Making citizens out of noncitizens has become a lucrative industry in the state. With a potential market of 400,000 foreigners, the illegal identity card (IC) business can be very profitable indeed.[46] Jeffrey Kitingan, a prominent Kadazandusun leader who was incarcerated under the Internal Security Act, says he was "privileged to meet fellow ISA [Internal Security Act] detainees...who were directly involved in the *project IC* (identity cards)—businessmen, government servants and Indonesians" (Kitingan 1997: 23). A local daily reported the arrest under the ISA of seven officials from the National Registration Department (NRD) for their involvement in the issuance of fake identity cards to foreigners (Kurus et al. 1998: 174).

It appears to Kadazandusuns and other natives that there is active involvement of some state officials in the process of legalizing illegal immigrants. In one court case (*Harris Mohd Salleh v. Ismail bin Majin*), the petitioner, Dr. Chong, told the court that a number of senior UMNO (the ruling Malay party) members from Sabah were detained under the ISA for their involvement in the falsification of ICs.[47] The list included the UMNO deputy chief of Tawau, Shamsul Alang, as well as other members of the UMNO. Some NRD officers and businesspeople were also detained under ISA for their part in this operation. According to Hassnar, a former ISA detainee and a participant in this operation, a total of 130,000 illegal foreigners were issued blue ICs in 1985 alone.[48] Hassnar testified in court that he played a leading role in the operation, which was aimed at increasing the Muslim population in Sabah. He further alleged that this endeavor involved foreigners, government officials, and members of the ruling Barisan Nasional (BN) Party. The state not only tacitly condones illegal immigration for the purpose of party politics; it is actively involved and invested in shaping political outcomes through the manipulation of documentary citizenship.

The largely Muslim makeup of this illegal immigration into Sabah is viewed as an instrument for changing the voting pattern of Sabah to benefit Malay parties such as the UMNO. The motive is to increase UMNO voters. The UMNO's obvious goal is to override the Kadazandusuns and Muruts in favor of a coalition of Muslim groups represented and led by the UMNO. Natives of Sabah feel threatened by the "presence of a large number of Filipino illegal immigrants who are being issued with blue (citizenship) identity cards and being registered as voters" (Kitingan 1997: 31–32). Just before the state elections of 1999, the PBS submitted a list of 49,270 illegal immigrants who had been issued ICs, enabling them to vote (Loh 1999: 35). A bestselling book about illegal immigrants has identified hundreds who have fake ICs and may have voted in elections.[49] It lists their IC numbers and their affiliation to the UMNO, provides photographs of these individuals, and in some cases, even lists their foreign passports (Mutalib 1999).

In response to this involvement, the former chief minister of Sabah, Joseph Pairin, urged the government to stop allowing holders of temporary identity documents, such as JPN 1/9, JPN 1/11, and JPN 1/22, to vote in elections (*Borneo Post* 1999f).[50] All are temporary documents, yet persons with such documents are allowed to vote. Dr. Chong, a PBS (the non-Muslim regional party) candidate from

Likas, submitted evidence alleging the misuse of these temporary documents (*Borneo Post* 1999g).[51] These were documents surrendered to him by anonymous individuals after the Sabah state elections in March 1999. As a result, the High Court declared the election result in Likas to be null and void, ruling that "non-citizens had cast their votes in the polls" (*Daily Express* 2001).[52] Judge Awang of the High Court wrote:

> The instances of non-citizens and phantom voters in the electoral roll as disclosed during the trial may well be the *tip of the iceberg*....It is common knowledge that an influx of illegal immigrants has plagued Sabah for some years. It is a well known fact as it had appeared in the local dailies too frequently. (emphasis mine; *Daily Express* 2001)

The judge noted in his decision[53] that people convicted of possessing fake identity cards in 1996 continued to appear on the electoral rolls of Likas in 1998. These immigrants included (*Harris Mohd Salleh v. Ismail bin Majin*):

> Kassim Bin Ali: IC Number H0508335
> Anwar: IC Number H0512235
> Kadir Labak: IC Number H0454652

Muslim illegal immigrants with documentation continue to participate actively in the election process and favor parties which support their inclusion in Malay society (Hai 2005: 273).

Is voting by illegal immigrants ensuring the dominance of the ruling party in Sabah, Malaysia? The answer is in the affirmative. The incorporation of illegal immigrants through citizenship documents is connected to the electoral politics of Sabah. Legalizing illegal immigrants has become the preferred strategy of the dominant Malay parties when overt Malayization (through conversion, internal migration, etc.) does not proceed quickly enough.[54] The goal of the Malays, who dominate the federal government, is to change the demographic and political character of Sabah so that it becomes Malay Muslim–dominated; due to cultural and religious commonalties, these immigrant Indonesians and Filipinos can easily be Malayized over time, after which they will support Malay Muslim parties. In the late 1990s, one of Sabah's leading political figures saw the challenge of manipulating documentary citizenship to the advantage of certain political parties: "The Sabah problem is really about insecurity, the fear of losing control of their [non-Muslim natives'] political future, fear of neo-colonization, of domination by Malays from Peninsula Malaysia, etc." (Kitingan 1997: 5).[55]

The tacit support of fraudulent activities by sections of the federal government and by Malay elements in the state government produces an insidious politics: a section within the state is trying to undermine the political rights of the major ethnic groups in a regional state through illegal migration. According to Herman Luping (1994: 444), a former attorney general of Sabah, "The popular belief amongst Sabahans, of course, was that both the UMNO and USNO [the premier Malay parties] leaders wanted these people [illegal immigrants] to stay in Sabah and become citizens so that they could swell the votes for their Muslim based party."

While the fake documentation business is partly driven by sheer profit motives, many non-Muslim natives allege that there are indicators of a deliberate political strategy of demographic change. For example, the complicit officials are not put on trial because that would involve publicity, which risks the possibility of all the details of the "IC project" being made public in a court hearing. The ISA, under which these persons are interned, conveniently permits the government to hold these officials without trial and then release them after a few years. Current juridical practice permits the government to refrain from releasing reports or figures on these internments, which they would be required to do if these officials were charged in a court of law. Taken as a whole, these appear to be face-saving forms of support for a well-functioning IC-making machinery. Kitingan (1997: 23–24) alleges, "what the Malaysian Schemers are doing is tantamount to *selling out our birth rights to aliens*" (emphasis mine).

Many Kadazandusun and other natives feel that documentary citizenship is a deliberate political and demographic strategy. In an outburst after losing power in 1985, Harris Salleh, a former chief minister and one of the most prominent politicians of Sabah, acknowledged such a demographic strategy:

> The Kadazans will become like the Sikhs are now in India, a race forever under suspicion by the majority race. [T]here is no doubt that Sabah is moving towards being dominated by the Muslims who already make up more than 50% of the population. It all depends on the federal government, how fast the process continues. Remember we have nearly 300,000 Filipino and Indonesian refugees and workers here in Sabah and most of them are Muslims. Most have been here for many years and will become eligible for citizenship. They are happy living and working here and do not want to leave.... the federal government can register any of the refugees in three hours, three days, three months or three years. There is no law stating the time and *if the federal government wanted to alter forever the voting patterns of Sabah then it can do it as easily as signing the papers.* (emphasis mine; Raffaele 1986: 425)

Voting by illegal immigrants (i.e., suffraged noncitizens) is changing the political map of Sabah, Malaysia, in ways similar to the changing political landscape of Assam, India. They have become influential and direct political players. By voting, illegal immigrants lodge themselves inside the politics of the state, thus remaking the incentive structure to their advantage. Slowly, political players start protecting the citizenship status of current and future illegal immigrants, as it is clearly an advantage for the parties who wish to stay in power.

In short, documentary citizenship can push the politics of a nation to modify its vision to accommodate illegal immigration for the sake of getting votes to stay in power. If the PBS in Malaysia, like the AGP in India, does not accommodate the push from below, it will be run out of power. Since Malaysia, like India, is multinational, its national identity is fiercely contested, and the force of illegal immigration only makes the state less effective at enforcing a clear definition of national and territorial sovereignty.

Afghans and Bangladeshis in Pakistani Elections

Are illegal immigrants exercising suffrage in Pakistan, even as the state does a dangerous dance back and forth between dictatorship and democracy? Bangladeshis who came to Pakistan before Bangladesh's independence from Pakistan in 1971 are legitimate citizens of Pakistan. They number about 40,000.[56] The majority of the Bangladeshis, however, came to Pakistan illegally after 1971, most in the 1980s, many first crossing illegally into India and then crossing illegally from India to Pakistan. In fact, in both India and Pakistan, all Bangladeshi immigration after 1971—the year Bangladesh became independent—is illegal. Additionally, according to the amended Citizenship Act of 1978, all Bangladeshis, including those who came before 1971, are required to legally apply for citizenship. This means that, in spite of the varying interpretations of the law by political parties, most Bangladeshis—here, old residents are lumped together with recent arrivals—have to apply for Pakistani citizenship anew.[57]

Currently, many illegal immigrants are refusing to register with the National Aliens Registration Authority (NARA), instead demanding Pakistani citizenship directly (Ali 2004). Since most of them possess a Pakistani national identity card (NIC) and other official documentation, losing their right to vote and other privileges is a clear step back for them.[58] Additionally, they resist going through a registration process which involves a "possible" naturalization process, unreliable to say the least, when they can claim to have come before 1971 and make a bid for direct Pakistani citizenship. As a result, by 2003, only 18,500 Bangladeshis and 6,500 Afghans were registered.[59]

According to confidential field reports on Karachi, in the area formerly called District West, the illegal immigrant population is estimated to be around a million

(Mansoor 2002). In addition, the former District East has over a half million. Importantly, 150,000 Bangladeshis have acquired the NIC and "thousands" of Afghans and Burmese are documented enough to claim Pakistani citizenship (ibid.). Their votes are now consequential in three national assembly seats and five provincial assembly seats. With the boundaries between illegal and legal citizens fuzzy, the Bangladeshi immigrant vote is now being courted by several political parties. Documentary citizenship has converted illegal immigrants into a valuable political constituency. Political parties such as Pakistan Tehrik-i-Insaf (PTI), Pakistan Awami Tehrik (PAT), and the Millat Party see an advantage in wooing the Bangladeshis, given that many of them can vote in spite of having entered Pakistan illegally. For example, Ejaz Shafi, a Pakistan Muslim League, Nawaz (PML-N) leader is contesting for a constituency in Karachi which includes approximately 20,000 voters whom he views as Pakistani citizens.

Similar to the process undertaken by the political supporters of illegal immigrants in India and Malaysia, backdating the records of large numbers of illegal immigrants to a citizenship-eligible date is common for those who wish to court Bangladeshi voters in Pakistan. Supporters of illegal immigrant voters assert that they came to Pakistan before 1971 and hence if they can produce "any proof of having worked somewhere drawing a salary, or had obtained admission in any school, or have any record of registration," they can register and be eligible for Pakistani citizenship (Mansoor 2002). Pro–illegal immigrant political players will find justifications for assuming illegal immigrants to be eligible voters; it is in their interest not to look too closely if they desire greater political power. Various pro-immigrant political parties make the case of Pakistani citizenship for Bangladeshis and Afghans just as political parties do in India and Malaysia.

In contrast, political parties appealing to native voters oppose any political role for illegal immigrants. The Muttahida Qaumi Movement (MQM) has accused political parties of "getting aliens' names included in the voters lists" for their political advantage (Mansoor 2002). This includes the Islamic party, Jamaat-i-Islami (JI), which has transformed illegal Afghans into genuine voters in the former District Central in Karachi (ibid.). A similar accusation was made by a leader of the Muttahida Majlis-e-Amal (MMA), who protested the issuance of fake IDs to Afghan refugees in the Frontier province.[60] Those supporting Afghan voters justify them either as belonging to indigenous Pakistani Pashtun, Pathan, or Hazara communities or as long-standing refugees who legitimately acquired Pakistani citizenship. It is certainly clear that large numbers of Afghans and Bangladeshis have now fraudulently acquired state documents via networks of complicity, which allow these two immigrant groups to exercise suffrage and for that reason to be courted by different political parties.

Native Muslim versus Immigrant Muslim

Documentary citizenship is pitting Sindhi Muslims against illegal Muslim immigrants despite Pakistan having an Islamic ideology that is biased in favor of other Islamic nations and peoples. In Pakistan, various political parties view illegal immigrants as a vote reservoir to be recruited. Islamic parties are one such group that views Muslim illegal immigrants sympathetically. For example, the president of Jamiat Ulema-i-Pakistan (JUP), Shah Faridul Haq, opposes state harassment of Bengali Pakistanis because they possess a "Pakistani national identity card, passport, domicile and other necessary documents" indicating their citizenship.[61] In the Sindh assembly, both the MQM and the MMA have encouraged the state to issue new computerized national identity cards (CNICs) to illegal immigrants in Karachi since they already possess other citizenship-indicating documents.[62] Similarly, local leaders such as Farooque Ahmed Awan from the Pakistan Muslim League (PML) and Abdullah Baloch from the Pakistan People's Party (PPP), two competing political parties, have also supported illegal immigrants' citizenship claims (*Daily Times* 2004b). Both of them oppose any police action to harass such immigrants. Coming full circle, Baloch questioned the authorities' actions against illegal immigrants on the basis of their long residency and the fact that "at least 84 Bangla-speaking people had become elected councilors in the last local government elections" (ibid.). As is often the case, citizenship claims are made on the basis of a history of the exercise of citizenship rights (voting, employment, house ownership, etc.) which may or may not be based on real documents. Citizenship is now predicated on the exercise of rights associated with it, in effect reworking the traditional path to citizenship, where status was followed by rights.

These trends are not without negative repercussions. Increasing illegal immigration is leading to anti-immigrant tensions in Pakistan. For example, in the Sindh province, which also includes Pakistan's largest city, Karachi, resolutions have been submitted in the provincial assembly by regional parties and local branches of national parties demanding that illegal immigrants be deported back to their states. Proponents argue that illegal immigrants should not be granted Pakistani citizenship and that all "three million" of them should be deported (*Dawn* 2005g). National assembly members, such as Khalid Iqbal Memon from the PPP and Kishan Bhel from the PML-N, are not in favor of issuing ID cards to illegal immigrants and warn that such a trend will benefit other illegal immigrants living in Karachi.[63] Legalization for one group, such as the Bengalis, could open a Pandora's box for others, such as militant Afghans. Kishan Bhel cautioned against making "Sindh an orphanage for immigrants of different countries." Much like regional organizations in Sabah and Assam, activists of the Jeay Sindh Mahaz protested against the "issuing of national identity cards to three million illegal immigrants in Sindh" (*Dawn* 2005b).[64] Anti-immigrant fervor is feeding directly into regional nativist sentiments with a common refrain—an opposition to the enfranchisement of illegal immigrants.

However, so strong is the illegal immigrant lobby that after one such anti-immigrant resolution, NARA officials and officers began receiving death threats (Ali 2004). A senior state official views the activities of the illegal immigrants as further proof that they have political patronage. The illegal immigration of Bangladeshis and Afghans is feeding into long-standing interethnic rivalries among Mohajirs, Pathans, Sindhis, and Punjabis. Ethnic tensions among these communities erupted into large-scale violence that claimed 630 deaths per year between 1990 and 2000 (Chaudhry 2004). Another estimate puts the daily death rate at 10–20 individuals during 1995 and a total of 6,000 deaths in a matter of two years between 1994 and 1996, including 200 security personnel (Shafqat 1996: 671). Karachi was in chaos for much of the 1990s, and illegal Bangladeshis and Afghans added to those tensions. In fact, Afghan refugees have been competing economically and politically with Mohajirs (both are well armed) as Karachi was flooded with arms in the wake of the Afghan war in 1979 (Wright 1991: 305). Newly arrived Afghan Pathans and Pashtuns settled comfortably, but fed into the preexisting Pakistani Pathan-Mohajir cleavages. Similarly, newly arrived Bangladeshis were absorbed into preexisting rivalries between the Sindhis and Mohajirs. Sindhis, who claim native ownership of Sindh, including its largest city, Karachi, behaved much like the nativists in Sabah and Assam in their vehement opposition to illegal immigration. Theodore P. Wright, Jr. (1991: 303) concurs, "Sind is comparable to the state of Assam in India (inundated by Bengalis)" in that "a peripheral people feel in danger or actually have been swamped: numerically, economically, and culturally within their own land by newcomers or invaders." Clearly, animosity toward illegal immigrants rises significantly when illegal immigrants start claiming political power on the basis of fraudulent documents. In short, documentary citizenship and its consequences are only possible when citizenship rights are embodied in documents.

Public Office, Anyone?

The deepening impact of illegal immigrants on local politics is further exacerbated when concerns are raised about illegal immigrants holding public office. The right to get elected or to serve in public office in India, Malaysia, and Pakistan is confined to citizens, as is the case in most other states (Tiburcio 2001: 190–193). Citizenship is always assumed to be secure. The possibility that illegal immigrants have bypassed the checks and balances of the naturalization process and actually begun to hold public office, thus determining the use of state resources, poses a significant challenge to democratic citizenship. The *possibility* that illegal immigrants can occupy political office goes against traditional accounts of citizenship and democratic politics, which presume legal and constitutional barriers to any political representation by noncitizens.

In Assam, a leader of the national BJP, Palit Kumar Bora, claimed that "several Ministers" in the Assam government "were of Bangladeshi origin" (*Assam Tribune* 2004a). In the recent scrutiny of the political role of illegal immigrants in India, even legal immigrants who have acquired citizenship through naturalization face barriers to their political participation. Constitutionally, there is only one class of citizen in India. Once an individual has acquired citizenship through naturalization, he/she can stand for election to any public office, even member of Parliament, vice president, prime minister, or president. However, in practice, Sonia Gandhi, who is Italian by birth and therefore is a naturalized Indian, was unable to claim the powerful public office of the prime minister. This was despite her being the leader of the ruling Congress Party and the widow of Rajiv Gandhi, a former prime minister of India, because of opposition to her naturalized status.[65] So even though, constitutionally, India has liberal citizenship laws, in practice, political opposition can force even a naturalized member of the Indian "first family" to relinquish any desire to hold a top public office.

In contrast to India, both Malaysia and Pakistan limit the highest political offices of the president and prime minister to Muslims. Additionally, both Malaysia and Pakistan disallow naturalized citizens for the highest public offices. For example, the chief minister of Sabah cannot be a naturalized citizen, according to Article 6(4) of the Sabah constitution in Malaysia.[66] Illegal immigrants are not eligible for any office in all three states. To hold public office in India, Malaysia, or Pakistan, the elected or nominated official should be the possessor of unquestioned legal citizenship; they must be able to be safely called upon for the exercise of their official duty in times of emergency or war. The possibility that public offices can be held by illegal immigrants undermines the preservation of a secure citizenship. And yet, in one case, it was discovered that a councilor of the Tawau municipal council was a foreigner who had a fake blue identity card. Documentary citizenship opens public office to illegal immigrants. For three years, this illegal immigrant was a member of four municipal committees, namely, the street-lighting committee, town planning committee, rural development committee and beautification committee.[67] He was later sentenced to three months in jail and was fined by the local court. It seems that the demographic border of Filipino and Indonesian Muslims extends deep into Malaysian territory and that demographic and political borders do not coincide. No doubt, the aforementioned former government official is not alone; many illegal immigrants, through networks of complicity and access to documentary citizenship, are leading the lives of privileged natives.[68]

This is not an isolated incident. In Karachi, with a population of 12 million, a large number of illegal immigrants have been elected to different levels of the local government.[69] The election of illegal immigrants to local municipal positions has happened even as 9,000 judicial cases against these individuals under the Foreigners Act are moving through various local courts.[70] For example, despite arriving from Bangladesh in 1983 and having been arrested under the Foreigners Act of 1946 and Foreigners Registration Ordinance of 1951,[71] Dr. Allaudin was serving as a *nazim*, a local public official. He also was tried for submitting a forged school matriculation certificate; he is one of many such cases. According to a confidential report by NARA's Karachi office, at least 80 Bangladeshi illegal immigrants have been elected to twenty union councils, six of which they lead.[72] Others in the local government assert that the number is much higher; by their estimates, more than 130 Bangladeshi illegal immigrants have been elected to public office in Karachi.[73] According to Mazhar Shaikh, a director general of NARA, the detection and regulation of illegal immigrants is made impossible because a "number of them have become elected nazims and councillors" (Mansoor 2003). Immigration regulation authorities, such as NADRA, face an uphill battle as they review the submissions made by candidates in elections to detect "politicians who lack citizenship" (ibid.).

Once illegal immigrants are elected to local government bodies, they can be called upon to verify other individuals' local status during the citizenship process, further compromising the system of secure citizenship. According to news reports, document-wielding illegal immigrants have "got employment in the government, semi-government and autonomous bodies" in Pakistan (Ali 2004). In India, the High Court in Assam froze the appointment of 5,000 police constables selected by the government after allegations that many illegal immigrants from Bangladesh were on the final list of potential constables (Bora 2005). This has serious consequences. Local officials are often the backbone of the entire identification system; it is at the local level that the verification of background documents occurs. Local officials will confirm an individual's address, settlement history, local roots, and other markers of identity. When illegal immigrants are able to hold official government positions, every proof required by the state to confirm local identity is also available to them. The election of illegal migrants to offices in which they can certify the citizenship of others and provide jobs, such as police positions, is a very important consequence that again may provide a positive feedback loop that increases the likelihood of documentary citizenship. As a result of this office holding, many more illegal immigrants have accumulated citizenship-identifying documents, making it hard to question their local antecedents.

A nightmare haunts the native communities of India, Malaysia, and Pakistan; having acquired documentary citizenship, it is now possible for illegal immigrants to vote and to control political offices. For example, in India, a common refrain is that voting by illegal immigrants will eventually lead to a situation where "an illegal Bangladeshi immigrant" could become the chief minister of Assam (Talukdar 2006). In reality, illegal immigrants will be cautious, and therefore they are highly unlikely to openly vie for a political office which may raise questions about their citizenship. However, if they are in large numbers, and if documentary citizenship leads to political control, the breach in citizenship will be permanent. Alternatively, they could wait for future generations arising from documentary citizenship to be more proactive politically. After all, their numbers will have given them sufficient political strength. There is no secure wall between a citizen and an illegal immigrant, as theories based on developed Western states would like us to assume. The myth that suffrage and political office are secure from illegal immigrants has been exploded. Citizenship is never secure in practice.

Conclusion

The Indian, Malaysian, and Pakistani experiences documented in this chapter highlight three remarkable features of international migration: (a) illegal immigrants can vote; (b) documents enable their political participation as citizens; and (c) parties and immigrants both have an interest in preserving the irregularities of documentation and collaborate to that end. Leading scholars of the mobility of labor and capital have pointed out the transnational character of such flows but have ignored the critical role that documents play in enabling the mobility and incorporation of labor in developing countries (Sassen 1998). In actual practice, voting and political participation are not products of some abstract group membership, but rather are products of the documents an individual holds, documents that are plentiful wherever there is illegal immigration. Illegal immigrants in developing states are voting in large numbers because they are able to procure illegally the documents that allow them to enjoy all of the privileges of citizenship. The act of voting, while perhaps not politically significant for the illegal immigrants, may have a substantial impact on the political outcomes of the host country. Around the world, documents, fake as well as real, are facilitating the incorporation and absorption of illegal immigrants into the state, legitimating them as full citizens.

Electoral politics and control over regional political power are central to the debate about immigration and the conflict over citizenship in India, Malaysia, and Pakistan. It is difficult to monitor an illegal population which is being encouraged to come illegally to the country for domestic political goals by sections within the state. This is very unlike the concerns of, say, Germany or France, which are primarily concerned with the social impact (crime, alien culture) and economic burden of immigrants. The Turks and Algerians are "a problem" in an economic sense and a threat to the cultural stability of the nation as far as they retain or practice their "alien" Islamic rituals. Will they be assimilated? Can they be German enough? These are the issues that concern scholars and policymakers about Western European immigration. Scholars of immigration to Western Europe have shown that the distinction between a citizen and an immigrant is blurring as citizenship-like rights are extended to immigrant groups (Hammar 1990). But this has been followed by a tremendous backlash against immigrants in Western Europe and the increasing popularity of anti-immigrant nativist parties.

Yet, the granting of national and state voting rights to illegal immigrants was never part of the phenomenon in Western Europe. European states welcomed immigrants as guest workers when the economy needed them. Now, Western Europe is busy erecting barriers to immigration. Yet, in our cases, already settled illegal immigrants are determining who will control the region, a common concern among opposition parties and many natives. This is because in India, Malaysia, and Pakistan, citizenship rights such as voting are being exercised by illegal immigrants who have access to citizenship documents. And the process is facilitated by groups within the host state. In the cases examined here, the "illegals" are welcomed, both as economic workers and as political actors; this is only possible in developing states with documentary citizenship.

If millions of illegal immigrants are becoming a permanent and prominent feature of the electoral systems of receiving countries, this poses critical policy and theoretical challenges to democratic citizenship in the developing world. Leading scholars of transnational political participation by immigrants have largely ignored this form of political participation and immigrant incorporation in developing countries (Baubőck 2005; Hammar 1990). Clearly, our theories have not prepared us for a possible electoral role at the national level by illegal immigrants because we have assumed that states have secure and effective control over their territories and populations. Recall Rogers Brubaker's crucial insight that territoriality and nationality are two different ways of segmenting the political realm, of defining who is "us" and who is the "other." In pluralistic, multicultural, and multiethnic countries like India, Malaysia, and Pakistan, many individuals are terribly worked up about the impact of illegal immigrants on ethnic balance. Territorial exclusivity is violated by documentary citizenship in multiethnic states, and nationality is violated by giving those outside the nation a direct political voice in affairs of the state.

Has the exercise of citizenship rights by illegal immigrants in their host states devalued our conception of citizenship? The political realm is clearly divided between those who benefit and those who lose from the exercise of citizenship by illegal immigrants. Others would argue that, by breaking legal norms, by not following acceptable, legal paths to citizenship, illegal immigrants have violated the social contract underlying the formation of a polity, the nation (Schuck and Smith

1985). In their view, citizenship has been undermined and devalued, especially since illegal immigrants have failed to play by the rules. However, this reading ignores the fact that these are historical migrations; their illegality only became a factor on the eve of their states' independence when they decided to follow the post–Second World War model of the state—a sacrosanct line across a territory indicating the border and, within those lines, a card-possessing membership. It is only as developing countries increasingly defined and created a shell of national sovereignty that illegal immigrants became illegal. The push from below in the form of documentary citizenship allows these immigrants to continue these traditional historical migration patterns by circumventing the modern gatekeepers of borders and citizenship. Understood this way, citizenship is expanding across borders in developing countries.

Evidently, Western constructs of democratic citizenship have failed to anticipate documentary citizenship. This, in turn, has critical policy and theoretical implications if we are to grasp the future challenges to democratic citizenship in the developing world. If Western powers view democratic politics solely in terms of self-governing states composed of individuals with full membership, they are more likely to impose such conceptions of citizenship on weakly developed states, such as Afghanistan, Iraq, the Ivory Coast, and East Timor, without addressing the challenges that arise from such underlying conditions as blurred community membership and unsecured borders.

The kinds of underlying conditions described in this chapter raise questions for developing nations themselves as well. Is the Westphalian state appropriate for the diverse citizenry of developing countries? If developing countries absorb noncitizens so easily, what does this tell us about the drawbacks of the deep institutionalization of membership? Should policymakers encourage or discourage a deeper institutionalization of territory and membership in a time of increasing globalization?

Answering such questions is as vital today as it was in the first phase of decolonization after World War II, which created new citizens within new states. In raising these questions, this chapter has challenged traditional theories of immigrant and noncitizen participation. Perhaps it is time to rework our understanding of democratic citizenship in light of the experiences of developing countries such as India, Malaysia, and Pakistan.

6

Tough Ain't Enough

Documents and the Regulation of Immigration

The greater number of offences would not be committed, if the delinquents did not hope to remain unknown. Every thing which increases the facility of recognizing and finding individuals, adds to the general security. This is one reason why less is to be feared from those who have a fixed habitation, property, or a family. The danger arises from those who, from their indigence or their independence of all ties, can easily conceal their movements from the eye of justice.

—Jeremy Bentham[1]

WE HAVE WITNESSED HOW DOCUMENTARY CITIZENSHIP COMPROMISES national sovereignty by giving illegal immigrants access to suffrage. They not only have social, civic, and economic rights, but they have a say in the political process through their exercise of a national franchise. There is yet another feature of sovereignty that is violated by documentary citizenship: territoriality, or the ability of illegal immigrants to travel back and forth between different states. Having exercised the franchise in their host state, illegal immigrants can explore the possibility of traveling abroad from their newly adopted state.

The freedom of international movement which documentary citizenship enables is a direct challenge to the sovereignty and security of developing countries. The prospect of a worldwide trend of increasing documentary citizenship is raising serious security concerns regarding flows of people as tourists, travelers, illegal workers, businesspersons, and students (Sadiq 2005a). If, as the earlier chapters have demonstrated, illegal Indonesians can easily acquire Malaysian citizenship documents, then what prevents Al Qaeda terrorists from doing the same? Foreign terrorist groups in "neutral" states, such as India, Malaysia, Thailand, and the

Philippines, could fraudulently acquire the citizenship paperwork for these states and then get legitimate visas to enter the United States or any other target country. Alternatively, they could use documents from neutral states to enter other neutral states (such as those in Eastern Europe or Central and Latin America) before making an attempt to enter the United States or any other target country. After all, immigration officers in Western states are unlikely to know the difference between a Pashtun from Afghanistan, a Pashtun from Pakistan, or a Pathan from India. Can an Arab *jihadi* migrate from Afghanistan to Pakistan and then to Indian Kashmir and then pose as an Indian going abroad? Who in the West would be able to distinguish between the claimed origin and the real origin of such an individual? Cities such as Delhi, Karachi, and Bangkok produce large amounts of fraudulent passports and other identity paperwork that enable illegal immigrants to enter the restricted borders of Western European or North American states. If this is true, as I have demonstrated, what then are the implications of documentary citizenship for the "war on terrorism" and on the increasing human mobility which is part and parcel of globalization?

Proof that these are pressing questions came on September 11, 2001, when hijackers boarded flights with identification consisting of manipulated passports, visas, and driver's licenses and executed the most devastating terrorist act ever performed on American soil. This and subsequent terrorist acts have made clear how both false identity documents and real but fraudulently acquired identity documents ease the travel and settlement of illegal or unwanted immigrants. The following testimony by Ahmed Ressam, a terrorist convicted for conspiracy to blow up the Los Angeles International Airport in December 1999, reveals the critical role that fraudulent documentation plays in allowing illegal immigrants to travel:[2]

Q.   What was [*sic*] some of the things you were doing in those few months after you came back?

A.   First I put my papers in order, my documents.

Q.   What document[s] do you mean? Documents? What type of documents?

A.   My bank card, driver's license, and insurance card.

Q.   Under what name?

A.   In the name of Benni Noris [*sic*].

Q.   And why was it important to get those papers in order?

A.   To travel.

This testimony shows that, if one has the right documents, one can go and settle anywhere. This and other evidence shows that documentary citizenship is undermining an essential organizing feature of modern international relations: sovereignty over a state's territory and people (Andreas 2003; Andreas and Snyder 2000; Onuf 1991). In its current form, sovereignty is intractably linked to both people and territory: "The state is the land, the people, the organization of coercion and a majestic idea, each supporting and even defining the other, so that they [become] indivisible" (Onuf 1991: 437).

Documentary citizenship undermines the sovereignty of nation-states by breaching the boundaries of national territory. Since documentary citizenship allows individuals to travel abroad, it undermines the state's ability to police its borders, to regulate who is allowed entry and who is excluded. By making possible the entry of illegal immigrants, i.e., those unwanted or undesired by the state, documentary citizenship undermines territorial sovereignty. Additionally, it also allows individuals to travel abroad without the knowledge of state authorities. Hence, documentary citizenship breaches sovereignty in many forms.

But how and why does this happen? To answer this question, we have to analyze the connection between documents and security. Is national security enhanced with standardized documentation? In what ways does it filter unwanted or illegal immigrants? These are critical questions in a time of increasing emphasis on such documentation—paper or plastic—to secure states. The ability to use such documents and bypass state regulation is ubiquitous in developing countries. To understand the link between national security and standardized documentation, we have to analyze how and in what ways documents undermine sovereign control over territory and people and thus challenge the security of states. This issue is at the heart of all discussions on state security in international relations, and yet, very few scholars have analyzed the connection between documents and security, even as some of the most dangerous immigrants—terrorists and criminals—are appearing at the borders of Western states bearing identity documents that appear legal but are fraudulently acquired.[3] This problem is rampant in developing countries, where most migration, much of it illegal, takes place. If the world is to deal with this problem, then we must understand how fraudulently acquired documents are challenging the sovereignty and security of states by shaping and transforming the process of international migration in the immigrant-sending countries. Once unwanted immigrants enter a state with fraudulent, yet apparently legitimate, identity documents, they are able to acquire further documentation that legitimates their presence.

The Visible Immigrant

In the literature on international relations and migration, there is a presumed overlap between an individual's identity and the paperwork he/she holds. The international mobility of people becomes possible primarily as a result of the standardized paperwork (or plastic) an individual holds, which legitimizes his/her nationality and locality; the individual is said to belong to a certain territory and address and is of a certain anthropomorphic type, as validated by the sending state. Here, the primary assumption of documentation is that there will be only one document per person. There may be different *categories* of documents, but one individual will possess only one document of each type. Thus, documents work in the following ways: individual A gets identity document "A," which is unique and separate from identity document "B," which belongs to individual B. When individual A travels within a state or crosses international borders, he/she creates entries into different state records as "A." A was here today, A rented a car, A crossed the border from this town, and so on. Depending on the degree of institutionalization, individual A will be screened minimally or minutely. However, every verification exercise assumes a unique document representing A, as A travels or settles. Everywhere, state authorities know the ethnic identity, citizenship, and location of A through the documentary record he/she produces. There is a paper trail following the individual.

Standardized documents, therefore, are threat neutralizers; they create safe members of the polity, individuals who are nonthreatening to the security of the state. Standardized documents behave as international treaties/institutions; they work on trust and reciprocity and are grounded in international norms. Hence, no harm will come *from* the person who carries the document, and all rights will be extended *to* the individual based on the document. That is precisely why criminals and other lawbreakers may lose their travel rights and have their passports, visas, and other state-authenticated documents withdrawn. It is thus the norms located in the standardized documentation provided by states to individuals which facilitate international travel. All host states are expected to ensure the possession and use of standardized documentation to meet international norms and regulations. So, on the other side of the theory of documentation, a functioning and comprehensive civil registration system that can identify members of individual states is vital because it allows the host state to locate an individual's origin, ethnic identity, and lived history. If the sending state can locate a person and know who he/she is, then the host state can better determine that individual's identity and eligibility to enter. Trust in the information recorded in the registration system also facilitates transactions across borders. On this hangs the decision to allow legal entry. Bilateral treaties that allow dual citizenship, most-favored-country visa status, and no visa requirements are all based on comparable registration norms between states. Documents embody an individual's living record and, therefore, convey trust in the registration system of and between states.

Since ethnic markers are often the basis for ethnic and nationalist violence and civil wars, in multiethnic societies or homogeneous societies with rising diversity due to immigrant populations, one way to demarcate native citizens and their privileges from outsiders is to insist on standardized documentation. These are safe travelers, safe ethnic groups. The possession of such documents signals to society and the state at large that even if an individual is from an undesirable ethnic group—who normally would be weeded out through subtle racial and ethnic profiling—that person can get in because these documents provide a history of safe and secure travel and settlement. In short, standardized documents promise the safety of the state. This allows states to create safe members within their territories and at the same time to limit the presence and entry of safe but unwanted ethnic groups. The British identity card conveys a "Britishness" which conveys a secure and safe meaning to those policing the borders of other states. Until 9/11, whether one was Bangladeshi, Pakistani, Afghan, Punjabi, or Indian, as a British document holder, one conveyed a certain secure signal to the authorities of other states. Documentation was assumed to convey the validity and trustworthiness of the state to which the individual belonged. Since 9/11, however, if one is a British Pakistani or a French Arab identity card holder, one conveys a different sense of security and reliability to other states. Similarly, an Indian passport conveys a secure meaning to Nepal, Malaysia, Bahrain, Qatar, and Indonesia—but not to Pakistan. However, with increasing global migration, an individual's racial/ethnic profile in state records is no longer a true marker of his/her territory and location.[4] One can be a Bengali Muslim and yet hold a Pakistani, Indian, or Bangladeshi passport, or be a Punjabi and hold a British, Canadian, American, or Malaysian IC.

The horizontal equality between two individuals gained momentum with the rise of the welfare state, universal suffrage, and the increased emphasis on human rights after the Second World War. This meant that all individuals, irrespective of race, ethnicity, sex, and religion, were to be treated equally—a "social citizenship" we now associate with T. H. Marshall (Marshall and Bottomore 1996). Since state surveillance and policing functions require ethnic and racial profiling of suspect individuals, this was usually conducted subtly under the equalizing bureaucracy of a legal regime and standard paperwork. Hence, the spread of standardized documents meant that police were constantly performing a balancing act when monitoring domestic populations. They had to balance between, on the one hand, respecting the equality of individuals irrespective of their race, religion, ethnicity, and language, and on the other, conduct monitoring practices whereby individuals were often assessed by their anthropomorphic features and social identities.

This is important because states, even liberal states, use racial and ethnic profiling to weed out unwanted immigrants (Joppke 2005). This is one way of locating an individual who is suspected of being a security threat. Whether it is "criminal tribes" in the British India of the twentieth century or the current international criminal networks, such as the Chinese Triad, Albanian human traffickers, Pakistani Islamic terrorists, or Afghan and Indian drug smugglers—in all cases, the state monitors gangs and individuals by their ethnic and racial markers. Hence, the association between certain ethnic groups and perceived security threats is central. Second, the determination that a particular ethnic group is undesirable to the state's demographic profile and culture is part of a state security apparatus which seeks to maintain an ethnic balance between communities. Even liberal states prefer some ethnic groups over others. A hierarchy of ethnic groups determines immigration preferences.

But how does one racially or ethnically profile in the increasingly multiethnic environment of today's international system? Naturally, this can only be done through standardized documentation:

> In the absence of telltale markers such as language or skin color—which are themselves inconclusive as indicators of one's national identity, of course, but which nonetheless frequently have been taken as such—a person's nationality simply cannot be determined without recourse to documents. As an ascribed status, it cannot be read off a person's appearance. (Torpey 2001: 269)

Documentation makes visible the traveler as a composite of category markers—not just as an individual. Therefore, documents, paper or plastic, are increasingly imprinted with the identity and category markers of individuals. One does not have to look at the individual for confirmation of her/his identity, just look at her/his documents. This documentary process is the modern transformation that facilitates human mobility between states. Through documents, one determines whether an individual is actually a Pakistani or a Thai or an Indonesian or a Saudi. Documents thus allow states to conduct reliable ethnic/racial profiling while confirming legal nationality as well. They make visible the individual features of the immigrant. So, while state agents recognize the equality of all individual travelers, they also provide basic ethnic and nationality information, which monitoring states require in order to regulate immigration. Different states use different ethnic and racial markers: race (Indonesia, Malaysia), religion (Malaysia, Pakistan), nationality but not religion or caste (India), language (Latvia, Estonia), and so on. These markers are combined with anthropomorphic information—color of eyes, skin tone, height—which is combined with a photograph. So the host state, while expressing the equality of all individuals before the law, is at the same time looking for racial and ethnic information to make judgments about entry—a system of subtle ethnic and racial profiling.

The Invisible Immigrant

The system of a recorded and authenticated individual moving between states either breaks down or is insufficient in developing countries. This occurs when documents are no longer a reliable marker of an individual's ethnicity, identity, and record of movement—where he/she has traveled in recent years. As can be expected, security is compromised in such cases. If the international system is based on one identity and ethnic profile per person, then the entire system is compromised if individual A possesses documents containing information on individual B, while individual B may or may not possess such paperwork. Here, individual A will travel as individual B, and authorities depending on such documentation will assume that the individual is B, not A. Both fraudulent documents—fake documents or real documents fraudulently acquired—and the absence of documents are endemic to developing countries.

In contrast to "safe" immigrants are unwanted immigrants whom the state views as being dangerous criminals, terrorists, insurgents, or political or cultural demographic threats. The system of safe, secure ethnic and racial profiling through standardized documentation breaks down due to the presence of documentary citizenship, which enables both dangerous criminals and unwanted ethnic groups to enter state territories by posing as safe immigrants. Such documents hide, i.e., make invisible, the ethnic, racial, and location features that may threaten a receiving state.

Bentham recognized this threatening feature of illegal immigration very early. According to Bentham, the "danger" comes from those who can "conceal their movements" from the institutions of the state (Bowring 1962: 557).[5] Illegal immigration challenges national security because of its dual characteristics; it provides invisibility while facilitating movement. How is this invisibility achieved? Documents allow illegal immigrants to conceal their actual identities, to travel, and to settle down, thus bypassing state controls.[6] In figure 6.1, an individual has acquired documentary citizenship and, under this assumed identity, travels between state 1 and 2. If the individual is a member of a criminal organization out to funnel money or traffick human beings, the individual can keep doing business by traveling under the assumed identity without detection. The individual's real identity is invisible to the state. The same is true if the individual is doing business to raise funds for an insurgent organization, such as the Moro National Liberation Front (MNLF), or a terrorist organization, like Al Qaeda; the individual can again use the assumed identity given by documentary citizenship to travel between states 1 and 2. Remember, the individual may also possess real and legal documents acquired through fraudulent means. Documentary citizenship makes possible legitimate travel, with legitimate visas, except the person is not who she/he claims to be. Legal travel between two states occurs even as the real identity of the individual is invisible. Additionally, there could be an individual who is traveling between states 1 and 2 simply for nonthreatening purposes, such as economic benefits. How then does one distinguish between travelers with criminal or violent intent and travelers as economic migrants?

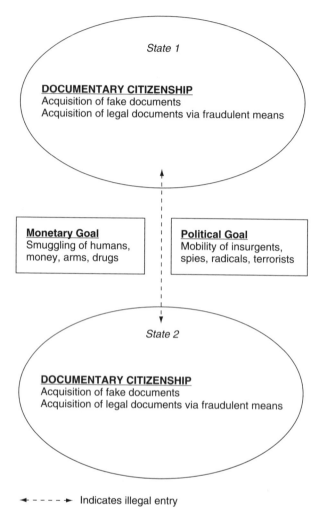

FIGURE 6.1. Invisible travel by illegal immigrants

The threat-neutralizer function of fake or real but fraudulently acquired standardized documents allows anyone in the possession of such documents to appear safe, secure, and legitimate. After all, illegal flows occur despite the best efforts of both sending and receiving states to document their populations accurately. Unlike the common argument of scholars that immigration and security have been closely tied, especially after 9/11, the problem is deeper. It is the civil registration system of individual states which identifies persons in all states. When such systems are unable to create one secure identity for every individual through documents, the entire system is undermined. Immigration is challenging states because of the variety and weakness, if not absence, of the identity documentation system in different states.

Additionally, there is the challenge of state capacity in sending states among developing countries. Specifically, resources for border control and a secure civil registration system are vital to the security of states. Yet, there is a range of state capacities and resources to enable the convergence between individual identity and paperwork. International relations theory presumes a complete convergence based on the recent history of the Western developed states, and therefore it assumes that it is possible to secure territory from unwanted immigrants and other foreigners. For an exact match between individual identities and documents, however, all members within a territory have to possess state-authenticated legitimate documentation. Such surveillance and monitoring, as well as the resources required for such a scheme, are only present in developed states where the security of territory and membership are assumed. In developing countries, this is not the case, and the exact match never occurs completely. Varieties of documents cover different sections of the society, with some paperwork reaching more members of the population than others.

Putting a Name to a Face

If the state has a monopoly over the use of force and is acceptable to a majority of the population, then the security apparatus represents the state. However, the political goals of the state may be contrary to those of a disaffected or marginalized minority or regional group. International minority ethnic networks, complicit sections within the state that are critical of policy, and blurred membership among marginalized minority groups may help disaffected groups to bypass state monitoring. Therefore, there is also a normative aspect to fake or real but fraudulently acquired standardized documents. Documentary citizenship undermines policies of oppression, ethnic suppression, and genocide. Natives seeking to escape tyrannical regimes (Iraqi Kurds under Saddam), totalitarian communist regimes (North Korea, Cuba, the former East Germany, Romania, etc.), genocidal regimes (Yugoslavia under Milosevic, Rwanda), functioning democratic states with severe prejudice against specific minorities (the Chakma minority in Bangladesh), and repressive regimes (Saudi Arabia) all have used documents to escape discrimination and repression. The most obvious historical example is that of the stateless people created as a result of the Holocaust, many of whom at some point used fake or fraudulently acquired documents to escape their tormentors and to settle in other states. Stories such as that of the Von Trapp family escaping Nazi Austria (fictionalized in *The Sound of Music*) abound, and yet hidden in them is the role of documents, real or fake. In such conditions, fraudulent documents have a mitigating role as they open alternative doors to otherwise persecuted groups. By undermining the security goals of such genocidal or totalitarian regimes, documents are the great equalizer—increasing individuals' security while undermining the security goals of a genocidal regime.

Conversely, the use of standardized documents is not always for lawbreaking purposes but can have a law-maintaining function, especially as states seek to survive, maintain stability, and preserve order. States may spy or gather intelligence on other states which threaten their national interest by using anonymous identities created through standardized documents. In short, because standardized documents give anonymity, native authenticity, and occupational legitimacy, they are essential to international criminal organizations, insurgents, and terrorist organizations as well as to states conducting covert intelligence-gathering activities.

If standardized documents are so critical to the functioning of the state security apparatus and to organizations challenging such a state, we should also examine the multiplier effect that documents have. When both legal and illegal flows rely on standardized documentation of some kind, we have created incentives by which new networks are generated and earlier networks are strengthened. Since these documents facilitate both the mobility and settlement of people, especially in areas vital to state economy and security, they also provide a target for groups challenging the state. Marginalized groups, insurgents, radicals, and terrorists all know that they can sustain themselves by plugging into these documentary circuits created by the state. Such documentary circuits are viewed by the state as safe, secure, and vital to its economic, social, and political survival. New flows become possible as a result of the circulation of standardized documentation.

Since standardized documents verify one's ethnic identity and travel record internally, internationally they bring foreign states within one's reach. An aspiring illegal traveler carries another piece of territory with him/her when in possession of another state's standardized documentation. This is an unrecognized form of extraterritoriality where both national and territorial sovereignty are transgressed as a result of paperwork; the individual is authorized to travel and settle while claiming to be from another nation-state. After all, a travel document, such as a passport, in the possession of an individual is actually the property of the state issuing the document; she/he has the privilege of carrying this document only as a right bestowed by the state. Since standardized documentation creates individual legitimacy and personal history instantly, it opens the door to other states, including their institutions, society, polity, security, and economy. In this way, standardized documentation represents an individual by sending signals of legitimacy, approval, and authenticity to the state. On the other hand, a real document fraudulently acquired bypasses the state by sending false signals of legitimacy and approval.

Traveling Abroad

Since September 11, 2001, there has been an intensification of border controls and a tightening of visa regulations, and yet states are confronted with ever smarter and sophisticated document-producing networks that enable travel for unwanted immigrants. Relying on fake asylum claims, amnesties, and marriages in an overall plan to acquire more and more legitimate documentation as a means to gain entry to a state further legitimates documentary travel and citizenship. In such a system, for those unwanted immigrants seeking international travel, such as insurgents from the Liberation Tigers of Tamil Eelam (LTTE) or Al Qaeda terrorists from Afghanistan, a passport is the most useful document. Indeed, Al Qaeda ran a "travel office" at the Kandahar airport in Afghanistan in addition to imparting security training to fellow jihadists in the techniques of producing fake travel documents, especially passports (Zill 2001; Levine 2004). "They are the greatest tools that terrorists have in their arsenal," says Asa Hutchinson, undersecretary for border and transportation security in the U.S. Department of Homeland Security (Levine 2004).

A foreigner traveling abroad requires a range of secure identity documents, including a national passport. Hence, travel agents, postal employees, courier services, passport officials, police, airline workers, and embassy officials are all part of a network providing the necessary paperwork to overcome or bypass every checkpoint or gate designed to protect territorial and national sovereignty.[7] Importantly, entry occurs only with appropriate documents. Each screening gate either reconfirms an earlier document or requests a new document. Stamps and seals are all marks of authentication. Therefore, complicity occurs at the gates of entry or exit from the nation—at the boundaries of sovereignty.

Illegal immigration's challenge to sovereignty is well known to developing countries, where questions of immigration and citizenship are handled by the sections of the government that safeguard domestic national security, e.g., the Ministry of Home or Interior. The link between immigration and security is also well recognized by scholars and policymakers (Weiner 1995: 131–149; Andreas 2003: 78–111). The following are some of the ways that documented illegal immigrants in India, Malaysia, and Pakistan threaten the security of these states.

First, by acquiring documentary citizenship, illegal immigrants can gain access to suffrage and public office, thus posing a political threat to native groups by having a say in the distribution of resources (see chapter 5). Second, as a consequence, the increasing settlement of illegal immigrants leads to increasing anti-immigrant tensions, violence, massacres, and sometimes insurgency (see previous chapter for discussion). Examples include the large-scale massacre of Bangladeshi Muslim illegal immigrants in Nellie (Kimura 2003) and Kokrajhar in Assam and the large-scale urban violence between immigrant groups from Afghanistan and native communities in Karachi, Pakistan. The widespread anti-immigrant sentiment among native communities, such as the Kadazandusun and Muruts in Sabah, Malaysia, does not lead to violence because of the tight grip maintained on interethnic relations by the government of Malaysia.[8] However, deep anti-immigrant sentiment along with ethnic stereotyping is already present, and who knows what would occur if law and order institutions were to collapse in Malaysia. Third, illegal immigration intermingles with the activities of international criminal organizations involved in the smuggling of drugs, arms, humans, currencies, and goods. For example, these include Afghan drug smuggling via Pakistan, Iran, and India; arms smuggling between Afghanistan and Pakistan; Myanmarese drug gangs; the trafficking of women and children from Nepal and Bangladesh to India, and from Afghanistan to Pakistan; and the smuggling of counterfeit goods among Malaysia, the Philippines, and Indonesia. Separating legitimate Afghan immigrants from Afghan militants, Afghan opium smugglers, and Afghan human traffickers is difficult if not impossible if they all use similar networks, share resources, and reside in the same communities. Fourth, illegal immigration leads to increasing border clashes between the border security forces of the two countries and between the border security forces and illegal immigrants. The inability of Pakistani authorities to seal the border with Afghanistan is partly a function of the networks that immigrating groups of Pashtuns, Hazaras, and others have built over the decades, which has led to a thriving illegal trade in drugs, arms, women, and children. Conflicting views on borders and illegal immigration have led to exchanges of fire between Indian and Bangladeshi border security forces. For example, sixteen men from the border security force of India were killed by the Bangladesh military force that guards the Indo-Bangladeshi border.[9] This led to an escalation of tensions between the two countries. The Indian and Bangladeshi forces exchanged gunfire from heavy weapons amid claims and counterclaims over different parts of the territory on the Indo-Bangladeshi border.

Finally, there is the immediate threat of insurgents, militants, and terrorist groups as they go back and forth between two states. The illegal settlement of MNLF cadres and leaders in Sabah, Malaysia, is a cause for tension between Malaysia and the Philippines. Along with the southern Filipino insurgent groups, there are terrorist groups, such as Abu Sayyaf, that use documentary citizenship to move easily among the southern Philippines, Malaysia, and Indonesia. Rebel groups from Aceh in Indonesia and Pattani in southern Thailand are all supposed to have members among the immigrant communities in Malaysia. The Sri Lankan rebel organization, the LTTE, utilizes the wider network of Tamil immigrants in India, Malaysia, Canada, and Singapore to finance and arm itself. Sikh insurgents or Kashmiri terrorists on the Indian-Pakistani border in the west, and Bodo,

ULFA, Naga, and Mizo insurgents on the border between Bangladesh and Northeast India are a frequent source of tension between these states. Indeed, the rise of militant Islamic groups with a parallel mushrooming of religious schools called *madrassas* on the border between India and Bangladesh is a major security threat to India. Similarly, Taliban leaders and cadres along with other Islamic extremists find sanctuary in the border region between Northwest Pakistan and Afghanistan, thus creating tensions between two states that are ostensibly on the same side in a global war on terror.

All of the insurgent, militant, and terrorist groups in India, Malaysia, and Pakistan know that, for international travel, they can rely on a fraudulent passport network running from Peshawar to Karachi to Delhi to Mumbai to Kuala Lumpur to Bangkok to Dubai to Hong Kong, thus enabling regional travel and, ultimately, their ability to reach the West. They undermine the sovereignty and security of states by weakening the capacity of states to segment the political realm—to draw, monitor, and maintain borders around national and territorial sovereignty (Hall 1999; Brubaker 1992). Common to all of these groups challenging state security, then, is the use of fake citizenship-affirming documents, such as birth certificates, high school certificates, national identity cards, receipts for national identity numbers, electoral receipts, and passports. While some lawbreakers may come from the pool of illegal immigrants, others come from local native groups. Both utilize documentary citizenship to conduct their operations.[10] These days, illegal travel is as necessary for terrorists, insurgents, opposition groups, militant groups, traffickers, and criminal organizations as it is for illegal immigrants who desire to settle down and earn a livelihood. They both share a desire to keep their real identities invisible so as to bypass the state's regulatory mechanisms.

Since documentary citizenship sustains the flow not only of economic migrants but also of international criminal gangs, violent groups, and terrorist organizations, it has a direct relationship to international security. Elsewhere, I have shown that networks of complicity and the condition of blurred membership allow illegal immigrants to enter and mingle with local populations. These conditions are available not only to illegal immigrants but also to any criminals, terrorists, insurgents, and political activists who may want to utilize the same networks and conditions to bypass the state security apparatus. Since developing countries have a higher level of complicity by sections within the state and widespread blurred membership, it is possible for criminal organizations to acquire documentary citizenship in these countries for unmarked regional travel to neighboring states or international travel to Western states. Moreover, since the poor, landless, and desperate illegal immigrants come from the same pool of economically or culturally marginalized groups that produce criminal networks, they also produce political networks of insurgents, opposition groups, and terrorists. Ethnic networks that facilitate illegal entry and standardized documentation can also be utilized by those with a political or violent goal.

As can be seen by the foregoing discussion, bypassing state monitoring is the key to these groups' ability to raise funds, acquire recruits and arms, and plan and carry out international terrorist events or criminal activities (Zill 2001). Hence, at the center of their international networks are operatives who specialize in travel documentation. If this is the case, how do insurgents, terrorists, and criminals acquire passports and other documentation to carry out their operations?

The recent focus on terrorism has revealed that passports are used for international travel *to* the highly documented developed states. Criminal or terrorist networks can use their members' real identities or aliases to purchase authentic passports from complicit state officials. Or, they can buy forged passports. The underground market in Indian, Thai, Pakistani, and Malaysian passports thrives due to the collusion of government officials. State cooperation notwithstanding, one can also alter the personal data and photograph on an existing authentic or fraudulent passport; this is particularly common among passports which already have genuine visa stamps from Western states. This significantly contributes to the inability of immigration officials to separate real from fake documents. In Gujarat, India, one can pay 100,000 rupees to "borrow" a passport with a valid American visa (Mukherjee 2004: 9). For example, Babuben Patel traveled abroad on the passport of Sakina Ahmad (B 3312631) from the state of Bihar. Law enforcement in India caught an agent who was modifying Yunus Ramaiya's passport (A 9689198) to send abroad an illegal immigrant. It had been successfully utilized earlier by another individual to reach the United States (ibid.). Advancements in counterfeiting technology, the increasing involvement of professional forgers, and the slow pace of global standardization undermine the capacity of state officials to separate real from fake documents (Zill 2001).

Bangladeshis in India, or Indonesians in Malaysia, or Afghans in Pakistan may not initially intend to travel abroad, but they have the ability to do so. So, can illegal immigrants traveling between developing countries use documentary citizenship to enter Western states? The answer is absolutely yes. Afghans in Pakistan can and do join the rest of the Pakistanis going abroad by posing as Pakistanis. Indonesians can and do join other Malaysians traveling abroad by posing as Malaysians, or they could choose to travel to a third country, such as Mexico or Thailand, acquire documentary citizenship, and travel abroad under that citizenship. A similar trail of fraudulent documents marked the path that Ressam, one of the Algerian terrorists, pursued when trying to enter the United States as a Canadian. He flew

> from France to Montreal using a photo-substituted French passport under
> a false name. . . . Ressam eventually obtained a genuine Canadian passport

TABLE 6.1. Indian passports by issuing city

	Applications received	Passports issued
Ahmedabad	252,131	311,938
Bangalore	189,486	191,314
Bareilly	47,400	40,970
Bhopal	52,750	48,336
Bhubaneshwar	25,362	22,178
Chandigarh	218,096	213,561
Chennai	273,037	260,379
Cochin	204,029	195,917
Delhi	218,049	195,705
Gawhati	20,354	20,571
Ghaziabad	51,801	43,577
Hyderabad	331,614	321,899
Jaipur	154,314	119,732
Jalandhar	201,572	201,649
Jammu	14,582	11,147
Kolkata	131,584	124,312
Kozhikode	283,895	239,105
Lucknow	183,728	151,642
Mumbai	256,969	233,542
Nagpur	27,237	25,356
Panaji	34,500	33,273
Patna	69,642	41,859
Pune	69,653	65,336
Ranchi	20,032	13,565
Srinagar	12,060	12,627
Surat	38,926	16,690
Thane	96,310	92,025
Trichy	316,807	284,383
Trivandrum	152,656	143,745
Vishakhapatnam	73,095	66,578
Total	4,021,671	3,742,911

Source: Government of India (2004b: 164).

through a document vendor who stole a blank baptismal certificate from a Catholic church. With this document he was able to obtain a Canadian passport under the name of Benni Antoine Norris. This enabled him to travel to Pakistan, and from there to Afghanistan for his training, and then return to Canada.[11]

Traveling abroad under a newly adopted nationality and citizenship, conferred by the possession of a passport, trumps most verification systems, cursory background checks, and, importantly, gives immediate access to any visa-free entry arrangement that the adopted country may have with other states. In short, by covering one's ethnic identity and citizenship with a neutral identity and travel documents, the individual ensures smooth international travel. The individual becomes invisible and, hence, secure from the surveillance institutions of the host state.

How prevalent is documentary citizenship among illegal immigrants from India, Malaysia, and Pakistan who travel abroad? India, with a total population of over 1 billion, had only 20 million registered passport holders worldwide by 2001 (Jha 2001).[12] By 2003, the figure had increased to 25 million (Baruah 2003). In effect, only about 2 percent of individuals commonly categorized as "Indians" can be identified by their Indian passport.[13] As India liberalizes its economy with a large middle class looking outward, it is very likely that a majority of these passport holders do not live in India. It is likely that Indians working overseas, or those needing to travel abroad for other reasons, hold a large percentage of these passports. Table 6.1 summarizes the figures for Indian passport applications and those finally issued passports after state verification between January 2003 and March 2004. In the table, we notice that, in India, in just fifteen months, 3,742,911 passports were issued. According to news sources, currently over 2.5 million passports are issued by the Indian government every year. Somewhat worryingly, approximately 10,000 passports are lost every year. Replace a photograph, a name, personal details, travel history, and one has an entirely new person traveling abroad. Figures on the number of individuals detected with forged documents and deportees from abroad based on data from five major international airports in India for 2002–2005 are in table 6.2. This is just the tip of the iceberg, considering that these events cover individuals traveling abroad via airports who were actually caught. Most are not caught, which explains the successful movement of illegal immigrants from India to varieties of destinations abroad.

With standards that are in compliance with International Civil Aviation Organization (ICAO) guidelines, one would assume that Malaysian citizenship is secure. It is not. Documentary citizenship is clearly evident when "Malaysians" travel abroad. According to a Canadian government report, Malaysian citizenship is accessed by noncitizens regularly (Government of Canada 2002):

> There is a high incidence of non-Malaysian nationals receiving Malaysian identity cards. Using the national ID card, these individuals subsequently gain access to Malaysian passports. Canadian and other officials continue to encounter a disconcerting number of improperly issued and improperly obtained Malaysian passports.

For example, the incidence of Malaysian passports being used by noncitizens to gain access to Canada rose by 39 percent in one year, from 163 in 2000 to 228 in 2001.[14] The report anxiously suggests that this is only a portion of the total number

TABLE 6.2. Immigrant deportees with fraudulent documents

Year	Forgery in passport/visa detected in India	Indian deportees from abroad
2002	1,344	4,808
2003	1,079	5,214
2004	1,072	5,423
2005	852	3,148

Source: Minister of State Sriprakash Jaiswal in the Ministry of Home Affairs, in reply to an unstarred question (no. 868) in the Lok Sabha, Government of India, Ministry of Home Affairs, November 29, 2005, http://164.100.24.208/lsq14/quest.asp?qref=20245. Figures available through June 2005.

of Malaysian passports being used for such purposes, since many individuals either dispose of their documents en route to Canada or return the documents for reuse by other individuals. After all, lost or damaged passports have commonly been used by illegal immigrants, human-smuggling syndicates, and traffickers. The incidence of lost or damaged passports for the year 2000 was 35 percent higher than for 1999 in the case of Malaysia.[15] Malaysia distributed 761,575 passports in 2000; however, during the same year, 9,057 passports were reported lost and 1,973 were reported damaged.[16] Perhaps Malaysian citizenship will become impermeable with the new biometric e-passport, which was introduced to the country in 1998. It utilizes a chip-based technology to store two biometric identifiers: (a) a digitized photograph and (b) digitized fingerprints.[17] Today, 4.5 million such biometric passports are in circulation, making this Malaysian citizenship document one of the most technically advanced in the world.[18] The utilization of such a standardized high-tech passport is the future goal of many developing countries as they try to meet post–9/11 travel guidelines. India is trying to create a national identity card and a passport with biometric measures, and so is Pakistan. Yet, in contrast to India and Malaysia, the situation is absolutely critical in Pakistan.

The Pakistani Case: Guarding the State or Facilitating the Network

Pakistan illustrates the power of networks to corrode institutions that otherwise guard and regulate entry to the nation. Pakistan has acquired additional notoriety in that networks of complicity have undermined the sanctity of its embassies and the foreign office—agencies that issue and facilitate all manner of passports and related identity cards. Widespread cases of lost and stolen passports have resulted in the dismissal of several Pakistani diplomats.[19] Networks of complicity—in this case, immigration officials at the airport along with airline staff—have opened all of the gates of entry (and exit) at the airport, which is another institution guarding

TABLE 6.3. Afghans traveling on fraudulent Pakistani passports

Name	Passport No.	Issued	Place of issue	Returning from
Mohammad Amin	KB-850188	4/23/03	Parachinar, Pakistan	Dubai
Nafia Khel	K-881872	11/28/01	Abu Dhabi	Dubai
Mohammad Javed	G-674853	7/27/99	Abbottabad, Pakistan	Dubai
Imran Khan	K-937388	12/6/01	Peshawar, Pakistan	Dubai
Abdul Qadeer Khan	K-578108	8/24/01	Jeddah, Saudi Arabia	Dubai
Mohammad Musharraf Khan	K-578033	8/23/01	Jeddah, Saudi Arabia	Dubai
Mohammad Javed	KA-281654	4/24/02	Riyadh, Saudi Arabia	Abu Dhabi
Sherawar Din	G-510246	6/3/99	Jeddah, Saudi Arabia	Abu Dhabi

Source: Dawn (2003).

Pakistani national and territorial sovereignty. Afghans traveling on Pakistani passports can only acquire air tickets, boarding passes, and other stamps of approval if sympathetic network members staff the entire gamut of the screening process at the airport (*Dawn* 2005c).[20] Table 6.3 lists the cases of eight Afghans with fake Pakistani passports, which were acquired on the basis of Pakistani NICs—real or fake—who were caught at Pakistani airports while returning from destinations in the Middle East (*Dawn* 2003).

Illegal immigrants from Afghanistan, Bangladesh, and Burma with Pakistani national identity cards and passports are causing a great deal of concern for the Pakistani government, which is under close scrutiny after 9/11. Consequently, the Pakistani Federal Investigative Agency (FIA) has supplied the details of over 32,000 stolen or missing passports to Interpol (Jang 2003). Such passports are especially useful since one can insert alternate photographs, personal descriptions, and travel history, making individuals, like those in table 6.3, appear to be legitimate Pakistani document holders. In 2005 alone, the High Commission of the United Kingdom received over 3,400 visa applications with forged documents, according to the Visa Service director, Alex Pond (*Dawn* 2006). Most of the fake documents were submitted by student visa seekers. Meanwhile, 20,000 illegal immigrants from Pakistan in Greece had to be issued temporary Pakistani passports to allow them to take advantage of a Greek amnesty for illegal immigrants (*Dawn* 2005a). In 2004, the FIA of Pakistan caught 835 people traveling abroad on forged documents (*Dawn* 2004a). We know that the actual number is much higher as passports are manipulated for other uses as well. According to a report, 20,000 non-Pakistanis performed the *hajj*, the Muslim holy pilgrimage to Mecca, by posing as Pakistanis under the Pakistani quota (Masood 2003). Illegal immigrants are using Pakistani passports to smuggle heroin to Bangladesh, and Afghans are traveling on Pakistani passports to Europe and the Middle East—all challenging the integrity of Pakistani citizenship (*Daily Times* 2004a).

In addition, blank copies of passports have been stolen on a regular basis from different passport offices in Pakistan, resulting in over 41,000 blank copies stolen between 1990 and 2005, with about 21,000 blank passports stolen between 2000 and 2005 (Ijaz 2005). The frequency with which Pakistani blank passports are being stolen indicates that these documents are available to many wishing to travel abroad under assumed Pakistani identities. In a period of three years, 12,937 blank Pakistani passports were stolen (Ijaz 2005). In 1999, 185 blank passports from the Muzaffarabad passport office and 1,960 passports from the Dera Ismail Khan office were stolen. The next year, 1,112 blank passports from the Sialkot office, 2,200 from the Quetta office, and 2,160 copies from the Abbottabad office were illegally removed. In 2001, 2,120 blank passports from the Multan office, 1,000 blank passports from the Gujranwala office, and 2,200 passport books from the railway authorities in Peshawar went missing. The primary concern with stolen passports is that many "illegal immigrants from neighboring countries, notably Afghanistan," are traveling with Pakistani documents (Qaiser 2003). While the Pakistani Bureau of Emigration and Overseas Employment (BEOE) has canceled the licenses of some recruitment agencies, a majority of these agencies continue to thrive by sending Afghans abroad on Pakistani passports and other Pakistani identity documents (Ahmad 2004). The director general of BEOE, Ibrahim Khan, confirms this fact, saying, "Yes, it's true that a large number of Afghans [have] gone abroad on Pakistani passports." He recognizes the easy access that Afghans have to Pakistani citizenship (Ahmad 2004).

Ironically, many members of the Pakistani Hazara and Pashtun tribes have successfully settled in Australia by posing as Afghan asylum seekers (Ansari and Bucha 2002). They carry two passports on the journey, destroying the Pakistani passport at sea and then claiming political asylum on their Afghan passport (ibid.).[21] To the uneducated eyes of international immigration officials, it is impossible to tell the difference between a Pakistani and an Afghan Pashtun, or a Pakistani Hazara and an Afghan Hazara. During 2000–2001, the Pakistani government received Bangladeshis, Indians, and Iranians—all Pakistani passport holders—who were deported from other states (Ali 2004). Illegal immigrants included those who entered Pakistan in the 1980s and acquired Pakistani passports, only to fly overseas for employment (ibid.). According to reports, almost 169,729 Pakistani illegal immigrants were deported from sixty-four countries in just two years, and yet the interior minister filed cases of fraudulent passports against only 468 individuals, out of which only 33 were convicted.[22]

Since the 1970s, a national identity card has been utilized by various branches of the government in Pakistan. But given the ease with which people can get driver's licenses or birth certificates (fake or real but with appropriate details), it is unlikely that either the earlier or the current computerized effort at an NIC is effective. It is common among the elites in Pakistan to have multiple passports—one set for traveling to the Middle East or other Muslim countries, yet another for the United States and other Western countries.[23] Whenever travel information has to be hidden, a separate passport is a must. For example, after 9/11, a person traveling to the United States could avoid showing his/her travel history to Middle Eastern states by simply using a clean passport. All this entails is a slight modification of the name—from Rashid Malik to Syed Rashid Malik or to Rashed (with an *e*) Malik, and so on. Remember that these are all genuine, authorized passports bearing legitimate visas that have been issued by complicit national authorities. If Western states begin viewing every Muslim-majority state as a terrorist threat, such practices will become even more widespread.

For developed states, such as the United States, these practices pose additional problems. Passports from friendly states, especially those with which a country has bilateral visa-free arrangements, are increasingly in demand because immigration and police officials are more lax in monitoring visitors from such states. As Jan C. Ting, a former assistant commissioner with the U.S. Immigration and Naturalization Service, points out:

> Under visa waiver, Zacarias Moussaoui, sometimes referred to as the 20th hijacker, was able to enter the U.S. before 9/11 by showing his French passport. Richard Reid, the "shoe bomber," was able to board an airplane headed for the U.S. by showing his British passport. And one of the 1993 World Trade Center bombers, Ramsi Yusuf, was able to enter the U.S. through visa waiver by presenting a counterfeit European passport. (Ting 2005)[24]

Between June 1991 and February 2004, over 200 people with visa-waiver passports showed up on terrorist watch lists, according to the Department of Homeland Security inspector general, Clark Kent Ervin (Levine 2004). There are twenty-seven visa-waiver states whose citizens get smooth entry into the United States with the mere presentation of a passport. For both illegal immigrants seeking better living conditions and individuals attempting to undermine American national security, a passport from one of these countries is invaluable (Letzing 2005). Unfortunately for the security of the United States, acquiring these passports is not too hard, given that there are over 10 million lost and stolen travel documents circulating globally (Levine 2004). And more are being lost or stolen this very moment.

Conclusion

In a time of globalization, an increased emphasis on the speed of communication, travel, and financial transactions has resulted in a demand for multiple physical markers of authentication. The volume and speed at which the flow of money, goods, and people are taking place require an increasing amount of paperwork, technical sophistication, and level of authentication, e.g., at the bank, the airport, the border, or the market. As technological innovation reduces travel time, the demand for more sophisticated documents, either fraudulent or real, increases—both for states trying to assert their sovereignty and for poor residents trying to cope with this imposed boundary and its effect on their opportunity structures. All of this raises a question. If requiring multiple identity documents is on the rise in both developed states (due to increasingly sophisticated technology) and developing countries (documents proliferate due to a lack of resources), does it make states more secure? As I have argued, the increasing availability and use of authenticating documents does not ensure increased security. The increasing use of multiple documents, even technologically sophisticated ones such as biometric measures, only increases the number of times that various personal and physical markers of an individual (signature, fingerprint, retina scan, handprint, facial scan, scars, or DNA) are recorded on paper (or some material substitute). If documents ensure access to facilities, those excluded from such services (such as the poor, the landless, vagrants, beggars, or criminals) will do their best to acquire them fraudulently. Correspondingly, because of the push from below, those trying to escape poverty or persecution are willing to do anything to procure an official or official-looking document that enables their illegal immigration. In a sense, processes arising from the civil society, such as illegal immigration and documentary citizenship, have undermined states' sovereignty.

While the cost may be high, the adoption of advanced identity-authenticating technologies is a possibility for developing countries. Given the widespread identity thefts via the Internet and banking scams involving credit card and Social Security numbers, developed states are moving to multiple physical authentications of identity, such as retina scanning and DNA testing. These technologies, known as biometric systems, identify patterns in a person's irises, face, fingerprints, voice, and physical characteristics; they can be stored on a computer chip (Bergstein 2003). If this conversion succeeds, it will create a class of biometrically documented travelers, a system which can only be subverted by well-funded human-smuggling gangs. Meanwhile, most of the developing world, unable to generate sufficient resources, will continue to struggle with document-carrying illegal immigrants. While these measures will control entry at regulated gateways, Western governments will have to contend with the system being subverted by porous borders, collusion by sections within the state, and the cooperation extended by immigrant co-ethnics. If this scheme only partially succeeds, then the state will have only added to the multiplicity of physical authentications of national identity.

In these circumstances, it is difficult for state officials to determine the country of origin of an individual if the person has utilized several fake passports using multiple routes. Concealing one's place of origin or identity becomes extremely easy if individuals can acquire feeder documents, such as a birth certificate. Since birth certificates are the foundation on which identification systems of states are built, individuals can utilize them to acquire subsequent documents, such as school graduation certificates, passports, or national identity numbers. In this way, illegal immigrants can acquire new identities and make fake residency claims. Confronting this challenge is Interpol, which has a database of 13.3 million entries of lost or stolen documents from a hundred and twenty one states (Interpol 2007: 10). However, this effort is recent.[25]

There are many constraints in the operation and management of a global database of travel documents.[26] Access is a key issue; many state officials at the entry points, such as airports and borders, do not have access to the necessary information on a real-time basis. It is vital to receive updated identity information from global resources as an individual attempts entry. Immediate access to the latest identity information allows gatekeepers to regulate the entry of an unwanted individual. There is another lacuna: the data do not include biographical information on individuals. This considerably limits the ability of officials to distinguish real from fake document bearers. Such limitations arise primarily due to strict privacy laws meant to safeguard individual rights. The system is also highly reactive and depends on a state gatekeeper becoming suspicious about a travel document or an individual and responding appropriately. As we saw in chapter 2, most complicit networks have agents working from within gatekeeping sectors of the state. The entire system fails if an agent chooses not to report an individual with fraudulent documents. Even if the agent has access to a database, the onus to react against suspicious individuals and documents falls on the border agent, law enforcement official, and administrative staff—all of whom can be bribed, coerced, or manipulated. Human error and the supply of unreliable information further weaken this database. Finally, not all states may cooperate in developing a global database because states have varying interests; one state's militant or terrorist may be another state's freedom fighter.

States also seem to believe in technology as a solution to securing territorial borders and membership boundaries. However, the measures required for complete control, monitoring, and surveillance of individuals will entail removing the influence of complicit ethnic networks and the condition of blurred membership. This can only happen at the expense of liberal norms and democratic principles. This is why authoritarian, monarchical, and communist states are relatively successful in exercising such control over the entry and settlement of noncitizens. The Soviets, Cubans, and East Germans, much like their current counterparts, the Saudis, Syrians, and North Koreans, seek complete control over individuals—including their movement and location. It is interesting that the introduction of and advances in the new smart card are happening in states that are fixated with order as an ideology and therefore have some experience with authoritarian rule or single-party regimes, such as China (single-party communist rule), Thailand (military), Malaysia (single-party rule), and Singapore (single-party rule) (Lyon 2004: 7).

The push from the top, from the state, to exercise complete control over individuals and their movement as a result of the "war on terror" will encounter pressures from the civil society below, which through complicity, corruption, and civil/legal measures will once again bypass state measures. Total identity management is a chimera for liberal democratic states. States will have to reconcile themselves to having different classes of travelers—some biometrically enabled to fly on airplanes, others trying to bypass such technology, and the overwhelming majority living and traveling within developing societies without any standard identifiers.

In conclusion, confronting the challenges of illegal immigration to sovereignty and security involves a large global enterprise. It requires centralizing and standardizing entire civil registration systems so that identity and membership are no longer blurred in the developing states which send illegal immigrants to Western states. It implies the monitoring and surveillance of already existing ethnic immigrant communities so that ethnic kinship networks do not trump receiving states' control by providing instant membership through documentation. Finally, it entails eliminating all corruption, bribery, and political or ethnic sympathy as a result of which complicity may happen within states. What securing developing or developed states from illegal immigration involves is a major global social-engineering and institution-building project, to which self-interested but resource-constrained states—both rich and poor—are unlikely to commit. Until then, states can act tough, but tough just ain't enough.[27]

7

After Citizenship

EVEN STATES WITH TOUGH REGULATIONS ARE FORCED TO ACCEPT ILLEGAL immigrants. Indeed, they frequently make deals, offer amnesties, and employ regularization exercises to convert large numbers of illegal immigrants into a more authorized membership, thus creating a path to citizenship. No wonder a recent headline in the *New York Times* proclaims, "Deal Would Put Millions on Path to Citizenship," as if the only path to citizenship for illegal immigrants is the one bestowed by the state via naturalization (Swarns 2006). This is untrue for developing countries. Naturalization is not the only option in the developing world. Contrary to statist visions of citizenship, illegal immigrants are creating a paper trail to citizenship. They bypass state-mandated procedures by acquiring citizenship-indicating documents. This book has followed their documentary path to citizenship.

A focus on the role of documents explains the process and ease by which illegal immigrants continue to gain access to citizenship. I have shown how illegal immigrants obtain documentary citizenship, including the rights to vote and travel under their newly acquired nationality, in India, Malaysia, and Pakistan. When immigrants travel across international borders, these very documents enable their movement and incorporation into a new state. A focus on documents (whether fake or real but fraudulently acquired) challenges our current theories of immigrant incorporation, which continue to maintain the conceptual dichotomy between illegal immigrants and citizens. Documents have come to bridge the gap between the two.

Illegal immigrants' access to civil, social, and economic rights within the nation-state is acknowledged as the liberal tradition in the West. But political rights, especially those with importance for national identity and security, remain secure from nonmembers, i.e., those outside the boundaries of citizenship. National sovereignty in this sense is still secure. After all, the received wisdom concerning democratic states is that while legal immigrants have certain political rights, only citizens have *all* of the rights of citizenship, especially that of voting in national and state elections. This book has argued, in contrast, that electoral rights are being accessed by illegal immigrants, belying the conceptual distinction between immigrants and citizens while undermining the very meaning of "citizen" and the "states" to which they belong. National boundaries, the walls putatively separating citizens from immigrants, are being subverted by documentary citizenship even as the insistence on documentation to identify individuals is rising globally. I have shown that networks of complicity and the condition of blurred membership are two critical factors that enable the acquisition of state documents. Complicit networks bypass state regulations by providing documentation, thus easing the daily life and settlement of illegal immigrants. In my overall argument, the acquisition of citizenship-indicating documents gives illegal immigrants access to citizenship—*documentary* citizenship. If documentary citizenship is widespread, as I contend it is, then this is cause for a serious reworking of our understanding of the state, the nation, the citizen, the border, and the illegal immigrant as the ubiquitous outsider. The illegal immigrant has overcome the traditional notion of secure citizenship and is now among us as a citizen. It is the end of secure citizenship as we know it. They have become us.

To conclude, let us consider the implications of documentary citizenship for our understanding of immigration and citizenship in the developing world. Having uncovered the myth of a secure citizenship, I will now analyze its full impact on nations. By allowing illegal immigrants access to national suffrage and other political rights, documentary citizenship is a response from civil society to citizenship from above. After this discussion, I will examine documentary citizenship as a central attribute of globalization, further demonstrating its common occurrence in developing countries. Finally, I look at the tension between embracing documentary citizenship as an addition to the diversity of a state and viewing it as a threat with potentially serious implications for national sovereignty. Should we welcome documentary citizenship as another positive feature of globalization, or be fearful of its implications?

Citizenship Redefined

If we think of citizenship as a formal status granted by states, then there would seem to be three traditional approaches to granting citizenship: jus sanguinis, jus soli, and naturalization. We have added a fourth: documentary citizenship. What does this do to our traditional understanding of citizenship?

At the beginning of this book, I outlined the various ways in which citizenship is understood. The settlement of illegal immigrants through documentary citizenship in India, Malaysia, and Pakistan fundamentally challenges some of our conceptions of citizenship. First, the traditional understanding of citizenship has always associated the gaining of citizenship status with a bundle of rights. Documentary citizenship reverses this relationship. Cumulative practices of citizenship by illegal immigrants strengthen their citizenship claims, and over time lead to citizenship status. What is unique to my argument is the way that citizenship status is acquired without going through any state-mandated processes.[1] Citizenship conferred by documents without naturalization, birth, marriage, adoption, or transfer of territory opens a new path to citizenship.

Second, this kind of citizenship ceases to provide a common national identity. Documentary citizenship facilitates the adoption of a new national identity by an immigrant without any necessary dilution or compromise of an earlier national identity. Illegal immigrants are free to choose their mix of identity markers. Hence, an illegal immigrant can hide his/her minority ethnicity by adopting the features of the majority ethnic group. Filipino Christian women in Sabah who adopt Muslim names or Bangladeshi Muslim women who adopt Hindu names are examples of this "flexible citizenship" (Ong 1999). If an illegal immigrant belongs to the majority ethnic group then she/he can easily access the advantages of the preferred majority. Hindu Bangladeshis get favorable treatment in Indian West Bengal while Muslim groups from the southern Philippines (Sulus, Bajaus) have direct access to affirmative action policies as *bumiputera* in Malaysia. Citizenship no longer brings with it a concrete national identity to be adopted by the immigrant. At the same time, a national identity is harder to adopt if it is bereft of co-ethnics from the immigrating group. Bangladeshi Muslims will find it hard to adopt a secularized civic Indian national identity in contrast to their Bengali Muslim identity in Bangladesh. A more secular, less Islamicized vision of Pakistani identity will not be an easy sell for adoption by radicalized Afghanis. The link between a definite national identity and citizenship has been broken.

Third, citizenship ceases to be a privilege. When the focus of illegal immigrants is merely gaining access to citizenship rights, the duties and responsibilities that accompany citizenship tend to be correspondingly ignored. There is no sense of obligation to the state since rights come instantly with the acquisition of documents. Moreover, the self-created character of documentary citizenship allows its beneficiaries to pick and choose the elements of citizenship of which they want to avail themselves: typically, entitlements but not duties or responsibilities. In the most extreme cases, a very thin conception of citizenship becomes prevalent, and citizenship is completely devalued. Of course, the opposite tendency may exist as well. One might argue that, with the increasing accumulation of documents and the associated practice of rights, illegal immigrants may slowly begin to feel part of the community and begin to shoulder civic responsibilities. In this scenario, a civic virtue develops among illegal immigrants as they regularly practice citizenship rights in their adopted state. I would argue that both types of tendencies can and do exist. However, inasmuch as documentary citizenship brings to bear no obligations or sense of duty and is disconnected from national identity, it does tend to devalue citizenship. The assumed privilege of citizenship no longer exists in the traditional sense. In the end, documentary citizenship can erase the boundaries between a citizen and an illegal immigrant.

Erasing the Wall

The bounded nature of citizenship, where the nation-state was a container for all rights, has eroded because of its dependence on documents. Citizenship is no longer a secure political realm. Hence, documentary citizenship presents a serious problem for our understanding of the composition of states. The international system is based on distinct states having exclusive citizenries. According to international norms, a person can belong to only one state at a time, making naturalization the only path to citizenship with full political rights. In this system of norms, dual citizenship is possible only with the permission of both states. In sum, the political exclusion of noncitizens is the basis of a world politics that equates national interests with the interests of citizens only. But if noncitizens and citizens *both* gain access to state membership, then the traditional system of mutually exclusive citizenries needs considerable reconceptualization. This is tantamount to saying that being an illegal immigrant is, in many developing countries, no different from being a citizen.

Noncitizens come through porous borders and reside in unmarked populations. The acquisition of documents allows these illegal immigrants to access the status of citizens. The possession of identical documents erodes the sharp distinctions between citizens and noncitizens, allowing both equal access to political rights. And if illegal immigrants have access to citizenship, they have access to political suffrage, public office, and military service—all areas of national importance. In such circumstances, national interest becomes difficult to locate in one citizenry, one state. The reality of both citizens and illegal immigrants participating in weakly institutionalized political processes has serious political implications, and in developing states with blurred membership, this is precisely what we are witnessing.

Blurred membership and ethnic networks of complicity point toward the importance of the thick, complex, long-term environments within which documentary citizenship emerges and is functioning (Sassen 2007). The thick environments are responsible for the potency of documentary citizenship, due to which (a) the ethnic networks bypass the formal legal features of citizenship, and (b) ethnic politics prevail over the national republican project and override older attachments. Sovereignty is at stake in such a world view, and all regulatory measures are failing.

If we understand state sovereignty in terms of its ability to exercise authority and control (Sassen 1996), then there are several ways in which the state has lost sovereignty due to documentary citizenship. It gives access to the political community by opening national citizenship rights to any document holder. From locally issued documents to the accumulation of national-level documentation, such as a national identity card, citizenship as practiced in developing countries is completely accessible to illegal immigrants. Each document brings with it the practice and privilege of a right conferred on a citizen. Importantly, citizenship brings with it political representation and public office—decision-making bodies involved in the construction of national identity and membership. The authority over who enters and settles within the body politic resides in law-making institutions of the state. However, state agencies dealing with immigration and/or citizenship are ineffective against the entry and settlement of millions of illegal immigrants.

Sovereignty is compromised in terms of territory as well. State authority is barely in existence as unauthorized immigrants cross territorial boundaries. Even as India, Malaysia, and Pakistan increase border checkpoints, fencing, and new border technologies, their continued loss of territorial authority points to the corrosive effect of documentary citizenship.

What happens when the state incorporates illegal immigrants through some process, say, an amnesty? An *amnesty* means state approval of illegal immigrant entry and access to local rights. In such conditions, the state reclaims control and authority over illegal immigrants by making them visible through official documentation, which enhances its power to monitor the individual more closely. Here the state regains sovereignty as a result of a compromise with the documentary citizenship of illegal immigrants.

In such circumstances, the indivisible allegiance to the state is compromised.[2] If social, economic, or political conditions deteriorate, documentary citizens will have a de facto escape clause whereby they will be able to return to their homelands, claiming their original citizenship on the basis of nationality. However, official citizens do not have this option: good times or bad times, they owe their loyalty to their state. The national encasing of citizenship carries with it duties and obligations, among them an insoluble allegiance of the individual to the sovereign state. Documentary citizenship is not conditional on loyalty to either the political community or the territory. Both political and territorial sovereignty yield to the power of documentary citizenship.

Expanding Subjects

There is another truth buried in documentary citizenship. At long last, here is a phenomenon that actually expands citizenship to illegal immigrants, not just local- or
municipal-level rights but actual full citizenship rights. The entrenched liberal values
of Western states only bring local voting rights, while documentary citizenship deliv-
ers instant national suffrage and the possibility of public office. National citizenship
can now be acquired in an irrevocable fashion based on citizenship-indicating fraudulent documents. Citizenship is no longer secure from any illegal immigrant as long
as he/she possesses documentary citizenship. In a perverse sense, our blind adherence
to traditional notions of citizenship have made us overlook this new path to citizenship, which is expanding citizenship norms in practice. Both liberal and illiberal
democracies allow democratic citizenship without any commitment to liberal values.
This means that the circle of individuals forming the polity, with equal rights, invisibly absorbs millions of illegal immigrants as fellow citizens in developing countries.
In this sense, sovereignty is expanding to embrace ever newer subjects.

Is citizenship elitist? Possibly. Since citizenship, for the state, is a legitimate
entitlement to social, economic, and civil benefits, it is no surprise that more and
more states are now insisting on the documentation of life events, such as birth,
marriage, and death, as a way to identify an individual. On these authenticated
documents depend the exercise of citizenship rights by individuals in a state. Such
a state-mandated citizenship, fully inscribed on a document, is elitist in many ways.
The lack of required documents excludes large sections of the population from
their citizenship rights. It is no surprise that traditional regimes of citizenship, with
their bag of citizenship goods, never benefit the masses of the poor in developing
countries. The poor just do not have the documents to access these citizenship
rights. While scholars of citizenship dissect civic, economic, cultural, political,
national, and postnational citizenship, in practice all of these citizenship rights have
remained outside the reach of large masses of the poor, while the illegal immigrant
travels back and forth between developing countries. Even today, developing states
continue to follow the top-down citizenship model implemented across the Atlantic
by documenting identity and centralizing databases and by using a piece of paper
(or plastic) to confer a combination of citizenship rights. However, as governments
implement citizenship from above, civil society is adapting from below. Illegal
immigrants have discovered that access to any citizenship right is contingent on
them showing appropriate documents. Documents bring illegal immigrants (and
other noncitizens) into the circle of a political community. Documentary citizenship
is civil society's way of adapting to a citizenship model that previously only existed

for the middle classes and elites in developing countries. It expands and makes meaningful citizenship for large numbers of natives and illegal immigrants. With documents, they have access to welfare and public assistance, i.e., social citizenship, and to full political citizenship, which is understood as equal political rights under the law. With resident illegal immigrants having a *full* say in the political community, equal citizenship as a goal is well within reach. Documentary citizenship expands both the notion of citizenship and its actual practice in democratic countries. While it may unnerve some to learn that documentary citizenship has stealthily opened the doors of secure citizenship to illegal immigrants, others may see it as a welcome feature of globalization.

Globalization of Citizenship

Since documentary citizenship pierces the "crustacean" framing of national citizenship, is this postnational membership a sign of increasing globalization? We have conceptualized the membership of immigrants, legal and illegal, as postnational membership (Soysal 1994), denizenship (Hammar 1990), transnational citizenship (Bauböck 2003; Ong 1999), etc. Like postnational membership, documentary citizenship too bypasses the state. It both escapes and manipulates state authority. However, unlike denizenship and postnational membership, it is not an incomplete membership. Many immigrants, students, travelers, tourists, and refugees are aspirants to citizenship. They become subjects of postnational membership and denizenship on the path to full citizenship. A range of rights becomes available to them as a result of expanding notions of membership, mainly in the European context. Yet, they are excluded from secure citizenship rights, like national voting, public office, and other rights crucial to national governance. In contrast, documentary citizenship brings full de jure citizenship to illegal immigrants. Documented citizens acquire full citizenship when they possess such markers of unquestioned citizenship as a NIC and a passport. In this way, the traditional idea of a secure citizenship has given way to a fluid citizenship. Documentary citizenship transmutes membership. It has no boundaries, no end. Multiple documents can bring multiple memberships. In this sense, it accentuates globalization. Increasing state reliance on documents expands the possibilities for travel and absorption.

Documentary citizenship is a central feature of globalization. As states increasingly divert resources to the documentation of individual identity through birth registration, marriage certificates, national identity cards, and passports, documentary citizenship will only increase. At the same time, documentary citizenship reveals several emerging characteristics of globalization (Sassen 2006). First, it should not be forgotten that the thick environments that produce documentary citizenship are localized, because the processes occur in subnational settings. The process leading to the formation of documentary citizens inhabits and is constituted inside the national container, at the local site (Sassen 2007). The individual illegal immigrant is reconstituted with one local framing layered on top of another, while claiming authenticity from multiple national authorities. It has denationalized citizenship and more (ibid.). Second, local networks are directly connected to global circuits and represent the localization of the global. The sole purpose of these local-global circuits is to bypass the national surveillance and monitoring that has been the focus of the Westphalian state ever since the late nineteenth century. The same circuits that make it possible for an illegal immigrant from Indonesia or the Philippines to get absorbed in Malaysia will also point them to other circuits which will enable their further travel to Singapore, Australia, and member countries of the European Union. Third, these circuits are invisible, and so even as the nation-state increases its surveillance goals through NICs and biometric measures, there is an invisible absorption of targeted communities through the power of global circuits placed locally. The nation-state cannot see this illegal immigrant settlement because these circuits use the same technology that the state uses for surveillance—standardized documentation.

Finally, since surveillance has been a nation-state obsession, the rising recognition of documentary citizenship will lead to increased nativism against illegal immigrants and a push for surveillance at both the global and local levels. Individual states in conjunction with international institutions will collaborate to monitor documented illegal immigrants. We find evidence for this in the recent activity of Interpol in creating a global database of lost or stolen passports, which may in the future expand to include data on other travel and identity documents. Additionally, urgent funds are being directed through UNICEF and international NGOs (e.g., Plan International) to improve the birth registration coverage of developing countries. Post–9/11, such schemes have been launched in India, Bangladesh, Pakistan, Afghanistan, and Indonesia, along with many other developing countries. Birth registration and certification—the first identity document of any state—has acquired urgency in a time of terrorist travel. Parallel to this is the effort to create centralized national databases of citizens and immigrants in India, Pakistan, Indonesia, and Malaysia, along with other developing countries. Clearly, the nation-state is confronting the power of thick social environments where the global is localized and made invisible, thus bypassing national surveillance efforts. Documentary citizenship is erasing the wall between immigrants and citizens since states increasingly identify individuals through documentation. This is not peculiar to India, Malaysia, and Pakistan; it is a global phenomenon.

Widespread Documentary Citizenship

In what ways is documentary citizenship a global phenomenon? First, as we saw in chapter 1, there is substantial migration in developing countries (36.9 percent of all international migration).[3] The figures underestimate illegal immigration within developing countries, especially hiding the large population of illegal immigrants with documentary citizenship. According to the *World Migration Report* (United Nations and International Organization for Migration 2005: 396), the proportion of migrants is highest in Asia (25 percent) and is conspicuous in Africa (9.3 percent); illegal immigration takes place in large numbers in these regions (Ghosh 2000). The presence of large numbers of co-ethnic immigrants in Africa and Asia means that illegal immigrants may be gaining access to citizenship in those regions. Since these regions have been neglected by immigration scholarship, studying them should be a priority in the coming years. Moreover, these are also regions with some of the largest concentrations of poor, most of whom tend to immigrate illegally, given their lack of financial resources. The share of the poor in 1993 is highest in South Asia (43.1 percent) and sub-Saharan Africa (39.1 percent), followed by Latin America and the Caribbean (Ghosh 1998: 38, table 2.1).

Finally, poor countries are also likely to have weakly institutionalized citizenship, i.e., widespread blurred membership. According to UNICEF, the following countries, among others, have no data on birth registration, the very first instance of identification by the state: Benin, Bhutan, Burkina Faso, Central African Republic, Congo, Ecuador, Haiti, Iraq, Ivory Coast, Laos, Madagascar, Nepal, Nigeria, Senegal, South Africa, Tanzania, Togo, and Vietnam (UNICEF 1998a: 661). Those with low levels of birth registration (30–50 percent of births, or more, are not registered) include Afghanistan, Angola, Bangladesh, Bolivia, Botswana, Burundi, Cambodia, Cameroon, Chad, Eritrea, Ethiopia, Gambia, Ghana, Guinea, Guinea-Bissau, India, Indonesia, Kenya, Lesotho, Liberia, Malawi, Mali, Mauritania, Mozambique, Myanmar, Namibia, New Guinea, Nicaragua, Niger, Sudan, Rwanda, Sierra Leone, Somalia, Uganda, Yemen, Zambia, and Zimbabwe (UNICEF 1998a). Notice the preponderance of poor developing states from Africa, Asia, and parts of Latin and Central America. Other states may also have poor regions with weakly institutionalized citizenship and a correspondingly large supply of illegal immigrants. To the extent that these developing states have both blurred membership and a large stock of complicit networks, they are likely to experience widespread documentary citizenship.

Documentary citizenship is pervasive and makes possible the immigration of foreigners to host states by creating a paper trail of authenticity for individuals. In the Ivory Coast, a national identity card scheme was central to a national politics

that slid into civil war (BBC News 2002a). About 30 percent of its 16 million inhabitants are foreigners (Nyce 2003). Large numbers of immigrants, many Muslims
from Mali, Burkina Faso, and Guinea, came to the Ivory Coast in the 1960s, 1970s,
and 1980s to work in its cocoa industry (Hartill 2006). Over time, the north became
a stronghold of Muslims, largely unauthorized, while the Christian south claimed
native status. It is these immigrants and their children, many born in obscure villages, some with fake birth certificates, others with none, whose voting potential
southerners fear (ibid.). Since blurred membership is widespread, the state, with
the help of the United Nations, introduced a NIC which would also enable the
exercise of the franchise, i.e., standardized documentation from above. The government hopes to document every individual with certainty. On the other hand, government forces in control of the south have regularly destroyed or confiscated the
ICs of those with northern ethnic features or names—accusing them of being foreigners. Every case of a northerner possessing an Ivorian identity card is presumed
to be an instance of documentary citizenship.

The supporters of President Laurent Gbagbo, mainly in the south, regard the
northern region as filled with illegal immigrants, who are overwhelmingly Muslim,
whom they feel should not be allowed a say in the country's affairs through suffrage
(BBC News 2006). In short, the northerners' claims to NICs are illegal and their
possession of national identity cards is fraudulent. Among the immigrants who
were denied citizenship status is Alassane Ouattara, a former prime minister and a
Muslim, whose mother is from Burkina Faso. His nationality came into question,
including claims that his nationality certificate was a forgery, as he rose to national
power after his party won many seats in a local election (BBC News 2002b). The
southern fear was that a Muslim representing illegal immigrants was on the verge
of taking power in the Ivory Coast. Therefore, to fend off his challenge, former
Prime Minister Ouattara's citizenship certificate was delayed until 2002. This further reinforced the northern belief that any settlement should include the right to a
NIC and the accompanying right to vote. Anti-immigrant violence and war cost the
Ivory Coast dearly: approximately 400,000 foreigners left, including 200,000
Burkinabes, 70,000 Guineans, 48,000 Malians, and 44,000 Liberians (Nyce 2003).

The UN secretary general, Kofi Annan, intervened in an effort to restart the
peace process between the Ivory Coast's president and rebel leaders, who hold polar
opposite views on individuals with documentary citizenship. How does one document almost 3.5 million immigrants from neighboring countries, give them electoral rights and a say in the political affairs of the state, and yet avoid a large-scale
civil war? Clearly, not only has territorial sovereignty been undermined by documentary citizenship, but national sovereignty is also at stake: the political arena
where the nation is constituted and where nation-forming decisions are taken. In
mid-July 2006, the government dispatched mobile courts, including a judge, a

prosecutor, and a court reporter, to hold hearings which would determine people's eligibility for a birth certificate and nationality (Hartill 2006). Individuals can obtain NICs and the right to vote only after this screening process. However, a third of the population of the Ivory Coast are immigrants, many of whom have no proof of citizenship. Making citizenship claims thus involves proving their historical ties to the area, their location, their ethnic identity, etc. The Ivory Coast is experiencing the consequences of large-scale illegal immigration, which sections within the host state are now unwilling to absorb—and documentary citizenship is at the center of this civil war.

I have found other cases in the developing world where individual identity intertwines with documentation so that noncitizens can access citizenship. In Thailand, there are eighteen different national ID cards. Combined, they try to account for various hill tribes, ethnic groups, and people of varying immigrant status and religion. Half of the tribal people are Thai citizens of some sort, possessing some form of documentation, while the other half possess the telltale attributes of blurred membership.[4] Meanwhile, with large numbers of illegal immigrants from Myanmar, Laos, and most recently Pakistan, Bangkok—the Thai capital—has developed a reputation as the fake passport capital of the world (Nicol 2000). Today, the business in fake documents is as lucrative as the drug trade. Many individuals in Bangkok specialize in providing fake documents to all kinds of foreigners. One such individual claims to have sent over 700 Tamils to Western Europe on the basis of such documents (ibid.). Until recently, a fake Canadian passport could be bought on Khao San Road in Bangkok for US$1,500.

In Iraq, the fall of the Saddam regime has attracted all kinds of illegal immigrants—construction workers, other help for hire, mercenaries, Islamic terrorists—many of whom may not leave Iraq, but acquire documentary citizenship and become Iraqi. The business in fake identity cards is thriving during the civil war between the Shias and Sunnis. It is virtually impossible to distinguish between a Sunni and a Shia: their ethnic features, language, and religion are the same (Gamel 2006). In times of interethnic bloodshed, names and identities can only be confirmed through ICs, and so, "[t]hey are issuing Sunni IDs in the Shia areas and vice versa," says Interior Ministry major general Mahdi al-Gharawi (ibid.). Sunnis venturing into Shia areas are met with checkpoints, and the reverse is also true. Belonging to the wrong sect in the wrong neighborhood can cost one's life. Prices for fake identity cards range from 5,000 Iraqi dinars (US$3.50) for a Saddam era lookalike to 50,000 Iraqi dinars (US$35) for a more recent type (ibid.). As documents become a life-and-death issue, documentary citizenship is growing in Iraq. Many illegal immigrants from nearby states, such as Iran and Jordan, and more distant countries, such as Pakistan, India, and Bangladesh, are likely to be absorbed into Iraq with documentary citizenship. Or, they will migrate to neighboring states, such as Turkey or Iran, on their way to Europe or some other Western destination. After all, acquiring a new identity is as simple as acquiring new documents.

Raising the Stakes

Common documentary citizenship raises further questions about our engagement with immigrant incorporation. One of the big lessons that emerged with the explosion of citizenship studies (for example, García Bedolla 2006; Bosniak 2006; Chavez 1997, 2001; Koslowski 2000a; Motomura 2006; Smith 1997; Sassen 2006) is that citizenship is never a clear-cut, well-defined category. How to map the complexities of membership in a state presents a great challenge. The introduction of concepts like blurred membership and documentary citizenship, as distinguished from full official citizenship, begins this process, perhaps more adequately for the conditions in developing countries. We can finally begin to understand the varieties of ways in which citizenship is practiced in the world. The recognition that documentary citizenship is a common phenomenon constitutes one direction for future inquiry.

What other pathways to citizenship have we ignored by neglecting the study of membership in developing states? Neglecting the experiences of developing countries has clearly impoverished the theoretical understanding of citizenship. At the very least, it has restricted innovation in the ways in which states confront illegal immigration. Importantly, it has skewed our understanding of democratic politics, narrowing the range of participants in democratic states and the variety of ways in which democracy is practiced. The impact on democratic politics through suffraged illegal immigrants is, after all, direct.

Is it also possible that documentary citizenship is present in some form in the developed states? For example, are Mexican illegal immigrants in the United States, Moroccan illegal immigrants in Spain, Tamil illegal immigrants in Canada, and Pakistani illegal immigrants in Australia using documentary citizenship to settle down? More research is needed on the relationship between the ethnic preferences of Western states and documentary citizenship. Given the differing capacities of developed states, particularly their technologies of surveillance and bureaucratic control, documentary citizenship would undoubtedly work a bit differently in the developed world. If documentary citizenship does exist there, what does it say about the developed states' notion of a secure citizenship and, within that, a secure realm for democratic politics? As states move toward technologically advanced forms of identity regulation, such as biometric measures, will they be able to exert control over citizenship in a way that would decisively separate legal from documentary citizens? Or might these new technologies simply reiterate old problems in new, more complex forms? At stake here is the very question of whether membership can ever be unblurred, and whether legitimate citizens can ever be sharply distinguished from documentary imposters. This is surely a fundamental dilemma of our time.

Many liberal states do not want to be anti-immigrant. And the reality is that it is easy for unwanted immigrants to gain entry into states, as this book has shown conclusively. Sealing the borders is difficult if not impossible: multilateral action is needed, and even then one cannot stop the movement of global human capital. On the other hand, expanded, centralized government powers to register and monitor obviously raise Orwellian fears on a national, continental, and even global scale—yet that is where documentary citizenship may lead us. There is a quest to create more global forms of rule-of-law governance that do not sacrifice meaningful democracy and civil liberties in the process. With documentary citizenship, the balance between a meaningful democracy that protects civil liberties and a secure citizenship and borders is difficult to maintain. One slip, and we could end up in an Orwellian nightmare in which a "national ID card would be a ticket to the loss of much of your personal freedom" (Safire 2001: A15). Internal passports in the form of NICs or passports for international travel both involve monitoring individuals' movements, a slippery slope that could encourage a variety of discriminatory practices.

Alternately, we can welcome and absorb the new diversity of documentary citizens. A culture or history of living with diversity suggests an easy embrace of documentary citizenship as yet another addition to a multicultural polity. If India, Malaysia, and Pakistan teach us anything, it is the elusive character of secure citizenship. Accepting the inevitability of documentary citizenship implies going beyond legally determined categories of state and citizenship. This perhaps is one way of overcoming our dilemma: how do we confront the challenge of unwanted entry into states without increasing and strengthening everyday forms of identity surveillance?

Notes

1. A sari is a traditional garment worn by many women in South Asia.

2. Nepalis were another group of noncitizens in Delhi; they were employed in low-end jobs and were settled everywhere in Delhi. While Nepalis did not need visas to enter India, they were definitely not considered to be Indian citizens. Yet, approximately 3–5 million Nepalis have silently settled down, many with Indian documents.

3. At a weekly rural market on a plantation in Tawau, East Malaysia, I was shocked to see tall Afghans and Pakistani Pathans who were there illegally. They sold fabric and loaned money, going from village to village, benefiting from the poor natives, who accumulated large debts. Many of them possessed Malaysian identity cards, and sold textiles, loaned money, and even married the daughters of indebted indigenous people—a practice, no doubt, common to many communities in the Afghanistan-Pakistan cultural region.

4. Also see Bendix 1996; and Beiner 1995.

5. In contrast, Hiroshi Motomura has demonstrated that immigrants have historically been viewed as "future citizens" with an inevitable path to naturalization. This is an inclusionary account of immigration in contrast to the post–Second World War obsession with drawing boundaries to emphasize political membership in the nation-state. See Motomura 2006. Here, by "foreigner," I mean a person entering a state from outside, not someone born to foreign parents.

6. The conceptual wall does not promote physical separation; it prevents a thorough understanding of illegal immigrants' entry to citizenship.

7. In her excellent work, Bosniak interrogates citizenship through the lens of "alienage," thus providing a more nuanced understanding of membership.

8. In one immigration volume, a Polish scholar and policymaker asserts that "modern borders serve political purposes of establishing and confirming 'membership'" (Jesien 2000: 191).

9. This section owes much to the excellent work on citizenship by Rajeev Dhavan and his collaborators at the Public Interest and Legal Support and Research Centre. See Dhavan 2004; and Karnad et al. 2006.

10. Universal Law Publishing 2004: 1. The principal legislation is the Citizenship Act of 1955, which was amended in 1986, 1992, 2003, and 2005.

11. Section 3(1)(b) of the Citizenship Act of 1955 (Universal Law Publishing 2004: 4).

12. Universal Law Publishing 2004: 4–5.

13. Restricted public offices include those of the president, vice president, judge of the Supreme Court or High Court, member of Parliament (both Lok Sabha and Rajya Sabha), and member of the state legislative assembly or council.

14. See section 9 of the Citizenship Act of 1955. Indian citizenship may be lost through renouncement (section 8) or termination (section 9) (Dhavan 2004: 35).

15. Legal Research Board 1998: 21–33.

16. Unless the individual is on official Malaysian service or duty.

17. I have benefited enormously from Seyla Benhabib's reading of Arendt in *The Rights of Others*, especially chapter 2.

18. An overwhelming emphasis on rights and entitlements in citizenship is known as the "postwar orthodoxy" (Kymlicka and Norman 1994: 354).

19. I say this because most studies on immigration rely on state-supplied data—from either government agencies or international organizations. This tends to completely miss flows that bypass the state, where the state institutions, immigrant community representatives, individual researchers, NGOs, political leaders, and journalists are all making guesstimates, some of which may be wildly imaginative. See Sadiq 2005b.

20. For the various terms used to describe illegal immigrants, see Ghosh 1998: 1.

CHAPTER 1

1. Even critical work in the constructivist international relations mode adopts this South-North dichotomy to explain immigration's role in international relations. See Doty 1996.

2. Douglas Massey, while acknowledging the crucial role of the state in international migration, proceeds to outline the principal features of international migration: immigration from developing countries to developed countries.

3. United Nations and International Organization for Migration 2000: 6.

4. Theories of immigration also assume that the poorest do not move due to the high transaction costs involved in migration. Yet the fact is that the poor are moving—and in large numbers. Clearly, the dominant economic-incentives explanations are not sufficient to explain the process of illegal immigration between two developing countries. But this is a matter for another book.

5. The report says, "Migration often occurs within the same continent." Refugee flows are even more localized, largely taking place between neighboring countries.

6. "Poverty" refers to those living on less than US$1 a day (PPP 1993). PPP stands for purchasing power parity.

7. A close examination of many statistics put out by international organizations, regional organizations, nongovernmental organizations, firms, etc., will confirm that many are replicating statistics supplied by individual states.

8. For example, see the reconfiguration of ethnic categories in the Malaysian census to accommodate the rising illegal immigrant population (Regis 1989).

9. Private e-mail, March 3, 2003. See Smith 1997.

10. See Peil 1983: 73–77.

11. Namboodri et al. 1998.

12. *Times of India* 2003b; Jha 2003. Deputy Prime Minister L. K. Advani was inaugurating a conference of chief secretaries and director generals of police on January 7, 2003, in Delhi when he gave this estimate, linking it to national security concerns.

13. B. Raman is a retired additional secretary, Cabinet Secretariat, Government of India.

14. Law Commission of India 2000: 2, 6. The Law Commission of India is one of the highest legal bodies in the country, and it was asked to report on the matter of illegal immigration to India and to recommend changes to the Foreigners Act and the Citizenship Act.

15. Copy in possession of the author.

16. Outlook 2005. Interview with the chief minister of Maharashtra, Vilasrao Deshmukh.

17. Myron Weiner quoted in Hazarika 2000: 226.

18. Bose 2005: 371. Ashish Bose is a leading authority on the population in India. Most census commissioners of India have, at one time or another, consulted him. My sincere thanks to him for sharing his time and research with me.

19. Results of the 2001 census are available at http://www.censusindia.gov.in/

20. Unni 1999. See Census 2001 Assam district profiles at: www.censusindia.gov.in/ Tables_Published/Basic_Data_Sheet.aspx

21. The map showing the distribution of population clearly illustrates the heavy settlement in the Brahmaputra valley.

22. In contrast, the Hindus are more urban: 65.08 percent of the rural population are Hindu and 83.58 percent of the urban population are Hindu.

23. Only Barpeta and Nalbari have exchanged rankings.

24. The districts of Nagaon, Dhubri, Karimganj, and Barpeta, among others.

25. The entire data set is now available on CDs.

26. See various parts of the Migration Tables in D-1 to D-17.

27. As a consequence of this agreement, the head of the MNLF, Nur Misuari, became the governor of the autonomous region of Muslim Mindanao in the Philippines.

28. Even the United States, with its large resources, is unable to control illegal immigration. For a critical look at the effectiveness of immigration control measures on the U.S.–Mexican border, see Andreas 2000.

29. Based on the author's conversations with Filipino immigrants.

30. She arrived twelve years prior to the interview in 1999. Because of the sensitive nature of this research, I have changed the names of some of my interviewees.

31. The word *Bahasa* is Indian in origin and means "language" in Sanskrit.

32. *Daily Express* 2000b. Wilfred Tangau, a legislator, asked in the Parliament whether the government considers these illegal immigrant settlements to be a security threat.

33. Department of Statistics, Malaysia 1983. According to the *Population and Housing Census of Malaysia 1980*: 13–14, "The figures for the years prior to the formation of Malaysia in 1963 are aggregates of the census figures for Peninsular Malaysia, Sabah, and Sarawak. For

years where no census figures were available, the estimates were derived by using the intercensal growth rates of the region."

34. Department of Statistics, Malaysia 2000: 20.

35. Interview, June 13, 1999.

36. This is a report done by Bilson Kurus, Ramlan Goddos, and Richard T. Koh for the state think tank, the Institute for Development Studies, which was published in the *Borneo Review* (Kurus et al. 1998).

37. Department of Statistics, Malaysia 1983: 58–59.

38. Department of Statistics, Malaysia 1983. See table 5.2: 58.

39. Department of Statistics, Malaysia 1995: 144. See table 4.1.

40. PBS is the main Kadazandusun and Murut party. A confidential and comprehensive, almost census-like, study was done on these illegal immigrants when the PBS was in power from 1985 to 1994: the Transient Population Study, undertaken by the Chief Minister's Department, Kota Kinabalu (Government of Sabah 1988). The study covers statistics regarding immigration until the period 1988–1989. The author has a copy in his possession.

41. Interviews with leaders of the PBS during my stay in Sabah in 1999.

42. This comes from the first of a four-part report on Filipino illegal migration to Sabah by correspondent Jerry Esplanade. See *Philippine Daily Inquirer* 1999.

43. Interview with Maximus Ongkilli, vice president, PBS, July 9, 1999.

44. The name of this illegal immigrant has been changed.

45. United Nations High Commissioner for Refugees and Government of Pakistan 2005: 6.

46. Afghan Research and Evaluation Unit 2005: 2.

47. United Nations High Commissioner for Refugees and Government of Pakistan 2005: 1.

48. United Nations High Commissioner for Refugees and Government of Pakistan 2005: 4. The census/registration effort occurred in spite of all the difficulties associated with covering such an illegal population, such as (a) their hostility, as they did not want to be identified for deportation by the state; (b) a general lack of law and order in northern areas in Pakistan (such as Gilgit, Sakardu), which resulted in their noncoverage; and (c) the lack of self-confession of their true identity as Afghans, given that many had already illegally acquired Pakistani identity cards and passports.

49. United Nations High Commissioner for Refugees and Government of Pakistan 2005: 5.

50. I read Sassen's "thick social environment" to mean the web of kinship and community networks, an internal structure of rewards and punishments which fosters community trust, loyalty, and identity.

51. *Katchi abaadis* refer to makeshift shelters made by scavenging cardboard, plastic sheets, tin, other locally pilfered building materials, and mud. The characterization of these settlements as temporary depends on local police deportation or demolition campaigns, which may or may not occur. Hence, temporary settlements become permanent features of the landscape.

52. Afghan Research and Evaluation Unit 2005: 2.

53. Afghan Research and Evaluation Unit 2005: 4.

54. United Nations High Commissioner for Refugees and Government of Pakistan 2005: 20.

CHAPTER 2

1. Reports of complicity by official registration authorities are common. For example, Bangladeshi illegal immigrants purchase "fake national identity cards with the connivance of registration offices in Karachi" (see Siddiqui 1998). More recently, data entry operators working for NADRA have been caught preparing computerized national identity cards based on duplicate finger prints (see *Dawn* 2007).

2. If networks of complicity become a regular feature of how "legalization" is accomplished, then an entire community may be permeated with a culture of complicity. People will begin to think that this is how things are done in this group. Hence, a report on the Afghan judicial system notes that "[i]t can take one bribe to obtain a blank legal form and another to have a clerk stamp it" to ensure a range of legal claims—to land, a house, and so on. As Afghans are familiar and acculturated to networks of complicity in their own state, when they arrive in Pakistan and notice the same possibilities, they easily utilize their networks in the Pakistani state to acquire local documentation. See Watson 2006.

3. Interview in Hazarika 2000: 57.

4. In a landmark judgment on the role of illegal immigrants in elections (*Harris Mohd Salleh v. Ismail bin Majin* 1999), a senior judge of the Borneo High Court in Malaysia observed that he was pressured to throw out petitions dealing with the exercise of suffrage by illegal immigrants. See *Daily Express* 2001.

5. In our cases, Douglas Massey's "daughter communities" already existed at the creation of the modern state and the "geometric" expansion of immigrant networks has already occurred (Massey 1987: 737).

6. Many authors have referred to the historical migration flows in Assam and the neighboring areas. See Weiner 1978. Also see chapters 2 and 3 in Singh 1990.

7. Traditional seafaring groups, such as the Bajaus and Obians, are now joined by newer trading and traveling communities—the modern-day street hawkers—i.e., illegal immigrants from Indonesia and the Philippines in Malaysia (Johari and Kiob 1997: 53–54).

8. Afghan Research and Evaluation Unit 2005: 3–4.

9. Nordstrom 2000: 35–54.

10. According to Bruce Mazlish, while patronage marked the seventeenth century and connections were characteristic of nineteenth-century English society, today "networks" characterize society—distributing power, position, and identities in a more equitable manner.

11. Mazlish 2000: 13.

12. *Malay Mail* 2005b, 2005c.

13. Nordstrom 2000: 38. Also see Strange 1996.

14. Lin and Paul 1995: 8. Takas and rupees are the currencies of Bangladesh and India, respectively.

15. Pohit and Taneja 2003: 1198.

16. Pohit and Taneja 2003: 1198–1199.

17. Towns in East Malaysia, such as Kudat, Sandakan, Tawau, Lahad Datu, and Kota Kinabalu, are the cornerstone of a regional trade arrangement among Indonesia, the Philippines, Malaysia, and Brunei called BIMP-EAGA. BIMP = Brunei, Indonesia, Malaysia, Philippines; EAGA = East Asian Growth Area.

18. International Organization for Migration 2004.

19. According to a survey in West Bengal, India, by A. C. Nielsen Org-Marg and Times of India (TOI), roughly 75 percent of the respondents felt that the electoral rolls in West Bengal have a large number of fake voters to manipulate election results. Approximately 55 percent believed that illegal immigrants from Bangladesh are on Indian electoral rolls and play a crucial role in elections, both at the state and local levels, in districts bordering the neighboring state, Bangladesh (*Economic Times* 2004).

20. NIC refers to the national identity card in Pakistan.

21. Papu Khan, the travel agent arrested in this case, was a candidate for a councilor's seat in the local government election in 2005.

22. Law Commission of India 2000: 8.

23. In this case, 1,085 Afghans too were facing prosecution.

24. Pakistan Press International 2005b.

25. Pakistan Press International 2004b.

26. Alarmingly, since Pakistan and India are historic rivals that have fought three wars, the report discloses that, in a period of five years (1990–1995), 408,464 Indians entered Pakistan legitimately, but only 175,059 registered with the Foreigners Registration Offices in Pakistan while the rest have disappeared. One wonders when these Indians will forsake their invisibility and emerge as Pakistani citizens.

27. Law Commission of India 2000: 35. Also see Governor of Assam 1998: 31–32. Both reports cite the figure of 1,454 deportations over a period of fifteen years in Assam.

28. Ghosh 2006; *Statesman* 2006; *Telegraph* 2006a. Also see *Telegraph* 2006b and 2003a.

29. The public "confession" of some individuals involved in the illegal distribution of Malaysian identity cards to illegal immigrants from the Philippines has been extensively covered; see, for example, Tibin 2007; *Star* 2007; *Daily Express* 2007.

30. The author has several photographs of Kampung Pulau Gaya and has bought groceries and fish sold by Filipino street vendors from Pulau Gaya at the fresh food market near the sea front. Most native locals view Pulau Gaya as a major settlement of Filipino illegal immigrants.

31. With rising incidents of corruption involving both federal and local American officials, there are fears that a "culture of corruption" is taking over the entire border between the United States and Mexico. Reports indicate a steady rise in the number of these individuals in the United States: seventeen in 2004, thirty-five in 2005, and fifty-two reported by October 2006. See Vartabedian, Serrano, and Marosi 2006: A1. While I make no claims on the presence of networks of complicity in developed states, it will be an interesting issue for others to explore in light of the stronger institutions of accountability. Are networks of complicity entirely absent or less effective as a result of stronger accountability mechanisms in developed states?

CHAPTER 3

1. Interview with J. K. Banthia, census commissioner and registrar general of India, New Delhi, September 24, 2004. At the time, Mr. Banthia head the entire census and civil registration system in India.

2. In developed states, there are various things for which one can be eligible. Since developed states have more economic benefits to offer and more institutions to regulate the

distribution, segmented access to a range of rights make sense. For example, one can be eligible for a work permit, but not eligible to vote. Or, immigrants, if they are legal residents, can be eligible for some things, e.g., medical care or education, but not the right to vote. These demarcations are possible in a well-institutionalized citizenship system. In developing countries, weak institutions of citizenship are combined with minimal welfare benefits for immigrants who are legal residents.

3. Theories of citizenship based on the provision of welfare services often rely on the strict patrolling of the boundary between citizen and immigrant that is common to developed countries. See Joppke 2005; and Hollifield 1992.

4. Blurred membership is widespread in developing countries, which is reflected in the interest by international agencies, such as UNICEF and Plan International, in developing civil registration systems in developing countries. As a result of these efforts, for example, nearly 50 percent of the population of 6 million Cambodians have received birth certificates. See http://www.writemedown.org/news/6mcambodians. For Plan International, see http://www.writemedown.org.

5. Such rites of passage are perhaps more fundamentally attributed to Gannep 1960.

6. Those who are officially identified by the state through a proof of citizenship constitute about half the population, the rest of the Indians assume citizenship via descent.

7. UNICEF 1998b: 5. Unity Dow's landmark essay is perhaps the best enunciation of the importance of birth registration.

8. See the chapter on "Invisible Children," (UNICEF 2005a: 35–57).

9. The Sulu belong to the Sulu archipelago in the southern Philippines and are also known as Tausug in the Philippines. In Sabah, Malaysia, they are known as Suluk.

10. Office of the Registrar General of India 1998b: 58.

11. Office of the Registrar General of India 1998b: 1.

12. Office of the Registrar General of India 1998b: 1.

13. UNICEF Innocenti Research Centre 2002: 8.

14. Literacy rates for those seven years of age and above.

15. Government of India 2002: 59.

16. Confirmed in conversations with an activist of the leading Delhi-based NGO, Bal Vikas Dhara. See its *Report on Ragpickers, Delhi*; personal copy in possession of the author.

17. It is only imperative if they seek benefits from the state, or if they are displaced from their local or rural networks and thrown into city life, which again, has a more palpable relationship between an individual and services.

18. *Hindustan Times* 1999d. A Home Ministry official also admits as much: "Given ethnic and language similarities, it is difficult to identify Bangladeshis" (Bhushan 2001).

19. Kaur 2004; Bernama 2005a; *Malay Mail* 2003. Suhakam is the Human Rights Commission of Malaysia.

20. The Filipino laborer Amillusin Umar was jailed for four months for acquiring a high-quality fake identity card. The *Borneo Post* and other local newspapers carry news about illegal immigrants every day. Much of the local news reporting is devoted to illegal immigrants.

21. Poor Tamil workers, such as Mr. Sahadevan, who was born in Malaysia, raised by poor Malaysian parents, and spent his entire life on rubber plantations like other Tamil plantation workers, have no identity cards and face harassment. See *Malay Mail* 2003.

22. Bernama 2004a, 2004b.

23. As I wrote this section, the controversy surrounding the entry to Yale University of a former key official from the Taliban regime became public. Sayed Rahmatullah Hashemi, a twenty-two-year-old "roving ambassador" for the Taliban regime, had misreported his age as twenty-four years. Identifying the age and birth date of average Afghans is even more difficult, given the unavailability of records in that country. See Brown 2006.

24. Pakistan has been ranked among the top ten failed states.

25. Based on figures shared by the Pakistani government with UNICEF.

26. Pakistan Country Paper 2006: 3.

27. This discussion has benefited enormously from the Pakistan Country Paper on the state of birth registration there, presented in March 2006.

28. Pakistan Country Paper 2006: 9.

29. Pakistan Country Paper 2006: 6.

30. Pakistan Country Paper 2006: 9.

31. Pakistan Country Paper 2006: 6.

32. Pakistan Country Paper 2006: 5, 14.

33. This was the International NGO Forum on Indonesian Development (INFID) (Children's Human Rights First and HRWG 2006: 3–4).

34. BPS Statistics n.d.: xiv:

> MICS is a rapid survey method developed by UNICEF in cooperation with other international organizations. MICS 2000 was conducted under the name of Mother and Child Education and Health Survey (SPKIA). Both the 1995 SKIA and 2000 SPKIA were conducted by BPS Statistics Indonesia, in cooperation with UNICEF and the Ministry of Health. The sample size of the 1995 SKIA was approximately 18,000 households. The sample aimed to produce national-level estimates which are disaggregated between urban and rural areas, and the provincial level estimates for seven provinces where UNICEF–GOI cooperation is implemented. The sample size of the 2000 SPKIA was 10,000 households, and the results were only representative at the national level. Results were disaggregated for urban and rural areas.

35. BPS Statistics n.d.: xxv; also annex 1 (Child Rights).

36. BPS Statistics n.d.: xxv, 90. According to the survey, 69.4 percent of children under five have no official birth certificates.

37. United Nations Department of Economic and Social Affairs 1998: 27.

38. A UNICEF report indicates that the births of 44.9 percent of children below five years of age were unregistered in Indonesia (UNICEF 2005b: 28–31).

39. BSAF is a network of NGOs in Bangladesh working to protect the rights of children.

40. The lack of a civil registration system is one of the challenges to be met by any program fighting the extensive trafficking of women from Afghanistan.

41. United Nations Department of Economic and Social Affairs 1998: 35.

42. United Nations Department of Economic and Social Affairs 1998: 35.

43. United Nations Department of Economic and Social Affairs 1998. Confirmed in conversations with Mr. M. Vijayan Unni, deputy registrar general of India, Government of India, during my field trip to India in the summer and fall of 2004. In my conversation with

Mr. Unni, I became increasingly aware of how traditional beliefs and customs can provide obstacles to the standardization of a civil registration system, even one as flexible as India's.

44. Conversations with Mr. Unni. I also know this from personal experience, since my mother was known by a singular name and so are many of her relatives.

45. United Nations Department of Economic and Social Affairs 1998: 35.

46. United Nations Development Group 2000. See section 6.4.2.

47. In the case of Pakistan, the figure could be higher, since these are approximate figures (UNICEF 2005c).

48. Mahmood 2007; Scott, Tehranian, and Mathias 2002: 10.

49. UNICEF 1998b.

50. Tenaganita 2006: 40–41.

51. Children's Human Rights First and HRWG 2006: 2–3.

52. After the terrorist bombings in Bali, it was reported that Indonesia did not have a computerized database for immigrants. See *New York Times* 2002.

53. India, Pakistan, and Indonesia have all launched national ID schemes as part of a global emphasis on centralized civil registration systems.

54. The debate surrounding the surveillance of the phone records of millions of Americans for national security purposes is yet another example of the state's desire to monitor individuals within its borders. The impulse to identify and monitor individuals begins with birth registration and then moves to higher forms of identification and surveillance.

CHAPTER 4

1. "Write Me Down, Make Me Real" is the campaign slogan for the global birth registration initiative launched by Archbishop Desmond Tutu on behalf of Plan, a leading international NGO.

2. Special thanks to Prashant Bhushan. See *Abu Hanif alias Millan Master v. Police Commissioner of Delhi & Others*, which terminates the order accusing Abu Hanif to be a foreign national. Also see *Abu Hanif alias Millan Master v. Union of India and Others*, which seeks to set up a tribunal for illegal immigrants and the extension of the IMDT Act 1983, to Delhi.

3. John Torpey's book while excellent, is not focused on the role of fraudulent documentation—of various kinds—in facilitating the citizenship of illegal immigrants in developing countries. See Torpey 2000.

4. Arjun Appadurai notes that the Mughal Empire in India enumerated land holdings, etc. See Appadurai 1993.

5. Rudolph and Rudolph 1985; and Winichakul 1996b: 215.

6. Winichakul 1996b. Also see Wink 1986.

7. Even today in China and Russia, one cannot move around the country freely even if one is a citizen because of residence controls. Internal controls are characteristic of most communist and authoritarian regimes.

8. Noiriel 1996 and Torpey 2000 have followed Max Weber, who introduced the "iron cage" of bureaucratization to the modern social sciences. See Weber 1978.

9. Guha 2003 is a brilliant essay on the historical construction of identity through enumeration efforts in India.

10. I would argue that the identification of individuals to protect their human rights became the concern of the postcolonial state only much later.

11. The author quotes from Prakash 1992: 155–160; and Arnold 1985: 77.

12. Also see Mann 2006 on the development of "infrastructural power."

13. In principle, a birth certificate is bestowed by the state to a child as the first identifying document. In practice, however, this identifying document is often collected at a later point in life—as a youth or an adult.

14. Others may see these marginalized groups as having no citizenship or possessing a second-class status.

15. Some illegal immigrants enter bearing fake documents.

16. My argument here has affinities with Hannah Arendt's discussion of stateless people and their nonrecognition. See Arendt 1968: 269–290.

17. While my claims are made with regard to developing countries, the model could very well apply to many cases in the developed world.

18. In recent years, the following states have offered amnesties to illegal immigrants and conducted regularization exercises to accommodate large illegal immigrant populations: Argentina in 2004; Belgium in 2000; Costa Rica in 2000; France in 1981–1982 and 1997–1998; Greece in 1997–1998 and 2001; Italy in 1987–1988, 1990, 1996, 1998, 2002; Malaysia in 1989, 1991, 1996–1997; Portugal in 1992–1993, 1996, 2001; South Africa in 1996, 2000; Spain in 1985–1986, 1991, 1996, 2000, 2001; Thailand in 1999–2000; and the United States in 1986, 1997–1998, 2000. See United Nations 2004: table III.3, 85.

19. This quadrant (b-ii) could also include minor cases of illegal immigration *between* documented communist and authoritarian regimes, such as North Korea, China, Vietnam, Myanmar, Libya, or Cuba. These states have well-controlled borders and well-documented populations in which state complicity is strongly favorable to co-ethnics and communists. Illegal immigration may occur, but it is not too difficult for the state to identify and legalize fellow communists. Such immigration is de facto legal.

20. In Western countries, such as the United States, cards from national-level retail chains, insurance agencies, and health clubs are often used for identification purposes.

21. Government of India 2004a: 16.

22. Office of the Registrar General and Census Commissioner, India 2007 (www .censusindia.gov.in/Census_Data_2001/Census_data_finder/B_Series/Educational_ Level.htm).

23. Office of the Registrar General and Census Commissioner, India 2007 (www .censusindia.gov.in/Census_Data_2001/Census_data_finder/B_Series/Educational_ Level.htm).

24. Government of India 2005: 40–41.

25. Government of India 2005: 41.

26. Government of India 2005. Importantly, verification in the state most affected by documentary citizenship, Assam, has not been carried out.

27. Citizens Campaign for Preserving Democracy 2005.

28. Following are some of the court cases: *A. I. Lawyers Forum for Civil Liberties & Anr. v. Union of India & Others*, Writ Petition (Civil) No. 125/1998, Supreme Court of India; *S. Sonaval v. Union of India*, Writ Petition (Civil) No. 131/2000, Supreme Court of India; *Jamaith Ulema-e-Hind & Anr. v. Union of India & O[the]rs*, Writ Petition (Civil) No.

7/2001, Supreme Court of India; *Abu Hanif alias Millan Master v. Police Commissioner of Delhi & Others*, Special Leave Petition (Criminal) No. 3778/2000, Supreme Court of India; *Abu Hanif alias Millan Master v. Union of India and Others*, Civil Original Jurisdiction, Writ Petition (Civil) No. 418/2001, Supreme Court of India; *Shekh Molla v. S. H. O. Inderprastha Estate & Others*, Criminal Writ No. 382/1993, Delhi High Court; and *Chetan Dutt v. Union of India and Others*, Civil Writ No. 3170/2001, Delhi High Court. Citizens Campaign for Preserving Democracy 2005.

29. See Namboodri et al. 1998. This is a report on illegal immigrants. It is, therefore, no surprise that when a regional passport officer, A. K. Bhattacharya, screened 16,000 dubious passport applications, he found most of them to be bogus. On sending out confirmatory letters to the addresses of the passport applicants, he got an overwhelming number returned with the stamp "addressee not found." The identification of individuals requires a stable address, which is usually not available to domestic migrants, landless, homeless, and other poor native populations. Additionally, this works in favor of illegal immigrants and other refugees hoping to demonstrate a domestic location.

30. The last few years have seen increasing efforts to secure the passport system through computerization and other upgrades.

31. *Times of India* 2003a.

32. *New Straits Times* 2004. Statement by Deputy Home Affairs Minister Datuk Tan Chai Ho in response to another member of Parliament's query.

33. It is hard to trace a source in this documentary circuit, given that both the providers and users, state or private, are involved in a fraudulent activity. At what point documentary citizenship allows a noncitizen entry into the legal documentary circuit is difficult if not impossible to prove. The few cases that are caught by the state are often the tip of the iceberg.

34. Government of Sabah 1988. This confidential survey was led by Jeffrey G. Kitingan, who later emerged as a leading political figure in Sabah. Copy in possession of the author. Also, see Seng 1989 where some of the findings were published.

35. Government of Sabah 1988: 19–20.

36. Government of Sabah 1988: 24–25.

37. Government of Sabah 1988: 25.

38. Government of Sabah 1988: 25–26.

39. Government of Sabah 1988: 29, 31.

40. Government of Sabah 1988: 29, 31.

41. Government of Sabah 1988: 32, 37.

42. Government of Sabah 1988: 46–48.

43. The presence of Pakistani immigrants was also noted.

44. Government of Sabah 1988: 53–59.

45. In the late 1990s, another study noted the pervasive use of documentary citizenship and included the records of hundreds of illegal immigrants who had acquired Malaysian identity cards, sometimes multiple identity cards under different names, who became active members of local and national political parties based on these citizenship-indicating documents. See an excellent piece of investigative journalism in Mutalib 1999. "IC Palsu" in the title of the work means "fake identity card."

46. Mutalib 1999: 188–189.

47. Mutalib 1999: 191–192.

48. Jeffrey Kitingan is a leading politician of Sabah, Malaysia.

49. The earlier Malaysia identity card system was based on four different colors: blue IC for citizens; red IC for permanent residents; green IC for limited-stay residents; brown IC for lawbreakers. The blue IC indicating Malaysian citizenship was the most sought after.

50. *New Straits Times* 2003.

51. *New Straits Times* 2005.

52. *Malay Mail* 2006.

53. Bernama 2006a.

54. Bernama 2006b.

55. *New Straits Times* 2002a; Daily Express 2002a, 2002b; Bernama 2005b, 2005c.

56. Bernama 2005d. Also, see Bernama 2005b, 2005c.

57. Bernama 2006c.

58. See a copy of the legal case filed by Joshua Kong Yun Chee with the International Criminal Court of Justice, The Hague, Netherlands, August 2005, at http://www.freewebs .com/justknock/migsiccsabah.htm.

59. Pakistan Country Paper 2006.

60. Dawn Wire Service 2001.

61. Dawn Wire Service 2001.

62. The issue rose as a result of the increasing cases of cell phone snatching; further sale or use of such cell phones requires a fake identity card—a common practice.

63. *Business Recorder* 2005c, 2005b; *News* 2002b.

64. Afghan Research and Evaluation Unit 2005: 2.

65. Afghan Research and Evaluation Unit 2005: 12.

66. Afghan Research and Evaluation Unit 2005: 18.

67. The secretary of the Ministry for States and Frontier Regions, Sajid Hussain Chattha, said, "The Afghan refugees having illegal ID cards and passports are not Pakistani nationals and would be treated under the laws." He later added, "Most of these people [have] bogus documents, and are involved in illegal activities." See Associated Press of Pakistan News Agency 2005.

68. This was a special report done for the magazine that published it.

69. The production of fake identity cards is common during elections; such manipulation could not take place without the cooperation of the officials in the state agency responsible for issuing the NIC, i.e., NADRA.

70. Also see Government of India, Parliamentary Debates, Rajya Sabha, Written Answer to Unstarred Question Number 163 on "Multipurpose Identity Cards" by Minister of State in the Ministry of Home Affairs, I. D. Swami, November 20, 2002, 63.

71. Critics could argue that I am assuming a territorial sovereignty for developing countries that they never possessed. However, this assumption is standard in the studies of immigration to Western Europe, Australia, and North America. To the extent that states in developing countries aspire to a Westphalian model, they all have (certainly India, Pakistan, and Malaysia have): (i) huge resources allocated to guarding the border, including separate paramilitary forces; (ii) important and well-funded state departments handling questions of immigration and citizenship, e.g., the Ministry of Home or Interior; and (iii) national campaigns devoted to creating a nation via a national map, a national image, a sacrosanct border. In this sense, developing countries have territorial and national sovereignty in the same

forms as developed states do, although their ability to mobilize resources to the task may vary. But when it comes down to it, we can see from the examples of a variety of poor communist states during the cold war that they too can and will mobilize resources to guard their sovereignty closely.

72. According to recent scholarship, while passports are an indicator of states' desire to control movement (Torpey 2000; Salter 2003), national IDs are an attempt by the state to monopolize the "legitimate means of identification" (Lyon 2004).

CHAPTER 5

1. *Assam Tribune* 2004b. According to the reporter, Ali the rickshaw puller was speaking in the local dialect but with a heavy Bangladeshi accent. Like other rickshaw pullers, handcart pullers, and vegetable vendors who are Bangladeshi immigrants, Ali was rushing to vote in the Indian elections as a way of proving his "citizenship."

2. That day, I traveled with a friend to a few voting booths to observe the conduct of elections from the outside. For months afterward, local newspapers were filled with stories of illegal immigrants voting. Illegal immigrants were the central political issue at that time in Sabah, Malaysia.

3. For the exclusion of long-time residents in European democracies, see Koslowski 2000a.

4. *Noncitizen* includes the following categories: legal immigrant, illegal immigrant, refugee, and tourist.

5. Can one draw a parallel between what is happening today in India, Malaysia, and Pakistan and what happened in the United States during the nineteenth century? Some illegal European immigrants to America in this period stepped off the boats and were immediately permitted to vote by ethnic political machines. This occurred even as indigenous populations (i.e., Native Americans) were denied basic citizenship rights. The parallel is illuminating; however, the distinction between citizen and immigrant—and the regulatory structures for dealing with these two categories—only became deeply institutionalized after World War II. This book covers the post–Second World War period, when many of these states gained independence and exclusive sovereignty became the norm of modern statehood.

6. Specifically, the influx of immigrants into Western Europe prompted the states of that region to extend policies in the social and economic spheres to immigrants over time (Koslowski 2000a: 72–94). The extension of citizen-like rights, such as a local franchise for immigrants, in some developed states became an index of the collapse of the distinction between citizen and immigrant. The Netherlands and some Nordic countries have granted immigrants the right to vote in local elections (Rath 1990: 127). Since states have long associated voting with de jure citizenship, the extension of this right, along with many other rights and privileges traditionally enjoyed only by citizens, is seen as a reformulation of the traditional conception of the state under pressures of globalization and international human rights norms (see Jacobson 1997; Sassen 1998).

7. Naturalized citizens can go on to become elected officials, but naturalization entails meeting stringent eligibility requirements.

8. Contributions by Sassen 1999, 2006; Castles and Davidson 2000; and Koslowski 2000b, 2002, have challenged traditional notions about immigration and its impact on world politics, but these too have not addressed the phenomenon of illegal immigrant voting.

9. See the work by Lisa García Bedolla (2006) on legal immigrants' voting in the United States. Also see Bauböck 2003; and Rath 1990: 127–157.

10. Rocco 1997. A classic statement on this is Marshall and Bottomore 1996.

11. Thanks to Rodney Bruce Hall for pushing me in this direction; see his *National Collective Identity: Social Constructs and International Systems* (1999). Also see Smith 2003.

12. Ngai 2005: 9–11. Brubaker 1992 shows the differing processes of boundary making in France and Germany. Also see Smith 1997.

13. Based on the author's informal observations, which have been reaffirmed by regular coverage of the issue in the national and regional media in India, Pakistan, and Malaysia (also confirmed in the author's conversation with an illegal immigrant in Malaysia). It is not easy to get an illegal immigrant to acknowledge that she/he is illegal and voting.

14. Kohli 2001.

15. Shourie 1983: 54–66. This piece of investigative journalism covers the massacre of Bangladeshi immigrants by native Assamese from Northeast India. Thousands died and over a half million were displaced during 1979–1985. See Singh 1984: 1066–1067.

16. See the introduction for more on the weak/strong Indian state.

17. Both native-born and naturalized citizens are eligible for *all* citizenship rights in India.

18. Election Commission of India 2007a.

19. Election Commission of India 2007b. The Election Commission has posted the relevant constitutional provisions, acts of Parliament, and other rules pertaining to India's electoral laws at http://www.eci.gov.in/faq/Contesting.asp; http://www.eci.gov.in/ElectoralLaws/Judgements/LandmarkJudgementsVOLI.pdf.; and http://www.eci.gov.in/ElectoralLaws/electoral_law.asp

20. Punishable by imprisonment for as much as one year, a fine, or both.

21. Election Commission of India 2000b. The EC decided to introduce electoral identity cards in all states (except Jammu and Kashmir) and union territories.

22. Election Commission of India 2000b.

23. *Assam Tribune* 2006.

24. Moreover, any discrepancies in identification markers such as name, age, address, sex and serial number "may be ignored" according to directives sent from the Election Commission (see Hindu 2001). The emphasis on crafting an "inclusive" electoral process was in tension with measures guarding the political community of Indians.

25. Scheduled Castes (SCs) and Scheduled Tribes (STs) are historically discriminated Hindu groups who have been legally identified for preferential policies by the constitution.

26. Election Commission of India 2001. While an alert and active EC acted fast to clean the electoral rolls in this case, over the years, many cases may have gone undetected.

27. Election Commission of India 2001; and the Supreme Court in *Lal Babu Hussain v. Electoral Registration Officers & Others* (AIR 1995 SC 1189).

28. Election Commission of India 2000a: 265.

29. Election Commission of India 2000a: 265–266. The EC cited the Gauhati High Court orders dated January 28, 1994, and February 1, 1994, in *H. R. A. Chaudhury v. Election Commission of India and Others* (Civil Rule Nos. 1566, 1616, 1836, and 2814 of 1993). This judgment was upheld by the Supreme Court in its order dated May 5, 1994, in Civil Appeals Nos.

4171–4180 of 1994 and its order in the *Lal Babu Hussain v. Electoral Registration Officers & Others* case.

30. Order dated February 6, 1995, in *Lal Babu Hussain v. Electoral Registration Officers & Others* (1995 [3] SSC 100). See Election Commission of India 2000a: 266.

31. Over the last sixteen years (1986–2003) under the IMDT, only 1,501 illegal migrants have been deported even though almost 129 million rupees have been spent on these tribunals (figure quoted by Pankaj Bora, the minister in charge of the Assam Accord implementation, in the state assembly on March 13, 2003). See Routray 2003.

32. *Jamayat Ulema-e-Hind v. Election Commission of India and Others* (W.P. No. 45/1998). See Election Commission of India 2000a: 267.

33. For a thorough analysis of the anti-immigrant movement in the context of regionalism, see Baruah 1999.

34. Shourie 1983: 54–66. Shourie covers the government's culpability in a massacre of Bangladeshi immigrants that could have been avoided. He ties the mass murder to the Congress Party's determination to hold elections in Assam without any changes in the electoral rolls, which were allegedly filled with names of Bangladeshi illegal immigrants. Shourie was later made a minister in the Hindu nationalist government of the BJP.

35. The impact on Assam of the British colonial period and the historical migration of different groups is well documented in Baruah 1999: 21–68.

36. Kimura examines the multiple narratives surrounding the Nellie massacre. See Kimura 2003: 225–239. Also see Hazarika 2000: 45–46.

37. For an inside look at the issues surrounding illegal immigrants' access to the franchise along with details of the Assam Accord, see the book by Prafulla Kumar Mahanta (1986: 139–143), who was then leader of the AASU and also a signatory to the Assam Accord and future chief minister of Assam.

38. The implementation of the Assam Accord poses several challenges (see Baruah 1999: 160–164). There is an international aspect too. Having detected illegal immigrants and deleted their names from electoral rolls, how are Indian authorities to deport these documentless immigrants to Bangladesh if there is no proof of their Bangladeshi identity? In fact, Bangladeshi authorities have used this as an excuse not to accept deportees from India. Deportation, or for that matter any comprehensive immigration solution, requires the cooperation of the Bangladeshi state, which is not forthcoming: Bangladesh does not officially accept that it has any illegal immigrants in India. Fencing the border (*Assam Tribune* 2000), another aspect of the Assam Accord, requires coordination between the Indian and Bangladeshi border authorities, which is again dependent on the state of bilateral relations between the two countries. In short, immigration regulation is tied to broader bilateral relations between India and Bangladesh.

39. In 1998, Foreign Minister Abdus Samad Azad asserted the official Bangladeshi position that there are no "Bangladeshi nationals" illegally residing in India (*Hindustan Times* 1998).

40. Also see Hussain 1993: 126–129.

41. With increasing illegal immigration to West Bengal, Delhi, and other parts of Northeast India, the citizenship of illegal immigrants is now a national issue. Additionally, see report on the increase in voters due to the presence of illegal immigrants on electoral rolls in West Bengal (*Hindustan Times* 1999b).

42. Other Hindu nationalist organizations, such as the Vishva Hindu Parishad (VHP), have reiterated this message; the VHP central assistant secretary (Seva), Arabinda Bhattacharjee, expressed alarm at the "Bangladeshi infiltrators" for having changed the demography of Northeast India such that "13 out of 25 districts" of Assam were "Muslim-dominated"; he distinguished between Muslim Bangladeshis as "illegal foreigners" and yet said the "Hindus are refugees" (see *Assam Tribune* 2003).

43. The Congress Party performance in the state assembly elections (see table 5.2) shows the complete dominance of the party in voter percentage until 1978 (23.62 percent of the votes), when the country was swept by an opposition wave, and later in 1985 (23.23 percent of the votes) with the anti-immigrant movement.

44. Percetakan Nasional Malaysia 1997: 101.

45. The alien was identified as Sabturia, and the news report gave her identity card number.

46. *Daily Express* 1998. See the statement by Joseph Sitin Saang, vice president of Parti Democratic Sabah (PDS).

47. *Daily Express* 1999b; *Borneo Post* 1999b: A4. The author was present in Sabah for a period when the court hearings on this matter were taking place. Dr. Chong went on to win part of his petition, and the Likas constituency election result was nullified by the order of the judge on June 8, 2001. The judicial decision by the High Court judge was delivered despite pressure on him from "sources" to dismiss the petition (*Daily Express* 2001).

48. *Borneo Post* 1999b; *Harris Mohd Salleh v. Ismail bin Majin* (1999). Hassnar was a former district chief in Sandakan.

49. The electoral role of illegal immigrants is corroborated by the author's conversations and interviews with both immigrants and local natives.

50. JPN 1/9 is a document issued to new applicants for identity cards; JPN 1/11 is issued to those who report a loss of identity card; and JPN 1/22 is given to those who change their blue identity card to the *bunga raya* card (*Daily Express* 1999e).

51. Copy in the author's possession. The evidence includes eighteen pairs of receipts; each pair of receipts has the same photograph of a person but two different names and two different corresponding national registration numbers, which also appear on the electoral rolls. Among these thirty-six JPN receipts, three names with the corresponding IC numbers appear twice but with different photographs, different addresses, and different dates of birth. The news reports covering this issue include *Borneo Post* 1999h: A5; 1999i: A5; 1999g: A4; 1999d: A1; and 1999f: A2.

52. The High Court accepted Dr. Chong's submission that the 1998 electoral rolls of the N13 Likas electoral seat were illegal since they contained names of illegal immigrants and persons who had been convicted for possession of fraudulent identity cards. See *Harris Mohd Salleh v. Ismail bin Majin*.

53. This decision was an exception and not the rule, and in his decision, Judge Awang draws attention to the political pressure imposed on him to throw out these petitions: "In my view it is an insult to one's intelligence to be given a directive over the phone that these petitions should be struck off without a hearing" (*Daily Express* 2001).

54. There have been many attempts to convert Kadazandusun and other natives to Islam. The process is called *masuk melayu* or "entering Malayness." The "born-again" Muslims are called *saudara baru*. I thank Herman Luping, a former deputy chief minister and former

attorney general of Sabah, for this information. See his book *Sabah's Dilemma* (1994: 530–535, 564–567).

55. Jeffrey Kitingan shared the same sentiments with me in an interview during my stay in Malaysia in 1999.

56. Pakistan Press International 2003.

57. Pakistan Press International 2003, 2004b.

58. Pakistan Press International 2003.

59. Pakistan Press International 2003. By 2003, only 26,000 aliens were registered, including natives of Bangladesh, Afghanistan, India, China, Iraq, Somalia, Iran, Myanmar, the Philippines, and Sri Lanka.

60. Pakistan Press International 2004a.

61. Pakistan Press International 2005a.

62. Pakistan Press International 2004a.

63. Pakistan Press International 2004a.

64. Also see Pakistan Press International 2005b.

65. Sonia Gandhi's naturalized status was widely covered in the national media. Her supporters put forth their defense in a locally circulated book. See Jai and Jai 2004.

66. Government of Sabah 1996: 12.

67. *New Sabah Times* 1999a: 6; 1999b: 1.

68. A report in the newspaper *Daily Express* quotes two researchers from Universiti Malaysia Sabah making the same argument. W. Shawaluddin Hasan and Ramli Dollah argue that the "possession of original Identity Cards via forged documents among the immigrants indirectly resulted in the group gaining control of the economic affairs, education, politics and job opportunities and, most importantly, the rights of the Bumiputeras." They further said, "In this respect, we don't have the right anymore to question them because they have already become a part of the state natives due to the original and valid documents in their hands." See *Daily Express* 2002c.

69. Pakistan Press International 2004b; Mansoor 2003.

70. Pakistan Press International 2004b; Mansoor 2003.

71. Pakistan Press International 2004b.

72. *Daily Times* 2004b; Mansoor 2003.

73. Additionally, there are thirty to forty local councilors in the interior of Sindh who may be illegal immigrants. See Mansoor 2002, 2003.

CHAPTER 6

1. The epigraph can be found in Bowring 1962: 557.

2. Excerpts are from the testimony before the federal district court of the Southern District of New York. See PBS *Frontline* 2005.

3. See, for example, 9/11 Commission Staff Monograph on 9/11 and Terrorist Travel at http://www.9–11commission.gov/staff_statements/index.htm; Susan Ginsburg, *Countering Terrorist Mobility* (Migration Policy Institute, 2006) at http://www.migrationpolicy.org/pubs/MPI_TaskForce_Ginsburg.pdf; and Rey Koslowski, *Real Challenges for Virtual Borders: The Implementation of US-VISIT* (Migration Policy Institute, 2005), at http://www.migrationpolicy.org/pubs/Koslowski_Report.pdf.

4. Critics will point out that, for many states, a racial or ethnic profile is not part of a person's official identity documentation, that some states may include ethnic identity information in travel documents, but others do not. Not true. If one looks carefully into the trail of documents that finally lead to a passport, one will find detailed information on parents, grandparents, place of birth, and type of marriage ceremony (religious or civil), which directly or indirectly gives the gatekeepers all of the ethnic/racial information they need to screen the individual. So it is true that travel documents may not contain ethnic or racial information, but the background documents that accompany such national documents often provide the necessary ethnic/racial information. Police, immigration authorities, and the border patrol are all trained to look into the trail of documents for such information.

5. In a similar vein, Jan C. Ting, former assistant commissioner (1990–1993), U.S. Immigration and Naturalization Service, has argued that "the sea of incoming illegal aliens provides a cover and a culture in which terrorists can hide, and a reliable means of entry." See Ting 2005.

6. Estimates of illegal immigrants in the United States, much like those of India, range from 10 to 20 million. In Pakistan and Malaysia, a range of figures in the millions is often cited. A report by the Pew Hispanic Center notes that illegal immigration forms the largest component of migration to the United States in spite of the tighter border security measures and huge resources deployed by the most powerful state in the world. See Passel and Suro 2005.

7. For example, several reports will attest to widespread complicity in Pakistan; see *Dawn* 2004b, 2005f; Qaiser 2003.

8. For a historical account of regionalism in Sabah and Sarawak see Roff 1974.

9. *Times of India* 2001; *Hindustan Times* 2001.

10. Local natives utilize documentary citizenship when they adopt fictitious identities to travel between states.

11. 9/11 Commission 2004: 177–178; Cantwell 2004.

12. The figure of 20 million Indian passport holders excludes those who may have died or acquired other citizenships.

13. Notice in table 6.1 that there are many more passports issued in some places than applications received. This discrepancy can be attributed to a particular city issuing a large number of passports to those whose applications were submitted in another city. Such discrepancies can also involve real documents being issued fraudulently to individuals under assumed identities. In states where such data are never collected or never centrally organized and made public, the scope for passport-type documentary citizenship is enormous.

14. Government of Canada 2002.

15. Government of Canada 2002.

16. Government of Canada 2002.

17. Asia-Pacific Economic Cooperation 2004.

18. Asia-Pacific Economic Cooperation 2004.

19. *News* 2002a. While quick countermeasures were taken in this instance, cases of lost and stolen passports remain commonplace in Pakistani missions abroad, particularly in the United Kingdom and the Middle East. See *Dawn* 2004b.

20. See other reports in *Dawn* 2005h.

21. In a similar incident, a Pakistani individual tried to claim asylum after destroying a passport on arrival in Canada. See *Dawn* 2005f.

22. United Press International 2006.

23. Confirmed in conversations with various Pakistani elites.

24. Jan Ting is a former assistant commissioner of the U.S. Immigration and Naturalization Service, 1990–1993.

25. The United States began contributing information to this database only in May 2004 and then was followed by several other states.

26. Personal e-mail, Ambassador Cresencio Arcos, director of international affairs, Department of Homeland Security, U.S. government. Mr. Arcos has been a member of the president's Foreign Intelligence Board, a senior deputy assistant secretary for international narcotics and law enforcement, and a deputy assistant for Latin American affairs; he has also served in the White House and as ambassador to Honduras.

27. Quote from Clint Eastwood in the movie *Million Dollar Baby* (2004).

CHAPTER 7

1. In developing states, the repeated exercise of citizenship rights leads to citizenship status. On the other hand, in developed states, while citizenship rights may be acquired through documentation, legal citizenship may still not be gained since citizenship status is very tightly regulated.

2. Aleinikoff and Klusmeyer 2001: 164–169.

3. United Nations and International Organization for Migration 2005: 396.

4. Thanks to Rogers Smith, who on returning from a visit to Thailand brought this to my attention. See Lertcharoenchok 2001.

Bibliography

Aashray, Adhikar Abhiyan. 2002. *Basere ki Kahani: A Study of the Problems in the Night Shelters in Delhi Using Participatory Research.* January. Delhi: Aashray Adhikar Abhiyan. www.homelesspeople.in/

———. 2001. *The Capital's Homeless.* Delhi: Aashray Adhikar Abhiyan. www.homelesspeople.in/

Abu Hanif alias Millan Master v. Police Commissioner of Delhi & Others. 2000. Special Leave Petition (Criminal) No. 3778, Supreme Court of India.

Abu Hanif alias Millan Master v. Union of India and Others. 2001. Civil Original Jurisdiction, Writ Petition (Civil) No. 418, Supreme Court of India.

Afghan Research and Evaluation Unit. 2005. *Afghans in Karachi: Migration, Settlement and Social Networks.* March. Kabul: Afghan Research and Evaluation Unit. www.areu.org.af/

Ahmad, Shafiq. 2006. Peshawar: Fake Degrees, Passports Seized. *Dawn.* May 20.

———. 2004. Action Taken against Recruitment Firms: Afghans Being Sent Abroad on Green Passports. *Dawn.* January 2.

Aleinikoff, T. Alexander, and Douglas Klusmeyer. 2001. Plural Nationality: Facing the Future in a Migratory World. In *Demography and National Security,* edited by Myron Weiner and Sharon Stanton Russell, pp. 154–176. New York: Berghahn.

Ali, Azam. 2004. Alien Nations. *Jang.* December 5.

Anderson, Benedict. 1991. *Imagined Communities: Reflections on the Origin and Spread of Nationalism.* London: Verso.

Andreas, P. 2003. Redrawing the Line: Borders and Security in the Twenty-First Century. *International Security* 28 (2):78–111.

———. 2000. *Border Games: Policing the U.S.–Mexico Divide.* Ithaca, NY: Cornell University Press.

Andreas, Peter, and Timothy Snyder, eds. 2000. *The Wall around the West: State Borders and Immigration Controls in North America and Europe.* Boulder, CO: Rowman & Littlefield.

Ansari, Massoud, and Sanna Bucha. 2002. Perilous Journey. *Newsline* (Karachi). Special Report. March.

Appadurai, Arjun. 1993. Number in the Colonial Imagination. In *Orientalism and the Post-Colonial Predicament,* edited by Peter van der Veer and Carol Breckenridge, pp.314–336. Philadelphia: University of Pennsylvania Press.

Arendt, Hannah. 1968. *The Origins of Totalitarianism.* San Diego, CA: Harvest.

Arif, G. M., and Mohammad Irfan. 1997. Population Mobility across the Pakistani Border: Fifty Years Experience. *Pakistan Development Review* 36 (4) (Winter): 989–1009.

Arnold, David. 1985. Crime and Crime Control in Madras, 1858–1947. In *Crime and Criminality in British India,* edited by Anand Yang, pp.62–88. Ann Arbor, MI: Association for Asian Studies.

Asia-Pacific Economic Cooperation. 2004. The Malaysian Machine Readable Travel Document (MRTD). 2004/STAR II/MP/008. Second Conference on Secure Trade in APEC Region. Chile. March 5–6. Presentation by Hj. Che Mamat Abdullah, state director, Immigration Department, Malaysia.

Associated Press of Pakistan News Agency (Islamabad). 2005. Pakistan: Afghan Refugees with Bogus Documents to Be Treated according to Law. August 4.

Assam Tribune (Gawhati). 2006. 21 Voter Identity Documents: EC. March 22. http://www.assamtribune.com.

———. 2005. Gogoi Govt Encouraging Bangladeshis. March 8.

———. 2004a. Several State Ministers Are of Bangla Origin: BJP. July 21.

———. 2004b. Migrants Vote for Citizenship Rights. April 21.

———. 2003. VHP Warns against Bangla Influx. May 26.

———. 2000. Entire Indo-Bangla Border to Be Fenced. May 24.

Bal Vikas Dhara. n.d. "Report on Ragpickers." Delhi. Author's Copy.

Bangkuai, Joniston. 2001. A Million in Sabah Have No Birth Certs. *New Straits Times* (Kuala Lumpur). October 16.

Bangladesh Shishu Adhikar Forum. 1996. Situation of Children in Bangladesh 1996. November. Presented at 15th Session of NGO Group Convention on the Rights of the Child. Dhaka: Bangladesh. www.bsafchild.org/state_english.pdf. Accessed on June 23, 2008.

Baruah, Amit. 2003. Database Lists 25M Passport-Holders. *Hindu.* January 28.

Baruah, Sanjib. 1999. *India against Itself: Assam and the Politics of Nationality.* Philadelphia: University of Pennsylvania Press.

Bauböck, Rainer. 2005. Expansive Citizenship: Voting beyond Territory and Membership. *PS: Political Science & Politics* 38 (October): 683–687.

———. 2003. Towards a Political Theory of Migrant Transnationalism. *International Migration Review* 37 (3):700–723.

BBC News. 2006. Ivorian Party Threatens ID Move. July 14.

2005. India Bangladesh Border Shooting. August 30.

———. 2002a. Opposition Attacks Ivory Coast Poll. July 8.

———. 2002b. Ouattara Declared Ivorian Citizen. June 30.

Beiner, Ronald. 1995. *Theorizing Citizenship.* Albany: State University of New York Press.

Bendix, Reinhard. 1996. *Nation-Building and Citizenship: Studies of Our Changing Social Order.* New Brunswick, NJ: Transaction.

Benhabib, Seyla. 2004. *The Rights of Others: Aliens, Residents and Citizens.* Cambridge, MA: Cambridge University Press.

Bergstein, Brian. 2003. U.S. Demanding Biometric Technology in Passports, World May Not
    Be Ready. *CNEWS*. August 23. www.cnews.canoe.ca/ http://www.canoe.com/CNEWS/
    TechNews/2003/08/23/167410-ap.html. Accessed July 1, 2007.

Bernama (Malaysian National News Agency). 2006a. More than 700,000 MyKad Unclaimed,
    Govt Stands to Lose RM2.1 Million. January 3.

——. 2006b. More than 9,000 Apply for the Name Change in MyKad since 2001. March 23.

——. 2006c. Status withdrawn for PR without MyPR. June 13.

——. 2005a. 300 Penans without Documents of Identity, Says Suhakam. September 23.

——. 2005b. Sabah CM Calls for Probe into MyKad Issue. June 11.

——. 2005c. Ensuring Information Security. February 17.

——. 2005d. No Mercy for Traitors in the Civil Service, Says Abdullah. February 12.

——. 2004a. 7, 500 Paperless Locals Documented since 2001. December 10.

——. 2004b. Ranau Folks Get Personal Documents. October 13.

Bhushan, Ranjit. 2001. Immigrants: Identifying a Problem. *Outlook*. May 14.

——. 1996. The Alien Dilemma. *Outlook*. November 27.

Bora, Bijay Sankar. 2005. Cong at the Receiving End. *Statesman* (Calcutta). April 2.

Borneo Post (Kota Kinabalu). 1999a. Alien Confesses Voted in Five Polls. November 16: A1.

——. 1999b. Conspiracy in Issuing ICs to Foreigners. November 12: A4.

——. 1999c. Illegal Jailed after Entering State since 1979. October 6: A3.

——. 1999d. Phantom Voters Influenced Election. September 29: A1.

——. 1999e. 54 Years Without Birth Certificate. September 29: A4.

——. 1999f. Flush Out Fake Voters: Pairin to BN. September 23: A2.

——. 1999g. Sanctity of Electoral Rolls Challenged. September 23: A4.

——. 1999h. Police Report on Fake Documents. September 22: A5.

——. 1999i. Petitioner Alleges Illegality. September 22: A5.

——. 1999j. RM10 for Fake IC. August 18: A3.

Bose, Ashish. 2005. Beyond Hindu-Muslim Growth Rates: Understanding Socio-Economic
    Reality. *Economic and Political Weekly,* vol. 40, no.5. January 29: 370–374.

Bosniak, Linda. 2006. *The Citizen and the Alien: Dilemmas of Contemporary Membership*.
    Princeton, NJ: Princeton University Press.

Bowring, John, ed. 1962. *The Works of Jeremy Bentham, Vol. 1, Chapter XII, Problem IX,
    Principles of Penal Law*. Reproduced from the Bowring Edition of 1838–1843. New York:
    Russell and Russell, 1962.

Boyd, Monica. 1989. Family and Personal Networks in International Migration: Recent
    Developments and New Agendas. *International Migration Review* 23 (3):638–670.

BPS Statistics–Indonesia, UNICEF. n.d. End Decade Statistical Report: Data and Descriptive
    Analysis. BPS Catalogue No. 4124. http://www.childinfo.org/MICS2/newreports/
    indonesia/indonesia.pdf. Accessed February 26, 2008.

Brown, Chip. 2006. The Freshman. *New York Times*. February 26.

Brubaker, Rogers. 1992. *Citizenship and Nationhood in France and Germany*. Cambridge, MA:
    Harvard University Press.

Brysk, Alison, and Gershon Shafir. 2004. Conclusion: Globalizing Citizenship? In *People Out
    of Place: Globalization, Human Rights, and the Citizenship Gap,* edited by Alison Brysk
    and Gershon Shafir, pp.209–216. New York: Routledge.

Business Recorder (Karachi). 2006. Karachi Police to Computerise Records. March 8.

Business Recorder (Karachi). 2005a. Lahore to Have More Swift Centers for CNICs. December 13.

———. 2005b. Over Dozen Held for Preparing Fake NICs during Local Bodies' Polls. August 28.

———. 2005c. Three Held in Darra. September 24.

Cantwell, Maria. 2004. Testimony to the Senate Judiciary Committee on Biometric Passports. June 15. http://judiciary.senate.gov/member_statement.cfm?id=1226&wit_id=243. Accessed July 1, 2007.

Caplan, Jane and John Torpey, eds. 2001. *Documenting Individual Identity: The Development of State Practices in the Modern World*. Princeton, NJ: Princeton University Press.

Carens, Joseph H. 1987. Aliens and Citizens: The Case for Open Borders. *Review of Politics* 49 (2) (Spring): 251–273.

Castles, Stephen, and Alastair Davidson. 2000. *Citizenship and Migration: Globalization and the Politics of Belonging*. New York: Routledge.

Chaudhry, Lubna Nazir. 2004. Reconstituting Selves in the Karachi Conflict: Mohajir Women Survivors and Structural Violence. *Cultural Dynamics* 16 (2–3): 259–290.

Chavez, Leo R. 2001. *Covering Immigration: Popular Images and the Politics of the Nation*. Berkeley: University of California Press.

———. 1997. *Shadowed Lives: Undocumented Immigrants in American Society*. Belmont, CA: Wadsworth Thomas Learning.

Children's Human Rights First and HRWG. 2006. Written statement submitted by the International NGO Forum on Indonesia Development (INFID), a Non-Governmental Organization on Special Consultative Status. Item 13: Rights of the Child. http://www.infid.org/newinfid/old-docu/06-unhcr-item13.pdf. Accessed on June 18, 2008.

Citizens Campaign for Preserving Democracy. 2005. *Democracy, Citizens and Migrants: Nationalism in the Era of Globalisation*. Delhi. February 9. http://www.amanpanchayat.org/index.php?option=com_content&task=view&id=33&Itemid=112. Accessed July 1, 2007.

Cole, Simon. 2001. *Suspect Identities: A History of Fingerprinting and Criminal Identification*. Cambridge, MA: Harvard University Press.

Dahl, Robert A. 2005. What Political Institutions Does Large-Scale Democracy Require? *Political Science Quarterly* 120 (Summer): 187–197.

———. 1989. *Democracy and Its Critics*. New Haven, CT: Yale University Press.

Daily Express (Kota Kinabalu). 2007. Express Reports True. January 20. http://www.dailyexpress.com.my.

———. 2005. Enough Warnings to Ketuas on Documents: CM. August 3.

———. 2004. Rampant Fake ICs Making It Difficult for Real Bumis. March 1.

———. 2003. Authorities Urged to Screen Citizenship of Illegals. January 7.

———. 2002a. 10 Hi-Tech Fake ICs Seized Daily. July 17.

———. 2002b. Govt. Expecting Police Report on MyKads. July 18.

———. 2002c. Bumis Are the Real Losers. July 18.

———. 2001. Its By-Poll for Likas. June 9.

———. 2000a. No Foolproof Way of Stopping More Seizures. September 12.

———. 2000b. Govt Aware of Security Threat. October 25.

———. 1999a. Sabah Qualifies for Refugee State Status. August 1: 20.

———. 1999b. Foreigners Voted, BN Claim. September 29: 1.

——. 1999c. Three Categories of Phantom Voters: PBS. August 21: 3.

——. 1999d. Kudat DO Gave Me a RM200 Bribe. November 17: 2.

——. 1999e. Future Generations Will Not Forgive. October 8: 4.

——. 1998. Electoral Roll Worry. May 20.

Daily Times (Pakistan). 2005. Birth Registration as Low as 20% in Pakistan. February 18. http://www.dailytimes.com.pk.

——. 2004a. Foreigners Using Pakistani Passports in Drug Trafficking. October 24.

——. 2004b. PML, PPP Back Bangla-Speaking People. September 6.

Dasgupta, Anindita. 2000. Political Myth-Making in Postcolonial Assam. *Himal* (Katmandu). August.

Dasgupta, Jyotirindra. 1997. Community, Authenticity, and Autonomy: Insurgence and Institutional Development in India's Northeast. *Journal of Asian Studies* 56 (2) (May): 345–370.

Dawn (Karachi). 2007. NADRA Employees Caught in Fake ID Cards Racket. November 17. http://www.dawn.com.

——. 2006. 3,400 British Visa Applicants Submitted Forged Papers. May 11.

——. 2005a. 20,000 Illegal Pakistanis in Greece to Get Passports. October 31.

——. 2005b. Govt Slated for Issuing NICs to Aliens. July 6.

——. 2005c. UAE Deports Pakistani National, 5 Others: Human Trafficking. June 17.

——. 2005d. NADRA Official Arrested. June 17.

——. 2005e. NICs for Illegal Aliens Opposed. June 6.

——. 2005f. FIA Accused of Helping Man Travel on Fake Documents. June 3.

——. 2005g. Hyderabad: Call for Repatriation of Illegal Immigrants. March 21.

——. 2005h. Travel Agency Owner Arrested for Passport Forgery. February 26.

——. 2004a. 835 Held for Traveling on Forged Documents. September 1.

——. 2004b. Foreign Passports Seized; Two Held. May 1.

——. 2004c. NADRA Refuses to Withdraw Cases against Councilors. January 3.

——. 2003. Afghans with Fake NICs Get Passports. June 6.

——. 2002a. Larkana: Fake NICs Case Accused Changes Statement. December 11.

——. 2002b. Fake ID Cards Being Made for Rigging; PPP: MMA Wants NADRA Staff Suspended. October 3.

——. 2002c. Man Providing Fake ID Cards to Afghans Held. July 22.

Dawn Wire Service (Karachi). 2001. NADRA Warns Aliens Not to Apply for New Id Cards. September 1. http://www.dawn.com. Accessed July 1, 2007.

Department of Statistics (Malaysia). 2000. *Population and Housing Census of Malaysia 2000: Preliminary Count Report.*October.

——. 1998. *Migration Survey Report.* July.

——. 1995. *Population and Housing Census 1991, State Population Report: Sabah.* March.

——. 1983. *Population and Housing Census of Malaysia, vol.* 1. January.

Dhavan, Rajeev. 2004. *Refugee Law and Policy in India.* New Delhi: Public Interest and Legal Support and Research Centre.

Directorate of Census Operations (Assam). 1999a. *Census of India 1991. Series 4: Assam, Part XI, Census Atlas.* New Delhi: Government of India.

——. 1999b. *Census of India 1991. Series 4: Assam, Part IV-B (ii), Religion* (table C-9). New Delhi: Government of India.

Directorate of Census Operations (Assam). 1998. *Census of India 1991. Series 4: Assam, Part VA & VB-D Series, Migration Tables, vol.* 1. Delhi: Controller of Publications.

———. 1997. *Census of India 1991. Series 4: Assam, Part II-A, General Population Tables,* pp. 118–120. Delhi: Controller of Publications.

Doty, Roxanne Lynn. 1996. The Double-Writing of Statecraft: Exploring State Responses to Illegal Immigration. *Alternatives* 21 (2): 171–189.

Durkheim, Emile. 1954. *The Elementary Forms of the Religious Life.* New York: Free Press.

Eastwood, Clint, dir. 2004. *Million Dollar Baby.*

Economic Times. 2004. Polls in State Aren't Free & Fair, Cops Are Partisan. February 8.

Election Commission of India. 2007a. *FAQs—Contesting for Elections.* http://www.eci.gov.in/faq/Contesting.asp. Accessed October 18, 2007.

———.2007b.*Landmark Judgements*[*sic*] *on Election Law.*http://www.eci.gov.in/ElectoralLaws/Judgements/LandmarkJudgementsVOLI.pdf. Accessed October, 18, 2007.

———. 2007c. *Election Laws.* http://www.eci.gov.in/ElectoralLaws/electoral_law.asp. Accessed October 18, 2007.

———. 2001. Disciplinary Action against Officers for Dereliction of Duty during the Summary Revision of Electoral Roll of 35-Thakurdwara Assembly Constituency in Uttar Pradesh, with Reference to 1.1.2001 as Qualifying Date—regarding No. MCS/PN/15/2001. September 28.

———. 2000a. *Elections in India: Major Events & New Initiatives, 1996–2000.* New Delhi: Nirvachan Sadan, Election Commission.

———. 2000b. *Photo Identity Cards: Effective Use in General Election to the Legislative Assembly of Haryana.* February 10. http://www.eci.gov.in/press/current/PN10022000.pdf . Accessed July 1, 2007.

———. 1951–2001. *Statistical Report on General Election* [*Year*] *to the Legislative Assembly of Assam.* New Delhi.

Feldblum, Miriam. 2000. Managing Membership: New Trends in Citizenship and Nationality Policy. In *From Migrants to Citizens: Membership in a Changing World,* edited by T. Alexander Aleinikoff and Douglas Klusmeyer, pp.475–499. Washington, DC: Carnegie Endowment for International Peace.

Foreign Policy. 2006. The Failed States Index. May–June.

Foucault, Michel. 1991. Governmentality. In *The Foucault Effect: Studies in Governmentality,* edited by Graham Burchell, Colin Gordon, and Peter Miller, pp. 87–104. London: Harvest Wheatsheaf.

———. 1977. *Discipline and Punish: The Birth of the Prison,* translated by Alan Sheridan. New York: Vintage.

Gambetta, Diego. 1988. Can We Trust. In *Trust: Making and Breaking Cooperative Relations,* edited by Diego Gambetta, pp.213–237. Oxford: Basil Blackwell.

Gamel, Kim. 2006. Iraqis Turn to Fake IDs for Safety. Associated Press. July 10.

Gannep, Arnold Van. 1960. *The Rites of Passage.* Chicago: University of Chicago Press.

Garari, Kaniza. 2003. Fake Identities Up for Grabs! *Economic Times* (New Delhi). September 9.

García Bedolla, Lisa. 2006. Rethinking Citizenship: Noncitizen Voting and Immigrant Political Engagement in the United States. In *Transforming Politics, Transforming America: The Political and Civic Incorporation of Immigrants in the United States,* edited by Taeku Lee, Karthick Ramakrishnan, and Ricardo Ramírez, pp.51–70. Charlottesville: University of Virginia Press.

———. 2005. *Fluid Borders: Latino Power, Identity, and Politics in Los Angeles.* Berkeley: University of California Press.

Ghosh, Bimal. 2000. *Managing Migration: Time for a New International Regime?* Oxford: Oxford University Press.

———. 1998. *Huddled Masses and Uncertain Shores: Insights into Irregular Migration.* The Hague: Nijhoff.

Ghosh, Manash. 2006. Ration Card as Tool of Plunder. *Statesman.* January 22.

Gokhale, Nitin. 2001. An Election Gimmick? Or Is Vajpayee and the BJP Serious about Work-Permits for Illegal Immigrants? *Outlook.* May 8.

Goswami, Sandhya. 2001. Assam: Changing Electoral Trends. *Economic and Political Weekly.* vol. 36. no. 19. May 12: 1584–1586.

Government of Canada. 2002. Regulations Amending the Immigration and Refugee Protection Regulations. *Canada Gazette* 136 (21) (October 9). http://canadagazette.gc .ca/partII/2002/20021009/html/sor332-e.html. Accessed July 1, 2007.

Government of India. 2005. *Annual Report: 2005–2006.* Ministry of Home Affairs.

———. 2004a. *Annual Report: 2003–2004.* Department of Food and Public Distribution, Ministry of Consumer Affairs.

———. 2004b. *Annual Report: 1 January 2003–31 March 2004.* Ministry of External Affairs.

———. 2002. *The Foreigners Act, 1946: With Allied Acts, Rules and Order.* Allahabad: Law Publishers.

———. Various years. Parliamentary Debates, Rajya Sabha. www.rajyasabha.nic.in/

———. Various years. Parliamentary Debates, Lok Sabha. www.loksabha.nic.in/

Government of Pakistan. n.d. *National Report on Follow-Up to the World Summit for Children.* National Commission for Child Welfare and Development, Ministry of Women, Development, Social Welfare and Special Education. http://www.un.org.pk/gmc/edr_ pakistan_en.pdf. Accessed November 11, 2007.

Government of Sabah. 1996. *Constitution of the State of Sabah.* Sabah: Dicetak Di Jabatan Cetak Kerajaan.

———. 1988. *An Overview of the Transient Population in Sabah.* Sabah: Resettlement Division, Chief Minister's Department. August 3.

Governor of Assam. 1998. "Report on Illegal Migration into Assam Submitted to the President of India by the Governor of Assam." November 8. Author's Copy.

Griego, Manuel Garcia. 1987. International Migration Statistics in Mexico. *International Migration Review* 21 (4) (Winter): 1245–1257.

Guha, Sumit. 2003. The Politics of Identity and Enumeration in India c. 1600–1990. *Society for Comparative Study of Society and History* 45 (January): 148–167.

Habib, Irfan. 2001. *The Agrarian System of Mughal India, 1526–1707.* Delhi: Oxford University Press.

Hai, Lim Hong. 2005. Making the System Work: The Election Commission. In *Elections and Democracy in Malaysia,* edited by Mavis Puthucheary and Norani Othman, pp.249–291. Kuala Lumpur: Penerbit UKM.

Hall, Rodney. 1999. *National Collective Identity: Social Constructs and International Systems.* New York: Columbia University Press.

Hammar, Tomas. 1990. *Democracy and the Nation State: Aliens, Denizens and Citizens in a World of International Migration.* Aldershot, England: Avebury.

Harris Mohd Salleh v. Ismail bin Majin. 1999. Returning Officer, Election Petition Nos. k5 and k11. High Court (Kota Kinabalu). 2001–3 MLJ 433; 2001 MLJ Lexis (Lexis Nexis).

Hartill, Lane. 2006. Ivory Coast Struggles to ID Its Citizens. *Christian Science Monitor.* August 17.

Hazarika, Sanjoy. 2000. *Rites of Passage: Border Crossings, Imagined Homelands, India's East and Bangladesh.* New Delhi: Penguin.

Hindu (Chennai). 2005. CBI Seizes Fake Ration Cards for Kerosene. February 27. http://www.hinduonnet.com.

———. 2001. Voter ID Compulsory for May 10 Polls: EC. April 28.

Hindustan Times (New Delhi). 2001. Bangla Rifles Kill 16 BSF Men. April 19. http://www.hindustantimes.com.

———. 1999a. Bangladesh Migrants Are Flooding Assam: Thakre. June 20.

———. 1999b. Bengal Sees More Claimants for Inclusion in Voters' List. June 4.

———. 1999c. Gill Urged to Move Supreme Court against "Doubtful" Voters in Assam. May 1.

———. 1999d. It's Difficult to Identify Bangladeshis, West Bengal Govt Informs Apex Court. February 2.

———. 1998. Bid to Push Indian Nationals into Dhaka. August 27.

Hollifield, James. 1992. *Immigrants, Markets, and States: The Political Economy of Postwar Europe.* Cambridge, MA: Harvard University Press.

Hugo, Graeme. 2000. Labor Migration from East Indonesia to East Malaysia. *Revue Europeenne des Migrations Internationales* 16 (1):97–126.

———. 1997. Asia and the Pacific on the Move: Workers and Refugees, a Challenge to Nation States. *Asia Pacific Viewpoint* 38 (3): 267–286.

Hugo, Graeme, and A. Singhanetra-Renard. 1991. *International Migration of Contract Labor in Asia: Major Issues and Implications.* Ottawa: IRDC.

Human Rights Watch. 2004. Help Wanted: Abuses against Female Migrant Domestic Workers in Indonesia and Malaysia. *Human Rights Watch* 16 (9) (July): 1–91.

Huntington, Samuel P. 1991. *The Third Wave: Democratization in the Late Twentieth Century.* Norman: University of Oklahoma Press.

Hussain, Monirul. 1993. *The Assam Movement: Class, Ideology and Identity.* New Delhi: Manak.

Ijaz, Wajahat. 2005. Interpol Seeks Data about Lost, Stolen Passports. *Dawn.* August 5.

International Criminal Police Organization (Interpol). 2007. *Annual Report 2006: Connecting People, Securing the World.* Lyon, France: Interpol.

International Organization for Migration. 2004. *Trafficking in Persons: An Analysis of Afghanistan.* January.

Isin, Engin F., and Bryan S. Turner. 2002. Citizenship Studies: An Introduction. In *Handbook of Citizenship Studies,* edited by Engin F. Isin and Bryan S. Turner, pp.1–11. London: Sage.

Jacobson, David. 1997. *Rights across Borders: Immigration and the Decline of Citizenship.* Baltimore, MD: Johns Hopkins University Press.

Jaffrelot, Christophe. 2002. Introduction: Nationalism without a Nation: Pakistan Searching for Its Identity. In *Pakistan: Nationalism without a Nation?* edited by Christophe Jaffrelot, pp.7–48. New York: Palgrave.

Jahangir, Asma. 2002. Question and Answer Session with the Research Directorate. September 6. Immigration and Refugee Board of Canada, PAK40294.E, October 25. http://www .irb-cisr.gc.ca/en/research/ndp/ref/?action=view&doc=pak40294e. Accessed July 1, 2007.

Jai, Janak, and Rajiv Jai. 2004. *Sonia's Foreign Origin: A Non-Issue.* New Delhi: Regency.

Jaiswal, Sriprakash. 2005. Reply to an Unstarred Question (question number 868) in the Lok Sabha. Minister of State, Ministry of Home Affairs, Government of India. November 29. http://164.100.24.208/lsq14/quest.asp?qref=20245. Accessed July 1, 2007.

Jamayat Ulema-e-Hind v. Election Commission of India and Others. 1998. Civil Original Jurisdiction, Writ Petition (Civil) No. 45. Supreme Court of India..

Jang (Rawalpindi, Pakistan). 2003. *Revelation of Stealing of 32,000 Passports in Urdu.* September 9. Source: BBC Monitoring © British Broadcasting Corporation 2003, Record No. 0FECE3F9C7EDF5A6. http://docs.newsbank.com. Accessed June 15, 2006.

Jesien, Leszek. 2000. Border Controls and the Politics of EU Enlargement. In *The Wall around the West: State Borders and Immigration Controls in North America* and *Europe,* edited by Peter Andreas and Timothy Snyder, pp.185–202. Boulder, CO: Rowman & Littlefield.

Jha, Nilanjana Bhaduri. 2001. Government in No Position to Check Passport Fraud. *Times of India* (New Delhi). September 22.

Jha, Sanjay K. 2003. There Are No Bangladeshis In India! *Outlook.* February 4.

Johari, Mohd. Yaakub. 1992. *Development of Informal Sector in Sabah: A Case Study in the Conurbation of Kota Kinabalu: Final Report.* Kota Kinabalu, Sabah: Institute for Development Studies. September.

Johari, M., and Anthony Kiob. 1997. The Making of Sabah as a Regional Centre for Maritime Services. In *BIMP-EAGA Integration: Issues and Challenges,* edited by Mohd. Yaakub Hj. Johari, Bilson Kurus, and Janiah Zaini, pp.51–74. Sabah: Institute for Development Studies.

Joppke, Christian. 2005. *Selecting by Origin: Ethnic Migration in the Liberal State.* Cambridge, MA: Harvard University Press.

———. 1999. *Immigration and the Nation-State: The United States, Germany, and Great Britain.* New York: Oxford University Press.

Karnad, Raghu, Rajeev Dhavan, and Bhairav Acharya. 2006. *Protecting the Forgotten and Excluded: Statelessness in South Asia.* New Delhi: Public Interest Legal Support and Research Centre. www.pilsarc.org

Kassim, Azizah. 1998. International Migration and Its Impact on Malaysia. In *A Pacific Peace: Issues and Responses,* edited by M. J. Hassan, pp. 273–305. Kuala Lumpur: ISIS.

Kaur, Jaswinder. 2004. Life Is a Boat for Bajau Laut. *New Straits Times* (Kuala Lumpur). December 22.

Kertzer, David, and Dominique Arel. 2002. Census, Identity Formation, and the Struggle for Political Power. In *Census and Identity: The Politics of Race, Ethnicity, and Language in National Censuses,* edited by David Kertzer and Dominique Arel, pp.1–42. Cambridge: Cambridge University Press.

Khaleej Times (UAE). 2004. Karachi Letter: Bangla Illegal Immigrants Caught in Red Tape. January 19.

Khan, Ahmad Naeem. 2004. Illegal Immigrants Fear Registration Means Exit in Pakistan. *OneWorld South Asia*. February 10.

Khilnani, Sunil. 1997. *The Idea of India*. New York: Farrar, Straus and Giroux.

Kimura, Makiko. 2003. Memories of the Massacre: Violence and Collective Identity in the Narratives on the Nellie Incident. *Asian Ethnicity* 4 (2) (June):225–239.

Kitingan, Jeffrey. 1997. *The Sabah Problem: The Kamunting Papers*. Sabah: KDI.

Kohli, Atul, ed. 2001. *The Success of India's Democracy*. Cambridge: Cambridge University Press.

Kong Yun Chee, Joshua. 2005. *IC Case for ICC*. International Criminal Court of Justice, The Hague, Netherlands. August. http://www.freewebs.com/justknock/migsiccsabah.htm.

Koslowski, Rey. 2002. Human Migration and the Conceptualization of Pre-Modern World Politics. *International Studies Quarterly* 46 (3):375–399.

——. 2001. *Global Human Smuggling: Comparative Perspectives*. Baltimore, MD: Johns Hopkins University Press.

——. 2000a. *Migrants and Citizens: Demographic Change in the European State System*. Ithaca, NY: Cornell University Press.

——. 2000b. The Mobility Money Can Buy: Human Smuggling and Border Control in the European Union. In *The Wall around the West: State Borders and Immigration Controls in North America and Europe,* edited by Peter Andreas and Timothy Snyder, pp.203–218. Boulder, CO: Rowman & Littlefield.

Kurus, B., R. Goddos, and R. Koh. 1998. Migrant Labor Flows in the East Asian Region: Prospects and Challenges. *Borneo Review* (Kota Kinabalu) 9 (2):156–186.

Kymlicka, Will. 1995. *Multicultural Citizenship: A Liberal Theory of Minority Rights*. Oxford: Clarendon.

Kymlicka, Will, and Wayne Norman. 1994. Return of the Citizen: A Survey of Recent Work on Citizenship Theory. *Ethics* 104 (2) (January):352–381.

Latham, Robert. 2000. Social Sovereignty. *Theory, Culture and Society* 17 (4): 1–18.

Lal Babu Hussain v. Electoral Registration Officers & Others. 1995. AIR. SC 1189.

Law Commission of India. 2000. *One Hundred Seventy Fifth Report on the Foreigners (Amendment) Bill, 2000*. New Delhi: September.

Leete, Richard. 2007. *Malaysia: From Kampung to Twin Towers: 50 Years of Economic and Social Development*. Kuala Lumpur: Oxford Fajar.

Legal Research Board. 1998. *Federal Constitution*. Kuala Lumpur: International Law Book Services.

Lertcharoenchok, Yindee. 2001. Searching for Identity. *Step-by-Step*, no. 5 (Fourth Quarter). Newsletter from the UN Inter-Agency Project on Trafficking in Women and Children in the Mekong Sub-Region. http://www.un.or.th/TraffickingProject/volume5.pdf. Accessed July 1, 2007.

Letzing, John. 2005. Cross-Border Security: The Visa Loophole. *PBS Frontline*. http://www.pbs.org/wgbh/pages/frontline/shows/front/special/visa.html. Accessed July 1, 2007.

Levine, Samantha. 2004. Terror's Best Friend. *USNews.Com*. June 12. http://www.usnews.com/usnews/news/articles/041206/6passports.htm. Accessed July 1, 2007.

Lin, S. G., and M. C. Paul. 1995. Bangladeshi Migrants in Delhi: Social Insecurity, State Power, and Captive Vote Banks. *Bulletin of Concerned Asian Scholars* 27 (1):3–20.

Loh, Francis. 1999. The Sabah State Elections, 1999. *Aliran Monthly* 19 (3) (April): 33–40.

Lucassen, Leo. 2001. A Many-Headed Monster: The Evolution of the Passport System in the Netherlands and Germany in the Long Nineteenth Century. In *Documenting Individual Identity: The Development of State Practices in the Modern World*, edited by Jane Caplan and John Torpey, pp.235–255. Princeton, NJ: Princeton University Press.

Luping, Herman. 1994. *Sabah's Dilemma: The Political History of Sabah: 1960–1994*. Kuala Lumpur: Magnus.

Lyon, David. 2004. Identity Cards: Social Sorting by Database. *Oxford Internet Institute*. Brief No. 3. November.

Mahanta, Prafulla Kumar. 1986. *The Tussle between the Citizens and Foreigners in Assam*. New Delhi: Vikas.

Mahidin, Jad. 2005a. Kids Need Help to Get Birth Certs. *Malay Mail* (Kuala Lumpur). August 8.

——. 2005b. Immigration Officers Cleared. *Malay Mail* (Kuala Lumpur). May 9.

Mahmood, Tahir. 2007. Why Fear Marriage Registration? *Indian Express*. August 7.

Malay Mail (Kuala Lumpur). 2006. Govt to Decide Soon on Status of Old IC. March 10.

——. 2005a. NGOs: Give Them Their Identification Papers. July 18.

——. 2005b. End of the Road for Hong Kong 'Snakehead.' March 23.

——. 2005c. Was There an Inside Link? April 20.

——. 2003. Man with Red I.C. Woes. May 3.

Mann, Michael. 2006. *The Sources of Social Power*: vol. 2, *The Rise of Classes and Nation States 1760–1914*. Cambridge: Cambridge University Press.

Mansoor, Hasan. 2003. Illegal Lives: Karachi's Two Million Immigrants Face a Government Crackdown. *Himal* (Katmandu). July.

——. 2002. Politicians Eye Illegal Immigrants' Votes. *Daily Times*. September 22.

Marshall, T. H., and T. Bottomore. 1996. *Citizenship and Social Class*. London: Pluto.

Masood, Aisha. 2003. Week Left to Attain New ID Cards as VERISYS Sets Off. *Pakistan Times*. November 24. http://www.pakistantimes.net/2003/11/24/metro.htm. Accessed July 1, 2007.

Massey, Douglas. 1999. International Migration at the Dawn of the Twenty-First Century: The Role of the State. *Population and Development Review* 25 (2): 303–322.

——. 1987. The Social Process of International Migration. *Science* 237 (14): 733–738.

Mazlish, Bruce. 2000. Invisible Ties: From Patronage to Networks. *Theory, Culture and Society* 17 (2).

Mead, Lawrence M. 1986. *Beyond Entitlement: The Social Obligations of Leadership*. New York: Free Press.

Misra, Udayon. 1999. Immigration and Identity Transformation in Assam. *Economic and Political Weekly*, vol. 34, no. 21. May 22–28: 1264–1267.

Motomura, Hiroshi. 2006. *Americans in Waiting: The Lost Story of Immigration and Citizenship in the United States*. New York: Oxford University Press.

Mukherjee, Saurav. 2004. For Rs 1 Lakh, Get Passport with US Visa in Guajarat. *Times of India*. December 21.

Mutalib, M. D. 1999. *IC Palsu: Merampas Hak Anak Sabah,* 2nd ed. April. Lahad Datu: Abdul Mutalib B. Mohd. Daud.

Namboodri, Udayan, et al. 1998. Illegal Immigrants: Political Pawns. *India Today.* August 10. http://www.indiatoday.com.

Nandy, Vaskar. 2001. Assam: Crisis of Chauvinism. *Economic and Political Weekly,* vol. 36, no. 28. July 14: 2616–2618.

Naommy, P. C. 2004. Government to Reform Birth Registration System. *Jakarta Post.* July 15. http://thejakartapost.com.

News (Islamabad). 2002a. Pakistan Foreign Office Sacks Diplomats Involved in "Passport Scam." September 15.

——. 2002b. Pakistan to Launch Crackdown against Illegal Immigrants. April 21.

New Sabah Times (Kota Kinabalu). 1999a. CASH: View Foreigners' Infiltration Seriously. August 19: 6. http://www.newsabahtimes.com.my.

——. 1999b. Foreigners Made JKKK Chairmen? August 18: 1.

New Straits Times (Kuala Lumpur). 2005. 1 Million Yet to Apply for MyKad. December 31. http://www.nst.com.my.

——. 2004. 479,433 Applications. June 4.

——. 2003. Collect MyKad or You May Be Fined. June 6.

——. 2002a. DPM: Punish MYKD Scam Culprits. July 27.

——. 2002b. Registering Rural Folk. February 18.

New York Times. 2002. Threats and Responses: Southeast Asia; More Attacks on Westerners Are Expected in Indonesia. November 25: A15. http://nytimes.com.

Ngai, Mae. 2005. *Impossible Subjects: Illegal Aliens and the Making of Modern America.* Princeton, NJ: Princeton University Press.

Nicol, John. 2000. Passports for Sale. *Maclean's* 113 (14) (April 3).

9/11 Commission. 2004. *The 9/11 Commission Report: Final Report of the National Commission on Terrorist Attacks upon the United States.* New York: Norton.

Noiriel, Gerard. 1996. *The French Melting Pot: Immigration, Citizenship, and National Identity.* Minneapolis: University of Minnesota Press.

Nordstrom, Carolyn. 2000. Shadows and Sovereigns. *Theory, Culture and Society* 17 (4): 35–54.

Nyce, Sayre. 2003. Viewpoint: Government Must Curb Ivory Coast's Xenophobia. *Reuters.* June 23. http://www.alertnet.org/thefacts/reliefresources/nyceview.htm. Accessed July 1, 2007.

Office of the Registrar General and Census Commissioner (India). 2007. *Census of India 2001.* http://www.censusindia.gov.in/

——. 2003a. *National Conference of Chief Registrars of Births and Deaths: Proceedings of the Conference.* New Delhi: Government of India Press.

——. 2003b. *Multi-Purpose National Identity Card (MNIC) Pilot Project, 2003.*

——. 1998a. *State Profile 1991 India.* Delhi: Controller of Publications.

——. 1998b. *Handbook on Civil Registration.* New Delhi: Government of India Press.

Olson, Camilla. 2007. *Malaysia: Undocumented Children in Sabah Vulnerable to Statelessness.* http://www.refugeesinternational.org/content/article/detail/10044.

Ong, Aihwa. 1999. *Flexible Citizenship: The Cultural Logics of Transnationality.* Durham, NC: Duke University Press.

Onuf, Nicholas. 1991. Sovereignty: Outline of a Conceptual History. *Alternatives* 16: 425–446.

Outlook (India). 2005. Illegal Bangladeshis are a Threat. May 2. www.outlookindia.com

Pakistan Country Paper. 2006. Record, Recognize, Respect: Fourth Asia and Pacific Regional Conference on Universal Birth Registration, March 13–17, Bangkok, Thailand. http://www.plan-international.org/pdfs/pakistancp.pdf. Accessed July 1, 2007.

Pakistan Observer (Islamabad). 2006. Around 1.3M E-Passports Issued in Two Months. January 20.

Pakistan Press International (Karachi). 2005a. JUP Decries "Excesses on Bengali Pakistanis." June 22.

———. 2005b. Sindh Assembly: Treasury Benches, MMA Members Disallow PPP to Move Motion against Issuance of NICs to Aliens. March 16.

———. 2004a. MQM, MMA Join Hands on Issuing of ID Cards to Immigrants. March 30.

———. 2004b. NARA to Send Record of Registered Aliens to Police Stations and Other Agencies; List of Aliens Who Got Them Elected to Local Governments. February 4.

———. 2003. Only 26,000 Aliens Registered in Last 15 Months. March 28.

———. 2002. 1.9 Million Illegal Immigrants Live in Karachi. March 16.

Pakistan Tribune (Islamabad). 2005. Afghan "Refugees'" Pakistani Passports, Identity Cards Illegal: NA Told. November 17.

Passel, Jaffrey S., and Roberto Suro. 2005. *Rise, Peak, and Decline: Trends in U.S. Immigration 1992–2004*. Pew Hispanic Center Report. Washington, DC. September.

PBS. 2005. *Frontline: Trail of a Terrorist*. http://www.pbs.org/wgbh/pages/frontline/shows/trail/inside/testimony.html. Accessed July 1, 2007.

Peil, Margaret. 1983. Situational Variables. In *Social Research in Developing Countries: Surveys and Censuses in the Third World*, edited by Martin Bulmer and Donald Warwick, pp.71–89. Chichester, England: Wiley.

Percetakan Nasional Malaysia. 1997. *Federal Constitution*. Kuala Lumpur: Percetakan Nasional Malaysia Berhad.

Philippine Daily Inquirer (Manila). 1999. Filipino Illegals Swell in Sabah. October 30. http://www.inquirer.net.

Pioneer (New Delhi). 2004. HC Indicts Delhi Govt. for Not Evicting Alien. September 9. http://www.dailypioneer.com.

Plan. 2005a. *Universal Birth Registration: A Universal Responsibility*. Surrey. February. http://www.plan-international.org/pdfs/advocacyreport.pdf. Accessed July 1, 2007.

———. 2005b. Desmond Tutu Demands Action on Recording Births of More than Half a Billion "Lost" Children. Press Release. February 22. http://www.writemedown.org/news/newsarchive. Accessed July 1, 2007.

Pohit, Sanjib, and Nisha Taneja. 2003. India's Informal Trade with Bangladesh: A Qualitative Assessment. *World Economy* 26 (August):1187–1214.

Polanyi, Karl. 1944. *The Great Transformation: The Political and Economic Origins of Our Time*. Boston: Beacon.

Prakash, Gyan. 1992. Science "Gone Native" in Colonial India. *Representations* 40: 155–160.

Qaiser, Aileen. 2004. The Authenticity of Attestations. *Dawn*. May 25.

———. 2003. Strengthening Pakistan's Case against INS Regulations. *Dateline Islamabad*. January 8.

Quek, Kim. 2006. Demographic Implosion in Sabah? Really? http://www.Malaysiakini.com. February 9.

Raffaele, P. 1986. *Harris Salleh of Sabah*. Hong Kong: Condor.

Raman, B. 2003. Indo-Bangladesh Standoff. *South Asia Analysis Group*. http://saag.org/papers6/paper597.html. Accessed October 18, 2007.

Rath, J. 1990. Voting Rights. In *The Political Rights of Migrant Workers in Western Europe*, edited by Zig Layton-Henry, pp. 127–157. London: Sage.

Regis, Patricia. 1989. Demography. In *Sabah 25 Years Later: 1963–1988*, edited by Jeffrey Kitingan and Maximus Ongkilli, pp.405–448. Sabah: Institute for Development Studies.

Registrar General of India. 2004. *The First Report on Religion, Census of India 2001*. Delhi: Government of India.

Rocco, Raymond. 1997. Citizenship, Culture, and Community: Restructuring in Southeast Los Angeles. In *Latino Cultural Citizenship: Claiming Identity, Space, and Rights*, edited by William Flores and Rina Benmayor, pp.97–123. Boston: Beacon.

Roff, M. 1974. *The Politics of Belonging: Political Change in Sabah and Sarawak*. Kuala Lumpur: Oxford University Press.

Rosenberg Ruth, ed. 2005. *Trafficking of Women and Children in Indonesia*. Jakarta: International Catholic Migration Commission.

Routray, Bibhu Prasad. 2003. Assam: The IM(DT) Act—Of Aliens, Natives and Politics. *South Asian Intelligence Review, vol. 1, no. 44.* May 19.

Rudolph, Lloyd, and Susanne Rudolph. 1987. *In Pursuit of Lakshmi: The Political Economy of the Indian State*. Chicago: University of Chicago Press.

———. 1985. The Subcontinental Empire and the Regional Kingdom in Indian State Formation. In *Region and Nation in India*, edited by Paul Wallace, pp.40–56. New Delhi: Oxford University Press.

Rushdie, Salman. 1980. *Midnight's Children*. New York: Penguin.

Sadiq, Kamal. 2005a. When States Prefer Non-Citizens over Citizens: Conflict over Illegal Immigration into Malaysia. *International Studies Quarterly* 49 (March):101–122.

———. 2005b. Lost in Translation: The Challenges of State-Generated Data in Developing Countries. In *Perestroika: The Raucous Rebellion in Political Science*, edited by Kristin Monroe, pp.181–199. New Haven, CT: Yale University Press.

Safire, William. 2001. Threat of National ID. *New York Times*. December 24: A15.

Saigol, Rubina. 2003. His Rights/Her Duties: Citizen and Mother in the Civics Discourse. *Indian Journal of Gender Studies*, no. 10.

Salmi, Hanys. 2004. Delicate Problems in Indonesia-Malaysia Ties. *Jakarta Post*. May 31.

Salter, Mark B. 2003. *Rights of Passage: The Passport in International Relations*. Boulder, CO: Rienner.

Sassen, Saskia. 2007. Introduction: Deciphering the Global. In *Deciphering the Global: Its Spaces, Scalings, and Subjects*, edited by Saskia Sassen, pp.1–18. New York: Routledge.

———. 2006. *Territory, Authority, Rights: From Medieval to Global Assemblages*. Princeton, NJ: Princeton University Press.

———. 2002. Towards Post-National and Denationalized Citizenship. In *Handbook of Citizenship Studies*, edited by Engin Isin and Bryan Turner, pp.277–292. London: Sage.

———. 1999. *Guests and Aliens*. New York: New Press.

——.1998. *Globalization and Its Discontents.* New York: New Press.

——.1996. *Losing Control? Sovereignty in an Age of Globalization.* New York: Columbia University Press.

Schuck, P. H., and R. M. Smith. 1985. *Citizenship without Consent: Illegal Aliens in the American Polity.* New Haven, CT: Yale University Press.

Scott, James C. 1998. *Seeing Like a State: How Certain Schemes to Improve the Human Condition Have Failed.* New Haven, CT: Yale University Press.

Scott, James C., John Tehranian, and Jeremy Mathias. 2002. The Production of Legal Identities Proper to States: The Case of the Permanent Family Surname. *Comparative Study of Society and History* 44 (1) (January):4–44.

Seng, Ho Ting. 1989. International Migration and Urban Development: The Case of the Filipino Immigrants in Sabah. In *Urbanization and Development: Prospects and Policies for Sabah beyond 1990,* edited by Mohd. Yaakub Johari and Baldev Sidhu, pp.225–242. Sabah: Institute for Development Studies.

Sengoopta, Chandak. 2003. *Imprint of the Raj: How Fingerprinting Was Born in Colonial India.* London: Macmillan.

Shafqat, Saeed. 1996. Pakistan under Benazir Bhutto. *Asian Survey* 36 (7) (July): 655–672.

Shah, Sadia Qasim. 2004. Delinquent Attesters Escape Action: CNIC Applications. *Dawn.* November 23.

Shah, Shekhar. 1999. *Bangladesh: From Counting the Poor to Making the Poor Count.* Washington DC: World Bank.

Shamsul, A. B. 1996. Nations-of-Intent in Malaysia. In *Asian Forms of the Nation,* edited by Stein Tonnesson and Hans Antlöv, pp.323–347. Surrey, England: Curzon.

Shigri, A. 1996. "A Report on Illegal Immigrants and Afghan Refugees in Pakistan." Confidential Memo. Karachi.Authors Copy (digital).

Shourie, Arun. 1983. Come What May. *India Today.* May 15: 54–66.

Siddiqui, Tahir. 1998. Pakistani Passports "on Sale" in BD. Dawn Wire Service. February 7.

Singh, Jaswant. 1984. Assam's Crisis of Citizenship: An Examination of Political Errors. *Asian Survey* 24 (10) (October): 1056–1068.

Singh, Manju. 1990. *Assam: Politics of Migration and Quest for Identity.* Jaipur: Anita.

Smith, Rogers. 2003. *Stories of Peoplehood: The Politics and Morals of Political Membership.* Cambridge: Cambridge University Press.

——. 2002. Modern Citizenship. In *Handbook of Citizenship Studies,* edited by Engin Isin and Bryan Turner, pp.105–115. London: Sage.

——. 1997. *Civic Ideals: Conflicting Visions of Citizenship in U.S. History.* New Haven, CT: Yale University Press.

Solinger, Dorothy J. 1999. *Contesting Citizenship in Urban China: Peasant Migrants, the State, and the Logic of the Market.* Berkeley: University of California Press.

Soysal, Yasemin. 1994. *Limits of Citizenship: Migrants and Post National Membership in Europe.* Chicago: University of Chicago Press.

Spaan, Ernst. 1994. Taikongs and Calos: The Role of Middlemen and Brokers in Javanese International Migration. *International Migration Review* 28 (1):93–113.

Spiro, Peter J. 1998. "Embracing Dual Nationality." Carnegie Endowment for International Peace, International Migration Project, Occasional Paper No. 1. June. www.carnegieendowment.org/publications/

Srikanth, H. 1999. Communalising Assam: AGP's loss is BJP's gain. *Economic and Political Weekly, vol.* 34, no. 39. December 4: 3412–3414.

Star (Kuala Lumpur). 2007. Musa Wants Dept Officials to Explain IC Situation. January 14. http://www.thestar.com.my.

Statesman (Calcutta). 2006. CPM Fraudsters Arrested. January 20.

Strange, Susan. 1996. *The Retreat of the State: The Diffusions of Power in the World Economy.* Cambridge: Cambridge University Press.

Sun (Kuala Lumpur). 1999. Officially, These Folks Don't Exist. April 19: A12.

Swami, Praveen. 2003. On a Dangerous Journey. *Frontline* 20 (5) (March 1–14).

Swarns, Rachel L. 2006. Deal Would Put Millions on Path to Citizenship. *New York Times.* April 6.

Tahir, Zulqernain. 2005. MNA, Naib Nazim "Human Smugglers." *Dawn.* January 18.

Talukdar, Sushanta. 2006. Peaceful Battle. *Frontline* 23 (7) (April 8–21).

Telegraph (Calcutta). 2006a. Enter, the Election Boss. January 9. http://www.telegraphindia .com.

———. 2006b. Six Lakh Fake Ration Cards. January 8.

———. 2003a. Home in Bangladesh, Ration in India. December 10.

Tenaganita. 2006. Acting Today for Tomorrow's Generation: Regional Conference on Stateless/Undocumented Children in Sabah. November 16–18, 2005. Kuala Lumpur, Malaysia: Tenaganita Sdn. Bhd.

Thien, Tony. 2006. Sabah Facing Epic Problem. February 6. http://www.malaysiakini.com.

Tibin, Newmond. 2007. Project IC Boils Over in Sabah. *Bernama* (Malaysian National News Agency). January 19.

Tiburcio, Carmen. 2001. *The Human Rights of Aliens under International and Comparative Law.* The Hague: Kluwer Law International/Nijhoff.

Times of India (New Delhi). 2003a. Passport Brokers Strike a Deal. June 7. http://timesof-india.com.

———. 2003b. Advani Asks States to Deport Illegal Visitors. January 8.

———. 2001. Now Bangla Troops Occupy Assam Village. April 19.

———. 2000. CBI to Grill Postmen Who "Delivered" Passports at Fake Addresses. October 10.

Ting, Jan C. 2005. Immigration and National Security. *Foreign Policy Research Institute E-Note.* September 9. http://www.fpri.org/enotes/20050909.americawar.ting.immigra-tionnationalsecurity.html. Accessed July 1, 2007.

Tomiyuki, U. 2000. Migration and Ethnic Categorization at International Frontier: A Case of Sabah, East Malaysia. In *Population Movement in Southeast Asia: Changing Identities and Strategies for Survival,* edited by Abe Ken-ichi and Ishii Masako, pp.33–55. Osaka, Japan: Japan Center for Area Studies, National Museum of Ethnology.

Torpey, John. 2001. The Great War and the Birth of the Modern Passport System. In *Documenting Individual Identity: The Development of State Practices in the Modern World,* edited by Jane Caplan and John Torpey, pp.256–270. Princeton, NJ: Princeton University Press.

———. 2000. *The Invention of the Passport: Surveillance, Citizenship and the State.* Cambridge: Cambridge University Press.

UNICEF. 2005a. *The State of the World's Children 2006: Excluded and Invisible.* New York: UNICEF.

———. 2005b. *The "Rights" Start to Life: A Statistical Analysis of Birth Registration 2005*. New York: UNICEF.

———. 2005c. *Investing in the Children of the Islamic World*. New York: UNICEF.

———. 2001. *Multiple Indicator Survey (MICS-2000): India Summary Report*. New Delhi. December.

———. 1998a. UNICEF on Deficient Birth Registration in Developing Countries. *Population and Development Review* 24(3): 659–664.

———. 1998b. *The Progress of Nations*. New York: UNICEF.

UNICEF and Plan. 2003. A Child's First Right: Third Asia Regional Conference on Birth Registration, Bangkok, Thailand, January 6–9.

UNICEF Innocenti Research Centre. 2002. Birth Registration: Right from the Start. *Innocenti Digest, no.* 9 (March). Florence, Italy: UNICEF.

United Nations. 2004. *World Economic and Social Survey 2004: International Migration*. New York: United Nations.

United Nations Department of Economic and Social Affairs, Statistics Division. 1998. *Handbook on Civil Registration and Vital Statistics Systems: Developing Information, Education and Communication*. New York: United Nations.

United Nations Development Group. 2000. *Common Country Assessment: Bangladesh 2000*. http://www.undg.org/archive_docs/1707-Bangladesh_CCA__Bangladesh_2000.pdf . Accessed July 1, 2007.

United Nations Development Program. 2000. *Human Development Report 2000*. New York: Oxford University Press.

———. 2007. *Human Development Report 2007*. New York: Oxford University Press.

United Nations High Commissioner for Refugees and Government of Pakistan. 2005. *Census of Afghans in Pakistan*. Islamabad: Ministry of States and Frontier Regions and Population Census Organization, Government of Pakistan and UNHCR.

United Nations Human Settlements Programme. 2003. *The Challenge of Slums: Global Report on Human Settlements 2003*. London: Earthscan.

United Nations and International Organization for Migration. 2005. *World Migration Report: Costs and Benefits of International Migration 2005*. Geneva, Switzerland: International Organization for Migration.

———. 2000. *World Migration Report 2000*. Geneva, Switzerland: International Organization for Migration.

United Press International. 2006. Over 169,000 Illegal Pakistani Immigrants Deported in Two Years. June 12.

Unni, M. Vijayan. 1999. *Census of India 1991: Assam State District Profile 1991*. New Delhi: Controller of Publications.

Universal Law Publishing. 2004. *The Citizenship Act, 1955*. Delhi: Universal Law Publishing.

Vartabedian, Ralph, Richard A. Serrano, and Richard Marosi. 2006. Rise in Bribery Tests Integrity of U.S. Border. *Los Angeles Times*. October 23: A1.

Vu, Gwendolen. 1997. Barter Trade between Sabah, Philippines and Indonesia. In *BIMP-EAGA Integration: Issues and Challenges*, edited by Mohd. Yaakub Hj. Johari, Bilson Kurus, and Janiah Zaini, pp.45–50. Sabah: Institute for Development Studies.

Watson, Paul. 2006. In Afghanistan, Money Tips the Scales of Justice. *Los Angeles Times*. December 26: A1.

Weber, Max. 1978. *Economy and Society: An Outline of Interpretive Sociology*. Berkeley: University of California Press.

Weiner, Myron. 1995. *The Global Migration Crisis: Challenge to States and to Human Rights*. New York: HarperCollins.

———. 1978. *Sons of the Soil: Migration and Ethnic Conflict in India*. Delhi: Oxford University Press.

Wines, Michael. 2002. Sometimes in Pakistan It's One Voter, 2 ID Cards. *New York Times*. October 10.

Winichakul, Thongchai. 1996a. Maps and the Formation of the Geo-Body of Siam. In *Asian Forms of the Nation,* edited by Stein Tonnesson and Hans Antlöv, pp.67–92. Surrey, England: Curzon.

———. 1996b. Siam Mapped: The Making of Thai Nationhood. *Ecologist* 26 (5) (September–October): 215–221.

Wink, Andre. 1986. *Land and Sovereignty in India: Agrarian Society and Politics under the Eighteenth-Century Maratha Svarajya*. Cambridge: Cambridge University Press.

Wright, Theodore P. 1991. Center-Periphery Relations and Ethnic Conflict in Pakistan: Sindhis, Muhajirs, and Punjabis. *Comparative Politics* 23 (3) (April): 299–312.

Young, Iris Marion. 1990. *Justice and the Politics of Difference*. Princeton, NJ: Princeton University Press.

Zill, Oriana. 2001. Crossing Borders: How Terrorists Use Fake Passports, Visas, and Other Identity Documents. *PBS Frontline*. 2001. http://www.pbs.org/wgbh/pages/frontline/shows/trail/etc/fake.html. Accessed July 1, 2007.

Zlotnik, Hania. 1987. Introduction: Measuring International Migration: Theory and Practice. *International Migration Review* 21 (4): v–vii.

Zolberg, Aristide R. 2006. *A Nation by Design: Immigration Policy in the Fashioning of America*. New York: Russell Sage Foundation; Cambridge, Mass.: Harvard University Press.

Index